I0165923

BREAK EVERY BOND:
SARAH HELEN WHITMAN
IN PROVIDENCE

LITERARY ESSAYS
AND SELECTED POEMS

EDITED AND ANNOTATED
BY
BRETT RUTHERFORD

YOGH &
THORN
BOOKS

PITTSBURGH, PENNSYLVANIA

Copyright 2019 by Brett Rutherford
All Rights Reserved

ISBN 978-0-922558-00-1
This is the 237th publication of The Poet's Press
Ver 1.1

Yogh & Thorn Books is an imprint of
THE POET'S PRESS
2209 Murray Avenue #3
Pittsburgh, PA 15217-2338

TABLE OF CONTENTS

BREAK EVERY BOND: SARAH HELEN WHITMAN IN PROVIDENCE

SARAH HELEN WHITMAN
AS POET AND CRITIC
by Brett Rutherford

◇————————————————————————◇

SARAH HELEN WHITMAN (1803-1878), poet and critic, is best known for her brief engagement to Edgar Allan Poe in 1848, and for her role as Poe's posthumous defender in her 1860 book, *Edgar Poe and His Critics*. She is seldom treated as more than an incidental person in Poe biography, and no books of her own poetry were reprinted after 1916, the same year the only full-length biography of her, by Caroline Ticknor, appeared. The list of Whitman's critical writings, most published under pseudonyms, has only recently been correctly identified and attributed to her. A reassessment of Sarah Helen Whitman as poet places her squarely in the Romantic tradition; and, as critic, as a ground-breaking American defender of Poe, Shelley, Byron, Goethe, Alcott, and Emerson. Whitman's accomplishments were small but significant, given the limits placed upon her success by the social, gender and religious norms of the time and place in which she lived — Providence, Rhode Island in the antebellum decades, as well as in the 1870s, when she published little, but carried on an extensive literary correspondence and served as her city's artistic den mother.

PROVIDENCE AT MID-CENTURY

A glance at published statistics help give us a better feel for the Providence in which Whitman and her contemporaries lived and wrote, and the role women played. The demographics suggest a society with very distinct class and race boundaries, but still one in which females were often the heads of households. The Census of 1855[1] documented 8,260 households in the bustling port and mill town, of which 1,315 were headed by women (about one in six.) About one in five houses in the city consisted of family groupings or boarding houses in which there were no children. Of the population of 46,400, only 1,390 were listed as "colored," and the town fathers were in a state of perpetual alarm about foreigners: 22 percent of the residents were recent immigrants from Ireland.

Providence was a rich city. As the birthplace of America's industrial revolution, it contained six cotton mills and four textile printing works. More than 5,000 vessels arrived that year in the port, and the city was connected to Boston, New York, and to other parts of New England with railroads, steamboats, stagecoaches and an "express steamer." If anything,

---

[1] Published by Providence City Council, 1856.

<9>

Providence was more interconnected with the other cities of the Northeast than it is today.

A writer living in Providence, however, had few local outlets. Although, at the time of the 1855 Census, there were four daily newspapers and six weeklies, and one semi-weekly, literary magazines *per se* did not thrive in the city. Sylvester Southworth had edited a four-page weekly titled *The Literary Subaltern* from 1829 to 1833.[2] Albert Greene edited the short-lived title, *The Literary Journal, and Weekly Register of Science and the Arts* (1833-34), and efforts to establish another around 1840 were greeted with ridicule by locals.[3]

It was a culture that prioritized learning, but with a fierce element of intolerance. Many local men attended Brown University, but that institution exerted little influence on the literary life of the city, and the leading families were notoriously conservative in taste. Expressing a liking for the "wrong" kind of literature had a social cost. Poetry, novels, and drama were frowned upon. The first attempts to open a theater in the city were thwarted by Baptist mobs, and some amateur attempts at theater had to be disguised as poetry readings or moral lectures.[4] In the late 1870s, Whitman reported to John H. Ingram, her British correspondent: "Though called the wealthiest city of its size in the Union, it [i.e., Providence] has no magazine or other literary periodical. "[5]

Although Providence did not publish much, its citizens were avid readers. At 1860, the year Whitman published her defense of Poe, a tally of local libraries indicated that Brown University had 25,000 volumes accessible to students and "gentlemen."[6] The Providence Athenaeum Library, the city's only large library, was a membership library with 20,000 volumes.[7] The other resources were the 3,300 books at the Mechanics and Apprentices Library, and 1,000 volumes at the Providence YMCA. [8]

Books were sold at bookshops, although some some were stationers' establishments whose selection may have been limited. There were 12 booksellers/stationers in Providence in 1860, and seven bookbinders.[9]

---

[2] H. P. Smith compiled a thorough history of early printers and newspapers in Rhode Island. See *Field*, pp. 563-611. Virtually are were political, religious, and trade newspapers, as well as almanacs.

[3] "Our Goosy," p. 1.

[4] For the tortured history of theater in Providence, see Willard's *History of the Providence Stage, 1762-1891.*

[5] Miller, *Poe's Helen Remembers*, p. 32.

[6] Adams, *Rhode Island Register*, p. 73. For a thorough history of libraries in Rhode Island, see J. P. Smith's chapter, "The Growth of the Library" in Field, pp. 615-639. The Providence Athenaeum's history is ably conveyed in Jane Lancaster's *Inquire Within.*

[7] Ibid, p. 61.

[8] Ibid, pp. 61-62.

<10>

Since many books were sold unbound, bookbinders made custom bindings for their clientele. The city had nine printing establishments in 1860.[10]

The major vehicle of cultural transmission other than reading books and journals, was the extensive Lyceum movement, which brought authors and speakers on many topics to all the cities and large towns, where large audiences came to hear them lecture or read from their work.

SARAH HELEN WHITMAN'S FAMILY HISTORY & MARRIAGE

Just as it would be impossible to understand fully female writers like the Brontës (captives of class, geography, and familial stricture) without knowing their family history, we must look to Whitman's genealogy and family history to grasp some of the social and gender pressures against which she had to strive as a writer.

The following is mostly derived from the work of John Austin, published in 1889, the only known genealogy of her family. (A 1974 genealogy by Franklin Powers mostly repeats the facts gathered by Austin.)[11] I include genealogy here, despite its slight tediousness, because the information is, first of all, rather difficult to obtain, and, second, because it puts the Power family and its fortunes squarely in the "Triangle Trade" era.

The Powers were in Rhode Island almost from its beginning. There would be six Nicholas Powers in the family line, the last of them Sarah Helen Whitman's father.

The first Nicholas Power received a home lot in Providence in 1640. He was in trouble briefly with the authorities for trying to purchase Indian lands in Warwick (RI) — expressly forbidden in the treaties with the local tribes — and was "dismissed with an admonition."[12]

Nicholas died in 1657, leaving his widow, Jane Power; a daughter, Hope; and the next Nicholas Power. This Nicholas died in the catastrophic King Phillip's War in 1675. He is not found in lists of combatants, but Austin explains: "He was killed in The Great Swamp Fight in Narragansett, by a shot from the command in which he was serving."[13]

His son, Captain Nicholas Power, was born in 1673. This Nicholas's second wife was Mercy Tillinghast, daughter of the Rev. Pardon Tilling-

---

9 Ibid, p. 127.
10 Ibid, p. 158.
11 References to the Power family in city records are indexed in Bowen's *Index to the Early Records of the Town of Providence*.
12 Powers, Genealogy, p. 106.
13 Ibid, p. 18.

<11>

hast. Captain Power died in 1734. He had four slaves: Cuffy, Tony, Caesar, and Peg.

The next Nicholas Power was a merchant and distiller. He married Anne Tillinghast, and died in Surinam in 1744. He sold his estate and distillery in Dutch Guiana to Captain John Brown in 1743. A family that owned slaves *and* a distillery would almost certainly have been involved in the notorious Triangle Trade of rum, slaves, and molasses.

In the next generation, we have another Captain Nicholas Power, a merchant and rope-maker. He married Rebecca Corey, and died January 26, 1808. The records indicate he freed a slave named "Prince" in 1781. Rhode Island officially outlawed slavery in 1784, replacing a 1652 law that had never been enforced, with an anti-slavery law that gradually freed existing slaves and prohibited new ones. This did not end Rhode Island's involvement in the Triangle trade, however, which went on to as late as 1825.

Nicholas Power, Jr. (1771-1844)

The Nicholas who figures in our story is the sixth, known as Nicholas Power, Jr., born September 15, 1771. He married Anna Marsh, daughter of Daniel and Susanna (Wilkinson) Marsh on August 28, 1798, in Newport. He was a merchant, going by the title of Major for some part of his life.

His mercantile life was predominantly land-locked: he formed a partnership as "Blodgett and Power" and opened a store near Providence's Baptist Meeting House. The goods sold there began with fabrics, linens, threads (English, Indian and Scottish), then dry goods, hardware and groceries. From 1808 to 1810 the store ran auctions of goods. Then, in 1812, the partnership terminated. The war with the British almost certainly interrupted their trade.

Nicholas and Anna's first child, Rebecca, was born in 1800. Sarah Helen Power, our and Poe's "Helen," was the second daughter, born in Providence on January 19, 1803. The house where she was born was that of her grandfather, Captain Nicholas Power, at the corner of South Main and Transit Streets. They lived in this house until her grandfather's death in 1808.[14]

As Nicholas Power's fortunes ebbed and flowed, the young family moved to a succession of houses and lodgings: a house at the corner of

[14] Ticknor, p. 9.

<12>

Snow and Westminster (now a parking lot in a depressed corner of downtown Providence); "the Grinnell House," and "the Angell Tavern," which had a garden leading to the water.[15]

Nicholas Power was not present for the birth of this third daughter, Susan Anna, in 1813, for he had gone to sea to build back his fortune. He was captured by the British during the War of 1812 and was not released until 1815, at which time he did not return to Providence. As far as anyone in Rhode Island knew, he was "lost at sea."

Sarah Helen's younger sister, Susan Anna, was born in 1813. She would mature into a willful manic-depressive, the classic mad relative without whom no New England house seemed complete.[16] Since her mother was descended from the Wilkinson line that had produced the religious cult founder Jemima Wilkinson (1751-1819), there is the possibility of a genetic predisposition for bipolar disease if not schizophrenia. Jemima Wilkinson, declaring herself dead, resurrected, and genderless, took the name "Public Universal Friend" and persuaded a number of people to forsake community and property and go off to live with her in upstate New York, where she preached to Indians, led a sexless commune, and promised (but failed) to walk on water.[17]

After 1816, Mrs. Power, regarding herself as a widow, purchased the house at 76 Benefit Street (now No. 88) as a residence for herself and her daughters. It would be their home for more than four decades.[18] The family was well able to live on the stocks and mortgages Mrs. Power had inherited from her mother, funds happily untouched by the impecunious Major Power.

Although Benefit Street was then fashionable, it had been built over grave plots. The original settlers of Providence owned long, parallel strips of land starting at the river and running up over College Hill. Until 1710 or so, most families buried their dead on this hillside, and a lane that threaded among the family burial plots was ultimately straightened and paved to become Benefit Street. For some years, the street terminated with a gate, to ward off the denizens of the sinister North End.

With the creation of Benefit Street, the city fathers persuaded families to exhume and relocate their moldering ancestors to the North Burial Ground. A number of gloomy and derelict churchyards were also relocated there gradually, but St. John's churchyard remained, its wall abutting the Powers' rose garden. Like the Brontë sisters, the Power sisters' always had view of a graveyard.

---

[15] Ibid., p. 9.
[16] Miller, pp. 129-130.
[17] For accounts of Wilkinson, see Vanderhoof, pp. 107-132, and David Hudson's *Memoir of Jemima Wilkinson*.
[18] Ticknor, p. 10.

<13>

Although a proper Providence upbringing in those days was probably rather stifling, Sarah Helen had a few escapes during her younger years: she visited relatives on Long Island, New York and briefly attended a Quaker school.[19] Despite the Puritanical suspicions and prohibitions of her relatives, she developed an early passion for poetry. She mastered Latin and would later be sufficiently adept in languages to read and translate both German and French.

In 1821, Sarah Helen's older sister Rebecca married William E. Staples.[20] Two children were born to them in rapid succession. There is a Judge William Staples home just up the block from the Power house on Benefit Street, and this is probably where the couple lived.

Despite her mother's deep-set mistrust of men, Sarah Helen, too, was wooed and won away from the Benefit Street home. In 1824, during her twenty-first year, she was engaged to attorney John Winslow Whitman. Urged to assume the proper responsibilities of womanhood, Sarah Helen was pressured to put aside her literary ambitions. As Ticknor tells it, "Mrs. Whitman's taste for poetry was frowned upon by certain relatives...[She received] reproving letters, expressing the hope that she

---

[19] Ticknor, p. 11.
[20] Ibid, p. 11.

<14>

'did not read much poetry, as it was almost as pernicious as novel-reading'."[21]

John Whitman seemed a good match. He was not one of those lawyers whom Shakespeare would have us kill. The third son of Massachusetts Judge Kilborne Whitman, he graduated from Brown University in 1818. He started a law practice in Boston, and practiced later in Barnstable.

During their long engagement, in 1825, Sarah Helen's grandmother, Rebecca Corey Power, died. Then, sorrow struck again that year when Sarah Helen's older sister Rebecca died on September 14th. Rebecca had been married only four years, and then her two children, according to the Power family records, "died young." Was her death

John Winslow Whitman.

childbirth-related, or did a contagion such as tuberculosis ("the galloping consumption") sweep through the Staples home, taking the young mother and then the children? This tragedy must have made a deep impression on the poetical Sarah Helen, who would have followed four coffins to the North Burial Ground in swift succession.

Sarah Helen's respectably-delayed marriage took place in 1828, with a Long Island wedding held on July 10th at the home of her uncle, Cornelius Bogert.[22] A four-year engagement may seem excessive by today's standards, but John Whitman may also have needed time to establish his law practice and set up a suitable home.

John Whitman turned out to have a creative side, too. It is interesting to note that Sarah Helen Whitman's biographer, and most of Poe's, seem to know her husband only by his profession. John Winslow Whitman had another persona altogether: he seems to have had some involvement with the Boston-based magazine, *The Ladies' Album*. He was also, briefly, partner in a weekly Boston newspaper titled *The Times*.

The Ladies' Album published some of her poems, not as Sarah Helen Whitman, but under the name "Helen." Ticknor, incorrectly, writes that Whitman's first published poem was in that journal in 1829, a poem titled, "Retrospection." In fact, Whitman published two poems there in 1828, the year of her marriage. It is telling that her second published poem, "To the Spirit of Poetry," is a direct refutation of the religious

---

[21] Ibid, p. 12.
[22] Ibid, p. 12.

<15>

admonitions against poetry that her family and friends had pressed upon her, as these lines reveal:

> Thou art religion, virtue, faith;
> Through thee the martyr conquers death;
> Thy voice, like solemn music leads
> To godlike thoughts, and glorious deeds.
> Borne upwards on thy radiant wings,
> Man's soaring spirit heavenward springs,
> And burst the ignoble chains that bind
> To earth's dull dross the immortal mind.
>
> To thee alone, the power is given,
> To render earth a present heaven:
> Oh! may thine influence elevate
> My soul above the ills of date:
> May thy pure present ne'er depart,
> But, treasured deep within my heart,
> There may the spirit ever be,
> A beauty, and a mystery.[23]

Through her husband's Boston affiliations, she met and came to know the circle of Transcendentalists. She shared with Emerson and Margaret Fuller a fascination with Goethe and German idealist philosophy. And she clung to her early love of Byron and Shelley. Mrs. Whitman was clearly not going to vanish into the draperies, and she was fortunate to have a literary ally in her husband.

The Power genealogy notes, cryptically, that Nicholas Power "was absent from Providence much in later years."[24] It was a case of adventure followed by spousal desertion. Sometime in 1831-1832, he made a sudden return to make amends and presumably resume his family life. Indications are that his nineteen-year "widow" was aghast at his re-appearance and threw him out of the house. He took up residence in a Providence hotel, and, to the dismay of all, spent his remaining years in conspicuous dissolution, or happy bachelorhood, depending upon one's point-of-view. Legend has it that he had fled a second wife and family in the Carolinas.

Did the Major return in a remorseful state, wanting to make amends and restore his family's fortune? Or was he ruined again, returning to old haunts to nibble away at his wife's property? Mrs. Power would have none of him, but his daughters may have felt differently. Sarah Helen,

[23] *Ladies' Magazine* (1828-1829) October 1, 1828 (p. 458).
[24] Austin, Genealogy, p. 23.

<16>

married and living in Boston, had not seen her father since her ninth year, and still cherished a somewhat heroic image of him. Her younger sister, still at home, had never known her father at all.

Things did not go well in Boston. Sarah Helen's husband was not destined for commercial success. Money vanished into failed inventions, and several business ventures went belly-up. John Whitman even appears to have gone to jail for a few months in a legal upset involving a bad loan — not a happy career turn for a young attorney. His name also appears as co-author of a series of booklets that appear to be transcripts of controversial Boston lawsuits, including one libel suit that involved a clergyman.

Worse yet, John Whitman also turned out to have a frail constitution. He caught colds frequently, and one of them, contracted in 1833, lingered and worsened into a total collapse and sudden death.[25]

Much more needs to be learned about John Whitman. Biographer Ticknor disposes of Sarah Helen's youth and marriage in a mere 13 pages, and Whitman herself pulls a veil of silence over the subject for the rest of her life. Husband and wife were clearly partners in the literary life they found in Boston, and one can only assume that inordinate family pressures back in Providence created the virtual cover-up that ensued.

So then, in 1833, Whitman found herself a widow after only five years of marriage. She donned the official "widow's bonnet" and moved back in with her mother and younger sister on Benefit Street. Her defense of Shelley, published in Providence's only literary journal early in 1834, bore the Roman-Etruscan pseudonym of "Egeria."

Although she would resume the role of dutiful daughter, Whitman was now a published literary figure in her own right, confident in her worth and powers, and acquainted with many of the best minds of New England. Even if convention and respectability compelled her to hide behind initials and pseudonyms, she was known, and appreciated.

---

[25] Ticknor, p. 13.

<17>

FAMILY TROUBLES

MEANTIME, NICHOLAS POWER, rebuffed from the attractive red house on Benefit Street, had set up lodgings in a Providence hotel and began his new, disreputable existence, pursuing his passion for the theater, and for its actresses. The prejudice against theater people was so strong in America at this time that actors were routinely forbidden the use of churches for weddings and funerals, and associating with professional actors was highly suspect.

At this time, the Power-Whitman household probably assumed its frozen triangle of control, dependence and artistic defiance. Mrs. Anna Power held the purse strings. She would make certain that no man ever got near the modest fortune that had come their way through the Marsh family.

The younger sister, Susan Anna, careened between manic highs and long periods of sullen silence. One episode reportedly led her to a sanitarium stay, for "mania,"[26] but Mrs. Power evidently preferred the cheaper long-term solution of keeping her daughter at home, under constant supervision.

Mrs. Power probably established some stern rules about the extent to which Susan's mood swings would be humored — though after their mother's death, Whitman seemed to surrender control to her reclusive "patient." During Susan's depressive periods, the house would be darkened and visitors turned away. Her need for silence, darkness and solitude were pampered, and if visitors were by some necessity admitted, Susan would hide in a closet.[27] In her manic phases, Susan Anna collaborated on some well-wrought fairy-tale poems with Sarah Helen, and amused visitors with impromptu verses about the wandering Nicholas Power.

Although Whitman accepted the burden of living with her embittered mother — and helping to care for her sister — her own mind, and her own writing, were unfettered. She was with the gods — Goethe, Schiller, Shelley, Byron, Emerson. She studied occult lore and learned about mesmerism and (later) spiritualism, as interest in these phenomena swept across the New England states. And when universal male suffrage, women's suffrage, and the abolition of slavery became New England's predominant issues, Whitman was there. Séances, poetry, and political activism, all went hand-in-glove.

An avid reader, she frequented the wonderful Providence Athenaeum, a membership lending library which moved into its new

---

[26] Miller, pp. 129-130.
[27] Ticknor, pp. 18-19.

<18>

Greek-revival temple only a few blocks away on Benefit Street in 1838, successor to The Providence Library Company founded in 1753.[28] She became a local celebrity, and parties and salons at her home drew not only the locals, but visiting celebrities such as Emerson. John Hay, a young poet later famed as Abraham Lincoln's secretary, was a devotee at the Whitman salon, which came to be called "The Phalanstery."

She may also have formed a stronger bond with her father based on their mutual love of the theater, as well as suffrage-related politics. Conspicuously, Whitman did not write a poem for the Athenaeum library's dedication, where prominent families who disapproved of her literary tastes held sway. Instead, she wrote a passionate defense of the drama and had it read at the opening of Providence's first substantial theater, Shakespeare Hall, the autumn of that same year.

Nicholas Power also immersed himself in the Dorr Rebellion, a mini-civil war in Rhode Island, in favor of expanding voting rights to men who did not own property. For an electrifying interval, the state had two rival governments, with shots fired just blocks from the Whitman-Power home. It is not certain whether Power was captured in the Providence street fighting or in the second action which took place in rural Chepachet. We get a sense of his closeness to Thomas Dorr when a witness in Dorr's treason trial reports that when Dorr was told, in Chepachet, that Nicholas Power had been captured, "he said 'Then my sword is gone.'"[29] Another witness in Providence confirms the significance of Power in the suffrage conflict: "We talked of Nicholas Power. I said to Blodget, I heard he was used up at Dedham. He said, yes, they packed a Jury and convicted him."[30]

Sarah Helen may have made clandestine visits to her father while he was imprisoned from 1842; since the Dorr Rebellion was over the issue of universal (male) suffrage, she could only have looked on his role as heroic. (Women were certainly not going to get the vote if even a majority of men could not vote, either.)

Around that time, Nicholas Power got around to placing a marker on his mother's grave with an inscription lamenting the effect of his long absence on his parent's well-being. Rebecca Corey Power had died in 1825, and it is likely that she never knew what became of her son.

His prison term served and his filial duty performed, Nicholas Power, aged 73, died on April 28, 1844. The sixth of his name, of a family that had once owned slaves, he had taken to the streets in his 71st year, with gun and sword, to fight for the voting rights of propertyless Irish immigrants.

[28] Whitman was not a member/shareholder at the Athenaeum. She borrowed books on a male cousin's membership.

[29] Pitman, p. 54

[30] Ibid, p. 74.

<19>

WHITMAN'S FIRST BOOK, *Hours of Life and Other Poems,* published in 1853 (her fiftieth year), was printed by Knowles, Anthony & Company under the aegis of George H. Whitney, a Providence bookseller. The edition was small and the poet was still giving away copies twenty years later. The volume includes the major poems she had written to and about Poe. We will never know if the bookseller published and underwrote *Hours of Life,* as Helen insisted, "at his request"[31] or whether she subsidized the venture. She wrote to Poe's biographer Ingram many years later: "I am utterly & entirely ignorant of all transactions with publishers. I have no relations with any publishers & never made a contract in my life."[32] At another time, however, she wrote: "Mr. Whitney, the publisher, surrendered to me the copyright before he gave up business as bookseller and publisher. Mr. Carleton also gave up to me his copyright of *Edgar Poe and His Critics.*"[33]

One of her fine poems, "Proserpine, [On Earth,] To Pluto, In Hades" deserves special attention for its allegory of the characters in the Poe-Whitman-Mrs. Power love drama. The poet uses the familiar mythical story of Ceres' daughter, Proserpine (Persephone in Greek), who must spend six months of the year with her brooding husband, Pluto, lord of the dead, and six months of the year above ground. This ancient fable explaining and symbolizing the seasons is turned topsy-turvy by Whitman. Her Proserpine *loves* Pluto and prefers to sit by his throne in the dark underworld. Her angry mother Ceres comes in a chariot drawn by two dragons to reclaim her. Here we have a trio of archetypes: Helen, Poe, and the ever-angry Mrs. Power. The Proserpine symbolism even carried to Helen's funeral in 1878: her coffin was decorated with a green wreath, and a stalk of wheat.

Whitman's longest and most ambitious poem is "Hours of Life." Its middle section, "Noon," is a spiritual saga and romantic quest — the poet's search for meaning and truth through the realms of myth and antiquity. In this long poetic odyssey we see: Echoes of Goethe in a passage that is almost a paraphrase of the famous scene of Faust alone in his laboratory, before he makes the acquaintance of Mephistopheles ... A fascinatingly brief flirtation with the vengeful god of the Old Testament, whom she rejects ... A wise examination and rejection of the sad religion of the Hindu ... as well as the death-obsessed Egyptian ... A passionate, almost Shelleyan plunge into the world of Ancient Greece, where she obviously feels close to the very origins of myth and meaning.

---

[31] Miller, *Poe's Helen,* p. 97.
[32] Ibid, p. 29.
[33] Ibid, p. 97.

<20>

Her use of the Dionysian Maenads — fierce, wild, drunken women, running down the mountain slope toward her as in a nightmare, crying out *"Evoe — ah — Evoe!"* is the most elemental, and frankly terrifying thing in all her writing. Here she is throwing herself into the world of Euripides' *The Bacchae*, probably the most Chthonic and unnerving of all the texts to come down from antiquity.[34]

She wrests herself away from the refrain of the Maenads only by turning to Nature. Here she waxes almost Byronic in taking comfort from the rude, natural world. She finds that she can accept this transcendental, all-encompassing Nature, free of the eidolons of ancient gods.

One thing only troubles her, though — the doubt that would bring her back to a more conventional, if still highly individual, resolution, in the third part of the poem. What about the abyss after death? she asks. Nature is *not* enough if the spirit does not survive and transcend the body. Thus she leaves her quest, Faust-like, with no satisfaction from all she has seen on her journey.

The beauty and power of "Noon" is easily obscured by the more conventional opening, and the rather spiritualist closing of the longer poem of which it is part. But "Noon" itself is a remarkable production, a piece Romantic in the purest sense. Whatever the poem lacks in originality in its occasional mimicry of Shelley and Byron, it makes up for in its economy, intellect and power. George Ripley, founder of *The Dial*, here being quoted by Whitman's posthumous editors from a *New York Tribune* review, called it "remarkable for the life-like reality with which it weaves the recollections of a profound and intense experience into the natural materials of song. ... a taste ripened and enriched by exquisite culture ... uniting spontaneous grace and freshness with classical finish. ... Rich as it is in characteristics that would establish an enviable poetical fame for any writer..."[35]

Whitman's collected poems were issued in a memorial edition a year after her death, in 1879, by Houghton, Osgood and Company, printed by The Riverside Press, Cambridge, Massachusetts. The third and last printing was in 1916. Her poetry remained out of print until the present editor's publication of *Last Flowers: The Romance Poems of Edgar Allan Poe and Sarah Helen Whitman* in 1985.

Whitman left $2,000 in her estate for the posthumous publication of her poems. No doubt this sum was applied to the 1879 edition of her poems. The 1916 reprint, the same year as Caroline Ticknor's biography, *Poe's Helen*, was probably a spontaneous production.

The present volume includes a selection of Whitman's poetry, ranging beyond the Poe-related works included in *Last Flowers*. Posterity

---

[34] Euripides, p. 401.
[35] Whitman, *Poems* (1879), p. xi.

<21>

has been somewhat unkind to her reputation, both in dismissing her as the ether-sniffing "poetess" once engaged to Poe, and because her poetry is at times less original. That many poems were written for friends and for her literary circle, meant that she had no qualms about inserting a quoted line here and there from another poet (with quotation marks), assuming that her readers would understand her use of a familiar line or phrase. The ego of the male poet would seemingly never condone this kind of collaborative poesy. The footnotes in this edition identify all the sources for Whitman's unattributed quotations.

WHITMAN'S PUBLISHED CRITICISM

EDGAR POE AND His Critics was published in 1860, not coincidentally after her mother died. It is her only published criticism in book form. Mallarmé, discovering the slender volume in 1877, wrote to Whitman of the book's "unexpected charm and a penetrating beauty."[36] Arthur Hobson Quinn, in one of the best Poe biographies of the first half of the 20th century, appraised her book as "not only a convincing personal tribute, but also one of the most sympathetic and brilliant interpretations of his poetry and fiction."[37]

Poe's most recent biographer, Kenneth Silverman, was one of the first to acknowledge that Whitman was a formidable intellectual match for Poe. Unlike the mostly-dilettante female poets Poe knew in New York, Silverman observes, "Sarah Helen Whitman was a woman with sophisticated philosophical and literary interests — after her friend Margaret Fuller, perhaps the leading female literary critic in America."[38]

Although she had no opportunity for formal education other than a brief period at a Quaker school on Long Island, Whitman was a well-read classicist, and her critical articles put her squarely in the league of the Harvard-trained Boston writers and reviewers. She knew Virgil and other Latin authors. She read Shelley and the Romantics, and she translated German supernatural ballads, as well as Goethe, and, from the French, Victor Hugo. Her correspondents included Elizabeth Barrett Browning, Stephane Mallarmé and other British and continental writers, as well as domestic writers and editors.

Noelle Baker, in a dissertation on Whitman's critical articles, characterizes her subject thus: "[S]he should be studied with such established critics as William Ellery Channing, Ralph Waldo Emerson, Margaret Fuller, Frederic Henry Hedge and Edgar Allan Poe. Whitman

[36] Lloyd, p. 102.
[37] Quinn, p. 572.
[38] Silverman, p. 347.

<22>

explicates transcontinental idealism within the context of American considerations of immorality, pre-Darwinian evolution theory, German *Naturphilosophen*, and the occult in her essays on Emerson, Alcott, Goethe, Shelley and Poe. She argued that these writers utilize literature, science and philosophy to recover individual spirituality in a time of inadequate traditional theology and doctrinal malaise. Almost invariably, Whitman defends her subjects from American critics who consider the byproducts of this secular faith irreligious or immoral."[39]

Susan P. Conrad says that Whitman's essays "rank with those of Margaret Fuller and Elizabeth Peabody as the most important literary criticism produced by women — and men — in the period [1830-1860]."[40]

Choosing "Break every bond" as her motto,[41] Whitman intentionally chose some of the most controversial literary figures to write about. She deflected, if not defended, Shelley's atheism; refused to throw out Byron's poetry even if he did have an affair with his half-sister; and championed the writing of Goethe even if Werther and Faust did seem to approve of seduction, vice, suicide, and bargains with the Devil. As Baker is quick to note, Whitman beat a trail-blazing path to Goethe's writing: "Whitman read German, and with Margaret Fuller produced the only American women's published analyses of German language and literature at a time when even most male critics read the Germans through Coleridge and Carlyle."[42]

In her last years, Whitman admired Swinburne's poetry, and in her correspondence with Mallarmé she offered the French poet advice on translating "The Raven."[43] She became "one of the most important mediators Mallarmé found between himself and Poe."[44] The French poet advised Whitman on her own translation of his "Tomb of Edgar Poe."[45].

Baker calls Whitman's criticism "a minor woman writer's programmatic attempt to publish a deviant, male-gendered authorial identity,"[46] but Baker, perhaps, makes too much of Whitman's pseudonymous publications. Her commentary about Whitman's attempts to "pass" as a male critic seems off the mark to me on three counts: first, criticism of the period tended to be highly intellectualized and almost genderless. Critics did not write as men or as women but as critics.[47] Second, two of

[39] Baker, p. iii.
[40] Conrad, p. 223.
[41] Baker, p. 12.
[42] Baker, p. 3.
[43] Lloyd, p. 103.
[44] Ibid, p. 104,
[45] See Ticknor, pp. 268-270.
[46] Baker, p. iii.
[47] Although Whitman's essay on Genius refers to men of genius, and makes the reader assume that gender for the writer, the editor of *The Boston Pearl* adds a

<23>

Whitman's key essays were published with the female pseudonym "Egeria," and most of Whitman's articles were circulated in manuscript among the literati and her identity was well known.

The name "Egeria" comes from Roman history.[48] This is the name given to the prophetess (or, some say, consort) of the Roman king Numa Pompilius, the great Roman lawgiver. Since Whitman was the wife of a young Boston lawyer at the time, "Egeria" was a suitable name for the wife and muse of a young man who might hope some day to be a judge or lawmaker. Both articles by-lined "Egeria" appeared early in her widowhood, and this may have added to her reticence.

This raises yet again the question of the extent to which Whitman's literary fame was stifled or limited by her gender. The male writers and editors who encountered Whitman, from the Harvard circle, the Transcendentalist circle, and from New York, implored her to submit articles and poems for publication. According to Baker, Orestes Bronson "offered her an equal share in the profits of his *Boston Quarterly Review* if she would contribute an article to each number."[49]

The discouragement that Whitman received from family and Providence society seems to have been mostly of female origin. In fact, men are not mentioned much at all in the family history, except when a male is required for legal purposes, such as arranging property transfers. Ticknor, Whitman's first biographer, alludes to family pressures that discouraged Whitman in her early years. Two of the original documents are at the John Hay library at Brown University — two letters from an older cousin who had been a "second mother" to Whitman during her stays on Long Island. Here we can see, first-hand, the kind of admonishment that Whitman had to endure in her teens, precisely when her passion for poetry was reaching its apex:

> I am still as much your *mother* as ever. How do your studies
> come on? Do you go to school or not? if not, I hope that you
> study at home. Do not neglect this important facet of your life.
> It is now the springtime with you, my dear, and recollect that if
> you attend more to its enjoyments than its cares; if intent only
> on its flowers and birds, its fragrance and its harmony, you
> neglect the toilsome preparation and ... your summer will be
> without fruit and your winter dreary indeed.

---

notice about "Egeria," reading: "Our readers will welcome, as we do, this lady as a contributor to *The Pearl*. The article in this paper is worthy of attention." Whitman, "Attributes of Genius," p. 111.

[48] Livy, p. 54.

[49] Baker, p. 2.

<24>

Of this be certain, that the only earthly foundation for permanent satisfaction is the utilization of the intellectual and moral faculties. Devote yourself, in the first place, to God, read his book, pray unto him and endeavor to increase in his knowledge. This, my child, is the only safe refuge in affliction, the only firm support in prosperity as well as in adversity, the only course of temporal as well as eternal happiness.

In the next place, cultivate a taste for solid and substantial knowledge; this only will tend to make you the sort of character I wish you to be. Poetry and novels, delightful as they may be to a youthful mind, are not only nugatory, they are not only void of all useful instruction, but they positively contaminate, and they occupy the time that ought to be devoted to better things.[50]

Two months later, Whitman's cousin reinforces her argument in another letter:

I hear from your own account that you read too much poetry, dear Sarah. Indulged in to excess it becomes almost if not quite as pernicious as novels. Any kind of reading which tends to excite the fancy and raise up visions of romantic feelings unknown to this world is dangerous, except occasionally as a relaxation.[51]

This is the kind of regurgitated sermonizing that young Sarah Helen would have heard from her mother and the social circle of genteel old families into which she was born. Rebellion had its price, but the young poet was clearly drawn to the rebels' side. She exulted when her father, in his seventies, took up arms in the Dorr War and was briefly jailed. She chose a "conventional" husband, but her mother may not have known that John Winslow Whitman was, comparatively, a freethinker who had scandalized his class at Brown by giving a commencement address titled "The Atheist."

Following is a bibliography of the critical articles which Baker has established as Whitman's writing:

- Egeria (pseud. Sarah Helen Whitman). "Character and Writings of Shelley." *The Literary Journal, and Weekly Register of Science and the Arts.* 1:32 (By-lined as Providence, Sat Jan 11 1834), pp. 252-253.

---

[50] Marsh, MS 204, HA1388.
[51] Marsh, MS 204, HA1387.

<25>

- Egeria (pseud. Sarah Helen Whitman). "On the Nature and Attributes of Genius. *The Boston Pearl: A Gazette Devoted to Polite Literature.* 5:14 (Saturday, Dec 19 1835), pp. 107-108.

- Whitman, Sarah Helen. "Review of 'Conversations with Goethe in the Last Years of His Life' translated from the German of Eckermann." *Boston Quarterly Review.* January 1840. Vol. 3, pp. 20-57 [By-lined as 'Providence, August 15, 1839'].

- A Disciple (pseud. Sarah Helen Whitman). "Emerson's Essays, by a Disciple." *United States Magazine, and Democratic Review.* Vol 16 No 84. June 1845, pp. 589-602.

- Whitman, Sarah Helen. *Edgar Poe and His Critics.* 1860. New York: Rudd & Carleton.

- Whitman, Sarah Helen. "Tablets." [Review of Alcott]. *Providence Daily Journal.* Vol. 39 No 261. Friday morning, October 30, 1868.

- Whitman, Sarah Helen. "Byronism." *Providence Daily Journal.* Vol. 41 No 93. October 18, 1869.

Edgar Poe and His Critics, Whitman's only critical work to appear in book form, has been praised as a great work of literary vindication. Whitman had to wait until her mother's passing to publish her defense of Poe. Moulton, writing at the time of Whitman's death in 1878, noted the little book's continued high place: "a little volume of passionate and superb prose, in defense of the dead man ... remarkable for its self-restraint... criticism, not eulogy"[52]

Whitman's critical appreciation of Shelley, published in 1834, defends genius against religion, yet her defense is timid, reduced in essence to the argument that kind Christians should have remonstrated gently with the poet and brought him back into the fold, rather than casting him out for his atheism. This modest critical sally alone sufficed to make Whitman an outcast among some families in Benefit Street, and once the British blasphemy trial against Shelley's poetry took place in the following decade, the blacklisting would have been reinforced.

At the time Whitman wrote her appreciation of Goethe in 1840, the second part of *Faust* was little-known, and only those able to read German could plumb its depths (she and Margaret Fuller were among them). Earlier, Thomas Carlyle had lamented the lack of a worthy *Faust* translation, thus:

---

[52] Moulton, p. 804.

<26>

A suitable version of Faust would be a rich addition to our literature; but the difficulties which stand in the way of such an undertaking amount to almost an absolute veto. The merits of a good translation, especially in poetry, always bear some kindred, though humble, relation to those of the original; and in the case before us, that relation approaches more nearly to equality than in any other that we know of. To exhibit in a different tongue any tolerable copy of the external graces of this drama, — the marvelous felicity of its language, and the ever-varying, ever-expressive rhythm of its verse, would demand the exercise of all that is rarest and most valuable in a poet's art; while the requisite familiarity with such thoughts and feelings as it embodies, could not exist but in conjunction with nearly all that is rarest and most valuable in a poet's genius. A person so qualified is much more likely to write tragedies of his own, than to translate those of others: and thus Faust, we are afraid, must ever continue in many respects a sealed book to the mere English reader.[53]

The vigor and philosophical penetration of her thought come through most strikingly in her 1845 explication and defense of Emerson, an essay that must have dazzled Poe even if he recoiled from New England Transcendentalism. After a wide-ranging discussion of Emerson's influences and innovations, Whitman closes with a new self-confidence:

In asserting that the fontal idea of Emerson's writings, as of the philosophy of the age, is absolute identity, I have not been careful to avert from them the imputation of Pantheism, Platonism, Spinozism, &c., &c. It matters little how we designate this manner of interpreting the phenomena of being, since it contains an inherent vitality which alike survives neglect and defies ridicule.

Superficial and timid men may decry these ideas as unintelligible or profane; but what rational ground of faith is left to him who doubts that God is over all and in all, that evil is but the absence and privation of good, and that all apparent evil must give way before a fuller development of the life that *is* within us? Only when the knowledge that the highest dwells ever with us becomes "a sweet enveloping thought," shall we be enabled to lead a single and trustful life, "to live in thoughts and act with energies that are immortal."

---

[53] Thomas Carlyle, "Goethe's *Faust.*" (1822), pp. 317-318.

<27>

Sadly, her literary essays and letters, other than *Edgar Poe and His Critics,* remained unpublished in book form. Whitman left $1,000 in her estate for the publication of her prose works. Moulton confirmed this in the *London Athenaeum* obituary.[54] Baker found heavily annotated copies of the reviews prepared by Whitman and/or an amanuensis, so the manuscript was at hand. The prose volume never appeared. Why did Whitman not re-publish her miscellaneous criticism during her lifetime? The experience of Margaret Fuller might be instructive. Fuller, Whitman's friend and a one-time resident of Providence, had published her own critical essays on literature, *Papers on Literature and Art,* in 1846, but the timidity of her publishers, Wiley & Putnam, prevented this volume from containing the full range of her controversial political and social thinking. Judith Bean tells us, "Her proposed collection was cut in half for publication, obscuring her political critique and the range of her work as a critic."[55] The excisions included a review of Shelley's poetry, and Whitman could have anticipated a similar problem, since her own essays centered on Shelley, Byron and Goethe. A criminal conviction in England charging a publisher with blasphemy for reprinting Shelley's "Queen Mab" is one possible factor in this case of publisher's panic, and in 1844, two Edinburgh booksellers were imprisoned for selling works by Thomas Paine and Shelley.[56]

POE – BUT ONLY BRIEFLY

WHITMAN'S RELATIONSHIP WITH Poe began, and ended, with poems. In January 1848, Mrs. Anne Lynch, a Providence-born poet who had moved to New York, invited Whitman to contribute poetic greetings to a Valentine's Day party she was planning for the Manhattan *literati.* Whitman and her sister Susan both sent poems. Hers was addressed to Poe, an allusive parody of "The Raven" with some penetrating understanding of Poe's literary themes.

Only after the February 14 party was over did Whitman learn that Poe had *not* been invited, and was in fact *persona non grata.* Anne Lynch then submitted 42 poems that had been read at her party for publication in *The Home Journal.* Whitman's poem was not among them.

It took two more communications to a reluctant Anne Lynch to get her to pass along the Poe valentine for publication. The *Home Journal* published it separately.[57] This publication commenced the famous Poe-Whitman romance. If Poe had noticed Whitman's 1839 publication

---

[54] Moulton, p. 804.
[55] Bean, p. 26.
[56] Hetherington, p. 53.
[57] Whitman, "To Edgar Allan Poe." *Home Journal,* March 18, 1848.

<28>

of her translation of Bürger's "Leonora," — the most famous of all supernatural ballads from Germany — her name would already have been known to him.

Whitman revised her valentine poem substantially in later years, making its imagery encompass more details from Poe's tales.

In 1853, she published the poems she had written to and about Poe in her first book. In 1860, after the death of her Poe-hating mother, she published *Edgar Poe and His Critics*, as a book. Her loyalty to Poe and her unselfish help to Poe biographers over the decades helped turn the tide of popular opinion against those who had depicted him as an amoral villain. Whitman's achievement, triumphing over Rufus Griswold's defamation of Poe, is one of the great vindications in literary history.

In the years between Poe's death in 1849, and 1860, Whitman was generally silent about her relationship with Poe. She relied upon friends to defend her honor — and Poe's. After the infamous "memoir" of Poe published by Rufus Griswold circulated wild and exaggerated stories about Poe and his conduct, her friend and fellow-poet William Pabodie published a letter in *The New York Tribune* in 1852, refuting some of Griswold's slanderous and distorted history. When Griswold threatened Pabodie with a libel suit in return, Pabodie defied him and published another letter showing further falsehoods in Griswold's writing. (It is a touching irony that Griswold's later life would be ruined by Mrs. Ellet, who had been Poe's principal nemesis among the New York literary women.)

At the time of writing *Edgar Poe and His Critics* (the copyright page of the book is 1859), Whitman was as yet unaware of Poe's attention to another woman during their courtship, and of his torment over that conflicted state, so she quite naïvely regarded herself as Poe's last love, in effect his literary widow. Although she writes as his "friend," there is psychologically, and no doubt socially, much more at stake for her. (The day-by-day convolutions of the Poe-Whitman romance and engagement are provided in *Last Flowers: The Romance and Poetry of Edgar Allan Poe and Sarah Helen Whitman*.)

<29>

SUFFRAGIST, ABOLITIONIST, AND SPIRITUALIST

WHITMAN ALSO WROTE on abolitionism and women's rights, and was honored for her work at New York suffragist conventions in 1870 and 1871. In 1868, she was elected vice-president of The Rhode Island Suffrage Association.[58] Her writings on this and other political topics have apparently never been researched.

Whitman endorsed a refined and individual brand of spiritualism. She attended the first recorded séance in Providence in September 1850, an event described as "not successful."[59] Whitman did attend other séances, and contributed several highly intellectual letters and essays on the subject to *The New York Tribune* and to *The Spiritual Telegraph*. Their texts can be found in Capron's 1855 book, and the author-enthusiast characterizes her thus: "Among the friends of the spiritual cause of Providence no one has exhibited more firmness, and none more readiness to defend in public and private the spiritual *theory* [emphasis mine] of these manifestations, than Mrs. Sarah Helen Whitman, the poetess. ... She always writes with vigor when reasoning on any subject, and does not forget to fortify herself with a strong array of facts."[60] Both Capron and Whitman seem eager to distance themselves from the gospel-based spiritualism that seemed to come all too easily to fanatical Protestants.

Essentially, Whitman nodded assent with the Christians only on the issue of the immortality of the soul. But *her* afterlife is the realm of Emerson's Over-Soul, more pagan than Christian — a place where lovers are reunited, justice prevails, and punishment — that favorite bugaboo of Puritans — is not even mentioned. It is a benevolent vision of a "here and now" survival of souls — a comforting and harmless dream. She makes it clear in her poetry that she rejects the smiting God — the Old Testament Jehovah whose shadow still darkened New England. The metaphysics of 19th century spiritualism has many aspects that resemble latter-day "New Age" movements, including a startling tolerance for diversity of behavior (including a strong "free love" component.)

Although much has been made of Whitman's involvement with mediumship, the veracity or accuracy of some of these claims seem suspect. Richard P. Benton, for example, describes Whitman as already involved in séances at the time of her romance with Poe, wearing a wooden coffin around her neck as a *memento mori*.[61] This somewhat trivializes and ridicules her — in 1848, no séance had as yet occurred in Providence, and in fact the table-tapping Spiritualist movement was then

---

58 Baker, p. 37.
59 Capron, p. 226.
60 Ibid, pp. 234-235.
61 Benton, p. 17.

<30>

just starting in upstate New York. Whitman's interests in 1848 were purely literary and metaphysical.

Spiritualists like to claim Whitman as a celebrity member of their movement, and there is a famous photo of her with her face covered in a dark veil, in "séance attire." Her recognition in the field is from her occasional correspondence and journalism; yet I could not find her name among officers or attendees at various spiritualist conventions held in the Northeast. It is also significant that, even though she hosted and attended séances, she makes no claims of mediumship in her poetry, or in her correspondence with Poe's biographer Ingram. Not one syllable of her work is "dictated" by spirits.

This makes Eliza Richard's fascinating essay on Poe, women poets and spiritualism all the more problematic. Richards has Poe "dictating" ideas and images into Whitman poems that were written before they met, and turns Whitman's passing allusion to spiritualism in *Edgar Poe and His Critics*[62] into a claim that Poe was a medium himself, astonishing since Poe died in 1849, and there is little in Poe's writing or criticism to suggest such an attitude. Poe's fiction *does* deal with souls that might transmigrate, but he does not summon ghosts. In his "The Facts in the Case of M. Valdemar," a dead man's body imprisons his dead soul, and the "news" from beyond is not soothing, but horrifying.

When Richards asserts that "Whitman experimented with spirit channeling after Poe's death to forge an echoic poetry haunted by his ghost"[63] she ignores the major poetry Whitman wrote before meeting Poe, and denigrates Whitman's own talents. Except in the parody poem, "The Raven," Whitman in fact never imitates Poe in style, and her influences are British, Continental, and Classical through and through.

In Whitman's defense of Poe's character, she is cautious to fend off charges of atheism against Poe, and she goes to awkward lengths when she attempts to accept Poe's "Eureka" with its idea of the absolute annihilation of the soul, even while re-interpreting it in more hopeful Spiritualist terms. Her first assessment of how radical Poe's ideas were

---

[62] Whitman, *Edgar Poe and His Critics,* p. 81.
[63] Richards, p. 270.

<31>

showed that she understood him entirely; her attempt to explain it away is not convincing. When she writes, "[H]is works are, as if unconsciously, filled with an overwhelming sense of the power and majesty of Deity; they are even dark with reverential awe," she is not describing the Poe she knew, nor the Poe his readers experience. Just as she attempted to shield the atheist Shelley, she would place her Athena-aegis before Poe.

WHITMAN AS LITERARY PERSONALITY

BY THE 1830S, Whitman had already settled into the eccentric style of dress and speech that a friend, Sarah S. Jacobs, describes thus: "deep-set eyes that gazed over and beyond, but never at you ... her movements were very rapid, and she seemed to flutter like a bird. ... Her spell was on you from the moment she appeared... when she spoke, her empire was assured. She was wise, she was witty ... her quick, generous sympathy, her sweet, unworldly nature, her ready recognition of whatever feeble talent, or inferior worth another person possessed"[64] She had also been blessed with, "a succession of adorers."[65] Of her style, Ticknor tells us further, "[S]he loved silken draperies, lace scarves and floating veils, and was always shod in dainty slippers. She invariably carried a fan to shield her eyes from any glare, and her pleasant rooms were never pervaded by anything but a subdued light."[66]

The latter-day figure of Isadora Duncan comes to mind in this description, not surprisingly. Whitman identified with Athena, so it was only natural that she should don the goddess's helmet for an occasional party. Poe biographers have made sport of Whitman's appearance, describing how friends trailed her on the street, retrieving for her the various scarves and parts of her costume that always seemed to be falling off. Her pagan garb was pretty daring in a very conventional city.

Although, with the publication of the non-Poe articles in this volume, as well as the publication of Whitman's poems, and her letter-exchange with Julia Deane Freeman,[67] we can now perceive her as a keen observer of letters and politics and a friend of artists, suffragists, spiritualists, poets and musicians. She was keen in her enthusiasms, yet reticent to lend her name to outlandish ideas and claims. Despite this, the prevailing impression of her is that of Poe's literary widow, as exemplified by this passage from Thomas Wentworth Higginson:

---

[64] Ticknor, pp. 5-6.
[65] Ticknor, p. 7.
[66] Ticknor, p. 15.
[67] Catherine Kunce. *The Correspondence of Sarah Helen Whitman and Julia Deane Freeman* (2014).

<32>

Whitman's home on Benevolent Street, later moved to Power Street.

I like best to think of Poe as associated with his gifted betrothed, Sarah Helen Whitman, whom I saw sometimes in her later years. She had outlived her early friends and loves and hopes, and perhaps her literary fame, such as it was; she had certainly outlived her recognized ties with Poe, and all but his memory. There she dwelt in her little suite of rooms, bearing youth still in her heart and her voice, and on her hair also, and in her dress. Her dimly-lighted parlor was always decked, here and there, with scarlet; and she sat, robed in white, her back always to the light, with a discreetly-tinted shadow over her still thoughtful and noble face. She seemed a person embalmed while still alive; it was as if she might dwell forever there, prolonging into an indefinite future the tradition of a poet's love; and when we remembered that she had been Poe's betrothed, that his kisses had touched her lips, that she still believed in him and was his defender, all criticism might well, for her sake, be disarmed, and her saintly life atone for his stormy and sad career.[68]

For many years, Whitman's parlor was home for "The Phalanstery," a circle of artists, writers and musicians who were the Bohemia of Providence. Enlivening this circle of friends were the many visitors, from literary lions to dilettantes, who craved admission into this charmed circle in an otherwise drab and disapproving city. No non-academic literary

---

[68] Thomas Wentworth Higginson. "Poe." *Literary World,* March 15, 1879.

<33>

person in Providence, then or since, has achieved a similar esteem and centrality.

After Mrs. Power's death in 1858, Whitman and her sister purchased another house on Benevolent Street (moved in the 20th century from its original location to 140 Power Street). The home was Whitman's literary salon, séance parlor, and a sanitarium for her sister.

Although the Power family, through its inheritances and mortgages, had a comfortable income, there are indications that Whitman and her sister lived at the edge of desperation in the final years, a *Grey Gardens* if not a *Whatever Happened to Baby Jane* finale. Biographer Ticknor submits these understated words from a family friend, William Whitman Bailey: "The lights were always turned down. Bits of drapery hung about, gave a weird and sombre aspect to the apartment. Mrs. Whitman always wore a veil indoors. . . . She had a trick of inverting her lamp shades so that a flood of light would be thrown upon and suffuse some particular painting or print, leaving the rest of the room in darkness. ... She was always youthful in feeling though then seventy years of age . . . One never realized that she was an old lady. . . . The life of the artist appealed to her. She certainly loved Bohemians, even if they lived as she did, from hand to mouth. It was certainly wonderful and pitiful to know upon how little she and Miss Power could exist. They kept no cook or maid, and ate like the gods when there was food, not always nectar and ambrosia, and when they felt like it. Her affection for her sister, so long afflicted, was most tender and pathetic."[69]

Susan Anna Power — who seems to have drifted, like her forebear Jemima Wilkinson, into religious mania — lived until December 8, 1877. Sarah Helen Whitman fell ill shortly after her sister's death, and was moved to the home of friends on Bowen Street, where she died June 27, 1878. Providence had lost its Muse.

---

[69] Ticknor, pp. 281-282.

<34>

The Providence Athenaeum, site of the Poe-Whitman romance.

SOME NOTES ABOUT THIS BOOK

FOR THE PRESENT volume, the original newspaper and journal articles by Whitman have been transcribed and corrected. The rather damaged microfilm of *The Providence Journal* was in a few places hard to decipher. The other journal articles were very legible as scanned by various contributing libraries, and most can be found on the Internet Archive.

Since Whitman's revisions for her intended posthumous collection never saw print, I have chosen to present the texts as they were seen by readers at the time of publication. I have silently corrected obvious typographic errors, italicized titles of literary works for stylistic consistency, and modernized spelling in a few instances. Here and there Whitman quotes from memory and errs slightly, and where found, I have so noted.

The text of *Edgar Poe and His Critics* is from Whitman's revised edition, published posthumously in 1885. Her changes to the 1860 first printing were largely changes in punctuation.

Whitman seldom provided source citations for her many quotations, allusions, and references. For this edition, I have attempted to locate and cite all literary sources, making in some places my best guess about the editions that might have been available to her. I have also added historical and biographical notes, and notes about locations and works of art. All the footnotes are mine, except for a handful that she included in her

<35>

poems, which I have marked as "—SHW." I have used my initials only in those few footnotes that are intermixed with Whitman's.

The result of this obsessive annotation project is to demonstrate the remarkable breadth of Whitman's reading in literature, philosophy, history, and science. It will also serve today's student or scholar of U.S. Antebellum literature by illuminating the truly trans-Atlantic and Continental nature of the literary life of the 1830s to 1870s. Few today, except for scholars of Transcendentalism or professional philosophers, will have read all the German philosophers Whitman cites. The notes also connect the complex web formed by the reading of Goethe and the Germans among Whitman, Margaret Fuller, Emerson, and other American writers.

This introductory essay sprang from work that I did at University of Rhode Island with Jane Berard, and also re-purposes some research that I did for my 1985 book, *Last Flowers: The Romance and Poetry of Edgar Allan Poe and Sarah Helen Whitman.* I have treated the Poe-Whitman romance only briefly in the essay in this volume, so I refer readers to *Last Flowers,* where I provide a day-by-day account of Poe's tormented courtship of Providence's Athena.

The essay has perhaps more than most readers ever want to know about six generations of the Power family preceding Sarah Helen Whitman, but I had several reasons for doing so. First, it lays the background social history of Providence so that the reader sees Whitman's family emerging from a Puritanical, slave-trading society that was painfully evolving into a manufacturing city full of immigrants. A rebellious younger generation fomented new ideas including abolition, expanded suffrage, and women's rights. The political explosion of the Dorr Rebellion involved Whitman's father as a combatant. Transcendentalism and spiritualism undermined traditional theology. By the end of the 1840s, Providence was ready for a Eureka moment. Seeing what Whitman pushed against, and what she pushed toward, makes us understand her more clearly. A cursory reading of Ticknor's biography might lead one to see Whitman as a universally beloved, eccentric woman who was "Poe's literary widow." It might be closer to the truth to say that she and her ideas were disapproved of by many in high places, and that she did what she did anyway, right up to the end. The common thread between this volume and the previous *Last Flowers,* is the treatment of the subject in her own time and place, making Providence almost as much the subject as its landmark poet.

The second reason to treat Whitman's history in such detail is simply that this subject was disposed of in a mere 13 pages in Ticknor's 1916 biography, and with the matter in hand, I felt that it might not be done again. Adding statistics about Providence in the 1850-1860 decade also

<36>

rounds out the picture of the literary life, such as it was, in Rhode Island, when she met Poe and sought to publish her first book.

Because Whitman's *Edgar Poe and His Critics* is a response to two texts by Rufus Griswold, I decided that today's reader would be served by providing the full text of Griswold's Poe obituary (signed "Ludwig") and pertinent excerpts from Griswold's "Memoir of the Author." While the latter text would have been available to Whitman's readers in 1860, since it was affixed to Poe's work, today's reader needs to read what Griswold wrote. It is not all slander, all the more tragic since Griswold as a critic had a keen sense of Poe's worth.

I located two additional pieces about Poe from Whitman's pen, which were not included in Baker's bibliography. The first is "Poe, Critic, and Hobby," from *The New York Daily Tribune* in 1875. The second is the "Introductory Letter" for Didier's *The Life and Letters of Edgar Allan Poe* in 1877. For the most exhaustive latter-day recollections about Poe, the reader is directed to the correspondence between Whitman and John Ingram in John Carl Miller's *Poe's Helen Remembers*.

I have annotated Whitman's essays on Shelley, Goethe, Emerson, Alcott, and Byron, citing, wherever possible, editions it is most likely that Whitman read. The article on Byronism, in which she takes on Harriet Beecher Stowe's call for censorship, and defends her childhood love of Byron, shows Whitman still fully-armed for literary battle in her 66th year.

Whitman's newspaper account of a visit to Bath, a literary travelogue rather than a critical essay, was included in Ticknor's 1916 biography as an example of her writing, and it seemed a worthy inclusion not only for atmosphere, but as a sample of her response to British writers and the landscape in which they worked. We want to know that she visited Beckford's Gothic hide-out and that she was hypnotized by a painting depicting the Rape of Europa.

In *Last Flowers*, I had selected the poems that Poe and Whitman wrote for or about one another, and then selected the best of the poems I imagined they might have read to one another. For this volume, I have made a wider selection, adding some of her nature poems as well as her translations from French and German. Of special note are "Noon," the central portion of her most ambitious poem, "Hours of Life"; "The Drama," her poem composed for the dedication of the Shakespeare Hall Theater in 1838; her six sonnets to Poe, and the haunting Poe tribute "The Raven"; and her classical poem, "Proserpine, On Earth, to Pluto in Hades." Whitman's poem to "Roger Williams," the founder of Rhode Island who fled to the then-uncharted locale to escape the wrath of Massachusetts Puritans, might seem at first glance to be a simple occasional poem composed for the Rhode Island Historical Society. It

<37>

turns out that the opening stanzas are concerned with the fresh-in-memory Dorr Rebellion, yielding a subversive text that parallels Roger Williams with the liberation-seeking Thomas Dorr. It may have been an opportunity for Whitman to throw a gauntlet in her father's memory.

Since Spiritualism rears its head throughout this book, I could not resist including, as an Appendix, a journalist's account of an 1855 "Spiritualist Picnic" in Flushing, Queens, New York. This account, reporting some of the frauds and absurdities of the popular movement, may help to explain why Whitman did not attend spiritualist conventions or associate her name with such doings.

I lived in Providence for many of the years between 1985 and 2015, so the researches for this book spanned many of those years, from my first discovery of Whitman's poetry at the Providence Athenaeum. The kind and tolerant librarians there premiered *Last Flowers* in 1985 with a grand event featuring actors recreating the Poe-Helen romance amid the very books they touched and read from. Several visits to the John Hay Library at Brown University, just yards up College Hill from the Athenaeum, yielded some peeks into the Sarah Helen Whitman materials there, and the library of the Rhode Island Historical Society yielded up the published Power family histories and useful city directories and census data. Without the devotion and diligent conservancy of these libraries, we should know far less about Whitman and her contemporaries.

The nature of scholarship has changed radically, however, since the advent of the Internet Archive, and other resources such as Google Books and the Hathi Trust, they in turn empowered by the willingness of public, university and research libraries to digitize and share rare books and old journals. Thanks to these resources, I was able to obtain full text, and most often a complete PDF facsimile, of nearly all the articles and books needed for this project.

Thanks are also due to Jane Berard, for her helpful comments on the earliest version of this introduction, and to David Wulff, for assistance in obtaining microfilm prints of articles from *The Providence Journal*.

This part is done. The rest of Sarah Helen Whitman's writing still awaits the efforts of a compiler and editor.

—*Brett Rutherford*
Pittsburgh, Pennsylvania
January, 2019

<38>

EDGAR ALLAN POE

DEATH OF E. A. POE (1849)
by "Ludwig" (Rufus Griswold)

◇————————————————————◇

EDGAR ALLAN POE is dead. He died in Baltimore the day before yesterday. This announcement will startle many, but few will be grieved by it. The poet was well known, personally or by reputation, in all this country; he had readers in England, and in several of the states of Continental Europe; but he had few or no friends; and the regrets for his death will be suggested principally by the consideration that in him literary art has lost one of its most brilliant but erratic stars.

The family of Mr. Poe — we learn from Griswold's *Poets and Poetry of America,* from which a considerable portion of the facts in this notice are derived — was one of the oldest and most respectable in Baltimore. David Poe, his paternal grandfather, was a Quartermaster-General in the Maryland line during the Revolution, and the intimate friend of Lafayette, who, during his last visit to the United States, called personally upon the General's widow, and tendered her acknowledgments or the services rendered to him by her husband. His great-grandfather, John Poe, married in England, Jane, a daughter of Admiral James McBride, noted in British naval history, and claiming kindred with some of the most illustrious English families. His father and mother, — both of whom were in some way connected with the theater, and lived as precariously as their more gifted and more eminent son — died within a few weeks of each other, of consumption, leaving him an orphan, at two years of age. Mr. John Allan, a wealthy gentleman of Richmond, Virginia, took a fancy to him, and persuaded his grandfather to suffer him to adopt him. He was brought up in Mr. Allan's family; and as that gentleman had no other children, he was regarded as his son and heir. In 1816 he accompanied Mr. and Mrs. Allan to Great Britain, visited every portion of it, and afterward passed four or five years in a school kept at Stoke Newington, near London, by Rev. Dr. Bransby. He returned to America in 1822, and in 1825 went to the Jefferson University, at Charlottesville, in Virginia, where he led a very dissipated life, the manners of the college being at that time extremely dissolute. He took the first honors, however, and went home greatly in debt. Mr. Allan refused to pay some of his debts of honor, and he hastily quitted the country on a Quixotic expedition to join the Greeks, then struggling for liberty. He did not reach his original destination, however, but made his way to St. Petersburg, in Russia, when he became involved in difficulties, from which he was extricated by the late Mr. Henry Middleton, the American Minister at that Capital. He returned home in 1829, and immediately afterward entered the Military Academy at West-Point. In about eighteen months

<41>

from that time, Mr. Allan, who had lost his first wife while Mr. Poe was in Russia, married again. He was sixty-five years of age, and the lady was young; Poe quarreled with her, and the veteran husband, taking the part of his wife, addressed him an angry letter, which was answered in the same spirit. He died soon after, leaving an infant son the heir to his property, and bequeathed Poe nothing.

The army, in the opinion of the young cadet, was not a place for a poor man; so he left West-Point abruptly, and determined to maintain himself by authorship. He printed, in 1827, a small volume of poems, most of which were written in early youth. Some of these poems are quoted in a review by Margaret Fuller, in *The Tribune* in 1846, and are justly regarded as among the most wonderful exhibitions of the precocious development of genius. They illustrated the character of his abilities, and justified his anticipations of success. For a considerable time, however, though he wrote readily and brilliantly, his contributions to the journals attracted little attention, and his hopes of gaining a livelihood by the profession of literature were nearly ended at length in sickness, poverty and despair. But in 1831, the proprietor of a weekly gazette, in Baltimore, offered two premiums, one for the best story in prose, and the other for the best poem. — In due time Poe sent in two articles, and he waited anxiously for the decision. One of the Committee was the accomplished author of "Horseshoe Robinson," John P. Kennedy, and his associates were scarcely less eminent than he for wit and critical sagacity. Such matters are usually disposed of in a very off hand way: Committees to award literary prizes drink to the payer's health, in good wines, over the unexamined MSS, which they submit to the discretion of publishers, with permission to use their names in such a way as to promote the publisher's advantage. So it would have been in this case, but that one of the Committee, taking up a little book in such exquisite calligraphy as to seem like one of the finest issues of the press of Putnam, was tempted to read several pages, and being interested, he summoned the attention of the company to the half-dozen compositions in the volume. It was unanimously decided that the prizes should be paid to the first of geniuses who had written legibly. Not another MS. was unfolded. Immediately the 'confidential envelope' was opened, and the successful competitor was found to bear the scarcely known name of Poe.

The next day the publisher called to see Mr. Kennedy, and gave him an account of the author that excited his curiosity and sympathy, and caused him to request that he should be brought to his office. Accordingly he was introduced: the prize money had not yet been paid, and he was in the costume in which he had answered the advertisement of his good fortune. Thin, and pale even to ghastliness, his whole appearance indicated sickness and the utmost destitution. A tattered frock-coat

<42>

concealed the absence of a shirt, and the ruins of boots disclosed more than the want of stockings. But the eyes of the young man were luminous with intelligence and feeling, and his voice, and conversation, and manners, all won upon the lawyer's regard. Poe told his history, and his ambition, and it was determined that he should not want means for a suitable appearance in society, nor opportunity for a just display of his abilities in literature. Mr. Kennedy accompanied him to a clothing store, and purchased for him a respectable suit, with changes of linen, and sent him to a bath, from which he returned with the suddenly regained bearing of a gentleman.

The late Mr. Thomas W. White had then recently established *The Southern Literary Messenger,* at Richmond, and upon the warm recommendation of Mr. Kennedy, Poe was engaged, at a small salary — we believe of $500 a year — to be its editor. He entered upon his duties with letters full of expressions of the warmest gratitude to his friends in Baltimore, who in five or six weeks were astonished to learn that with characteristic recklessness of consequences, he was hurriedly married to a girl as poor as himself. Poe continued in this situation for about a year and a half, in which he wrote many brilliant articles, and raised the *Messenger* to the first rank of literary periodicals.

He next moved to Philadelphia, to assist William E. Burton in the editorship of the *Gentleman's Magazine,* a miscellany that in 1840 was merged in *Graham's Magazine,* of which Poe became one of the principal writers, particularly in criticism, in which his papers attracted much attention, by their careful and skillful analysis, and generally caustic severity. At this period, however, he appeared to have been more ambitious of securing distinction in romantic fiction, and a collection of his compositions in this department, published in 1841, under the title of *Tales of the Grotesque and Arabesque,* established his reputation for ingenuity, imagination and extraordinary power in tragical narration.

Near the end of 1844 Poe removed to New-York, where he conducted for several months a literary miscellany called *The Broadway Journal.* In 1845 he published a volume of "Tales" in Wiley and Putnam's Library of American Books, and in the same series a collection of his poems. Besides these volumes he was the author of *Arthur Gordon Pym,* a romance; "A New Theory of Versification;" *Eureka,* an essay on the spiritual and material universe, a work which he wished to have "judged as a poem; and several extended series of papers in the periodicals, the most noticeable of which are "Marginalia," embracing opinions of books and authors; "Secret Writing," "Autography," and "Sketches of the Literati of New-York."

His wife died in 1847, at Fordham, near this City, and some of our readers will remember the paragraphs in the papers of the time, upon

<43>

his destitute condition. His wants were supplied by the liberality of a few individuals. We remember that Col. Webb collected in a few moments fifty or sixty dollars for him at the Union Club; Mr. Lewis, of Brooklyn, sent a similar sum from one of the Courts, in which he was engaged when he saw the statement of the poet's poverty; and others illustrated in the same manner the effect of such an appeal to the popular heart.

Since that time Mr. Poe has lived quietly, and with an income from his literary labors sufficient for his support. A few weeks ago he proceeded to Richmond in Virginia, where he lectured upon the poetical character, &c.; and it was understood by some of his correspondents here that he was this week to be married, most advantageously, to a lady of that city: a widow, to whom he had been previously engaged while a student in the University.

THE CHARACTER OF Mr. Poe we cannot attempt to describe in this very hastily written article. We can but allude to some of its more striking phases. His conversation was at times almost supra-mortal in its eloquence. His voice was modulated with astonishing skill, and his large and variably expressive eyes looked repose[d] or shot fiery tumult into theirs who listened, while his own face glowed, or was changeless in pallor, as his imagination quickened his blood or drew it back frozen to his heart. His imagery was from the worlds which no mortal can see but with the vision of genius. Suddenly starting from a proposition exactly and sharply defined in terms of utmost simplicity and clearness, he rejected the forms of customary logic, and by a crystalline process of accretion, built up his ocular demonstrations in forms of gloomiest and ghastliest grandeur, or in those of the most airy and delicious beauty — so minutely, and distinctly, yet so rapidly, that the attention which was yielded to him was chained till it stood among his wonderful creations — till he himself dissolved the spell, and brought his hearers back to common and base existence, by vulgar fancies or by exhibitions of the ignoblest passion.

He was at all times a dreamer — dwelling in ideal realms — in heaven or hell — peopled with creatures and the accidents of his brain. He walked the streets, in madness or melancholy, with lips moving in indistinct curses, or with eyes upturned in passionate prayers, (never for himself, for he felt, or professed to feel, that he was already damned), but for their happiness who at the moment were objects of his idolatry — or, with his glances introverted to a heart gnawed with anguish, and with a face shrouded in gloom, he would brave the wildest storms; and all night, with drenched garments and arms wildly beating the winds and rains, he would speak as if to spirits that at such times only could be evoked by him from the Aidenn close by whose portals his disturbed soul sought

<44>

to forget the ills to which his constitution subjugated him — close by that Aidenn where were those he loved — the Aidenn which he might never see, but in fitful glimpses, as its gates opened to receive the less fiery and more happy natures whose destiny to sin did not involve the doom of death.

He seemed, except when some fitful pursuit subjected his will and engrossed his faculties, always to bear the memory of some controlling sorrow. The remarkable poem of The Raven was probably much more nearly than has been supposed, even by those who were very intimate with him, a reflexion and an echo of his own history. He was that bird's

> ——— Unhappy master,
> Whom unmerciful disaster
> Followed fast and followed faster,
> Till his songs the burden bore —
> Till the dirges of his hope, the
> Melancholy burden bore
> Of "Nevermore," of "Nevermore."

Every genuine author in a greater or less degree leaves in his works, whatever their design, traces of his personal character: elements of his immortal being, in which the individual survives the person. While we read the pages of "The Fall of the House of Usher," or of "Mesmeric Revelations," we see in the solemn and stately gloom which invests one, and in the subtle metaphysical analysis of both, indications of the idiosyncrasies, — of what was most remarkable and peculiar — in the author's intellectual nature. But we see here only the better phases of this nature, only the symbols of his juster action, for his harsh experience had deprived him of all faith in man or woman. He had made up his mind upon the numberless complexities of the social world, and the whole system with him was an imposture. This conviction gave a direction to his shrewd and naturally unamiable character. Still, though he regarded society as composed altogether of villains, the sharpness of his intellect was not of that kind which enabled him to cope with villainy, while it continually caused him by overshots to fail of the success of honesty. He was in many respects like Francis Vivian in Bulwer's novel of *The Caxtons*. "Passion, in him, comprehended many of the worst emotions which militate against human happiness. You could not contradict him, but you raised quick choler; you could not speak of wealth, but his cheek paled with gnawing envy. The astonishing natural advantages of this poor boy — his beauty, his readiness, the daring spirit that breathed around him like a fiery atmosphere — had raised his constitutional self-confidence into an arrogance that turned his very claims to admiration into prejudice against him. Irascible, envious — bad enough, but not the worst, for these

<45>

salient angles were all varnished over with a cold repellant cynicism, his passions vented themselves in sneers. There seemed to him no moral susceptibility; and, what was more remarkable in a proud nature, little or nothing of the true point of honor. He had, to a morbid excess, that desire to rise which is vulgarly called ambition, but no wish for the esteem or love of his species; only the hard wish to succeed — not shine, not serve — succeed, that he might have the right to despise a world which galled his self conceit."[1]

We have suggested the influence of his aims and vicissitudes upon his literature. It was more conspicuous in his later than his earlier writing. Nearly all that he wrote in the last two or three years — including much of his best poetry — was in some sense biographical; in draperies of his imagination, those who had taken the trouble to trace his steps, could perceive, but slightly concealed, the figure of himself.

There are perhaps some of our readers who will understand the allusions of the following beautiful poem. Mr. Poe presented it in MS. to the writer of these paragraphs, just before he left New-York recently, remarking that it was the last thing he had written:

ANNABEL LEE.

It was many and many a year ago,
In a kingdom by the sea
That a maiden there lived whom you may know
By the name of ANNABEL LEE;
And this maiden she lived with no other thought
Than to love and be loved by me.

I was a child and she was a child,
In this kingdom by the sea.
But we loved with a love that was more than love —
I and my ANNABEL LEE —
With a love that the wingèd seraphs of heaven
Coveted her and me.

And this was the reason that, long ago,
In this kingdom by the sea,
A wind blew out of a cloud, chilling
My beautiful ANNABEL LEE;
So that her highborn kinsmen came
And bore her away from me,

---

[1]Bulwer-Lytton. *The Caxtons,* pp. 330-331.

<46>

To shut her up in a sepulchre
In this kingdom by the sea.
The angels, not half so happy in heaven,
Went envying her and me —
Yes! — that was the reason (as all men know,
In this kingdom by the sea)
That the wind came out of the cloud by night,
Chilling and killing my ANNABEL LEE.

But our love it was stronger by far than the love
Of those who were older than we —
Of many far wiser than we —
And neither the angels in heaven above,
Nor the demons down under the sea,
Can ever dissever my soul from the soul
Of the beautiful ANNABEL LEE:

For the moon never beams, without bringing me dreams
Of the beautiful ANNABEL LEE;
And the stars never rise but I feel the bright eyes
Of the beautiful ANNABEL LEE,

And so, all the night-tide, I lie down by the side
Of my darling — my darling — my life and my bride,
In her sepulchre there by the sea —
In her tomb by the sounding sea.

WE MUST OMIT any particular criticism of Mr. Poe's works. As a writer of tales it will be admitted generally, that he was scarcely surpassed in ingenuity of construction or effective painting. As a critic, he was more remarkable as a dissecter of sentences than as a commentater upon ideas: he was little better than a carping grammarian. As a poet, he will retain a most honorable rank. Of his "Raven," Mr. Willis observes, that in his opinion "it is the most effective single example of fugitive poetry ever published in this country, and is unsurpassed in English poetry for subtle conception, masterly ingenuity of versification, and consistent sustaining of imaginative lift." In poetry, as in prose, he was most successful in the metaphysical treatment of the passions. His poems are constructed with wonderful ingenuity, and finished with consummate art. They illustrate a morbid sensitiveness of feeling, a shadowy and gloomy imagination, and a taste almost faultless in the apprehension of that sort of beauty most agreeable to his temper.

<47>

We have not learned of the circumstance of his death. It was sudden, and from the fact that it occurred in Baltimore, it is to be presumed that he was on his return to New-York. "After life's fitful fever he sleeps well."

— LUDWIG

<48>

Excerpts from
MEMOIR OF THE AUTHOR (1850)
by Rufus Griswold

◇————————————————————◇

IN 1822, HE returned to the United States, and after passing a few months at an Academy in Richmond, he entered the University at Charlottesville, where he led a very dissipated life; the manners which then prevailed there were extremely dissolute, and he was known as the wildest and most reckless student of his class; but his unusual opportunities, and the remarkable ease with which he mastered the most difficult studies kept him all the while in the first rank for scholarship, and he would have graduated with the highest honors, had not his gambling, intemperance, and other vices, induced his expulsion from the university.

At this period he was noted for feats of hardihood, strength and activity, and, on one occasion, in a hot day of June, he swam from Richmond to Warwick, seven miles and a half, against a tide running probably from two to three miles an hour. He was expert at fence, had some skill in drawing, and was a ready and eloquent conversationist and declaimer.

His allowance of money while at Charlottesville had been liberal, but he quitted the place very much in debt, and when Mr. Allan refused to accept some of the drafts with which he had paid losses in gaming, he wrote to him an abusive letter, quitted his house, and soon after left the country with the Quixotic intention of joining the Greeks, then in the midst of their struggle with the Turks. He never reached his destination, and we know but little of his adventures in Europe for nearly a year. By the end of this time he had made his way to St. Petersburgh, and our Minister, in that capital, the late Mr. Henry Middleton, of South Carolina, was summoned one morning to save him from penalties incurred in a drunken debauch. Through Mr. Middleton's kindness he was set at liberty and enabled to return to this country.

His meeting with Mr. Allan was not very cordial, but that gentleman declared himself willing to serve him any way that should seem judicious; and when Poe expressed some anxiety to enter the Military Academy, he induced Chief Justice Marshall, Andrew Stevenson, General Scott, and other eminent persons, to sign an application which secured his appointment to a scholarship in that institution. . . .

For weeks the cadet applied himself with much assiduity to his studies, and he became at once a favorite with his mess and with the officers and professors of the Academy; but his habits of dissipation were

<49>

renewed; he neglected his duties and disobeyed orders; and in ten months from his matriculation he was cashiered.

He went again to Richmond, and was received into the family of Mr. Allan, who was disposed still to be his friend, and in the event of his good behavior to treat him as a son; but it soon became necessary to close his doors against him forever. According to Poe's own statement he ridiculed the marriage of his patron with Miss Paterson, and had a quarrel with her; but a different story, scarcely suitable for repetition here, was told by the friends of the other party. Whatever the circumstances, they parted in anger, and Mr. Allan from that time declined to see or in any way to assist him. Mr. Allan died in the spring of 1834, in the fifty-fourth year of his age, leaving three children to share his property, of which not a mill was bequeathed to Poe. . . .

His contributions to the journals attracted little attention, and his hopes of gaining a living in this way being disappointed, he enlisted in the army as a private soldier. How long he remained in the service I have not been able to ascertain. He was recognized by officers who had known him at West Point, and efforts were made, privately, but with prospects of success, to obtain for him a commission, when it was discovered by his friends that he had deserted. . . .

On receiving a month's salary he gave himself up to habits which only necessity had restrained at Baltimore. For a week he was in a condition of brutish drunkenness, and Mr. White dismissed him. When he became sober, however, he had no resource but in reconciliation, and he wrote letters and induced acquaintances to call upon Mr. White with professions of repentance and promise of reformation. . . . A new contract was arranged, but Poe's irregularities frequently interrupted the kindness and finally exhausted the patience of his generous though methodical employer . . .

While in Richmond, with an income of but five hundred dollars a year, he had married his cousin, Virginia Clemm, a very amiable and lovely girl, who was as poor as himself, and little fitted, except by her gentle temper, to be the wife of such a person. He went from Richmond to Baltimore, and after a short time, to Philadelphia, and to New-York. . . . An awakened ambition and the healthful influence of a conviction that his works were appreciated, and that his fame was increasing, led him for a while to cheerful views of life, and to regular habits of conduct. He wrote to a friend, the author of "Edge Hill,"[2] in Richmond, that he

---

[2] James Ewell Heath (1792-1862), poet, novelist, playwright, historian, author of *Edge-Hill, or, The Family of the Fitzroyals* (1828). He was the first editor of the *Southern Literary Messenger*.

<50>

had quite overcome "the seductive and dangerous besetment" by which he had so often been prostrated, and to another friend that, incredible as it might seem, he had become a model of temperance," and of "other virtues," which it had sometimes been difficult for him to practise. Before the close of the summer, however, he relapsed into his former courses, and for weeks was regardless of everything but a morbid and insatiable appetite for the means of intoxication. . . .

I T WAS WHILE he resided in Philadelphia that I became acquainted with him. His manner, except during his fits of intoxication, was very quiet and gentlemanly; he was usually dressed with simplicity and elegance; and when once he sent for me to visit him, during a period of illness caused by protracted and anxious watching at the side of his sick wife, I was impressed by the singular neatness and the air of refinement in his home. It was in a small house, in one of the pleasant and silent neighborhoods far from the centre of the town, and though slightly and cheaply furnished, everything in it was so tasteful and so fitly disposed that it seemed altogether suitable for a man of genius. For this and for most of the comforts he enjoyed in his brightest as in his darkest years, he was chiefly indebted to his mother-in-law, who loved him with more than maternal devotion and constancy.

In New-York Poe entered upon a new sort of life. Heretofore, from the commencement of his literary career, he had resided in provincial towns. Now he was in a metropolis, and with a reputation which might have served as a passport to any society he could desire. For the first time he was received into circles capable of both the appreciation and the production of literature. He added to his fame soon after he came to the city by the publication of that remarkable composition "The Raven," of which Mr. Willis has observed that in his opinion "it is the most effective single example of fugitive poetry ever published in this country, and is unsurpassed in English poetry for subtle conception, masterly ingenuity of versification, and consistent sustaining of imaginative lift," and by that of one of the most extraordinary instances of the naturalness of detail — the verisimilitude of minute narrative — for which he was preeminently distinguished, his "Mesmeric Revelation," purporting to be the last conversation of a somnambule, held just before death with his magnetizer; which was followed by the yet more striking exhibition of abilities in the same way, entitled "The facts in the Case of M. Valdemar," in which the subject is represented as having been mesmerized *in articulo mortis*. These pieces were reprinted throughout the literary and philosophical world, in nearly all languages, everywhere causing sharp and curious speculation, and where readers could be persuaded that they were fables, challenging a reluctant but genuine admiration. . . .

<51>

Poe's cottage at Fordham, as it was in 1874.

As the autumn of 1846 wore on Poe's habits of frequent intoxication and big inattention to the means of support reduced him to much more than common destitution. He was now living at Fordham, several miles from the city, so that his necessities were not generally known even among his acquaintances; but when the dangerous illness of his wife was added to his misfortunes, and his dissipation and accumulated causes of anxiety had prostrated all his own energies, the subject was introduced into the journals. The "Express" said:

> We regret to learn that Edgar A. Poe and his wife are both dangerously ill with the consumption, and that the hand of misfortune lies heavy upon their temporal affairs. We are sorry to mention the fact that they are so far reduced as to be barely able to obtain the necessaries of life. This is indeed a hard lot, and we hope that the friends and admirers of Mr. Poe will come promptly to his assistance in his bitterest hour of need.

. . .

<52>

[From a letter Poe sent to Willis for publication:]

Of the facts, that I myself have been long and dangerously ill, and that my illness has been a well understood thing among my brethren of the press, the best evidence is afforded by the innumerable paragraphs of personal and of literary abuse with which I have been latterly assailed. This matter, however, will remedy itself. At the very first blush of my new prosperity, the gentlemen who toadied me in the old, will recollect themselves and toady me again. You, who know me, will comprehend that I speak of these things only as having served, in a measure, to lighten the gloom of unhappiness by a gentle and not unpleasant sentiment of mingled pity, merriment and contempt. That, as the inevitable consequence of so long an illness, I have been in want of money, it would be folly in me to deny — but that I have ever materially suffered from privation, beyond the extent of my capacity for suffering, is not altogether true. That I am 'without friends' is a gross calumny, which I am sure you never could have believed, and which a thousand noble hearted men would have good right never to forgive me for permitting to pass unnoticed and undenied. Even in the city of New York I could have no difficulty in naming a hundred persons, to each of whom — when the hour for speaking had arrived — I could and would have applied for aid with unbounded confidence, and with absolutely no sense of humiliation. I do not think, my dear Willis, that there is any need of my saying more. I am getting better, and may add — if it be any comfort to my enemies — that I have little fear of getting worse. The truth is, I have a great deal to do; and I have made up my mind not to die till it is done. Sincerely yours. December 30th, 1846. EDGAR A. POE.

This was written for effect. He had not been ill a great while, nor dangerously at all; there was no literary or personal abuse of him in the journals; and his friends in town had been applied to for money until their patience was nearly exhausted. His wife, however, was very sick, and in a few weeks she died. . . .

<53>

FOR NEARLY A year Mr. Poe was not often before the public, but he was as industrious, perhaps, as he had been at any time, and early in 1848 advertisement was made of his intention to deliver several lectures, with a view to obtain an amount of money sufficient to establish his so-long-contemplated monthly magazine. His first lecture — and only one at this period — was given at the Society Library, in New-York, on the ninth of February, and was upon the Cosmogony of the Universe; it was attended by an eminently intellectual auditory, and the reading of it occupied about two hours and a half; it was what he afterwards published under the title of "Eureka, a Prose Poem."

To the composition of this work he brought his subtlest and highest capacities, in their most perfect development. Denying that the arcana of the universe can be explored by induction, but informing his imagination with the various results of science, he entered with unhesitating boldness, though with no guide but the divinest instinct, — that sense of beauty, in which our great Edwards recognises the flowering of all truth — into the sea of speculation, and there built up of according laws and their phenomena, as under the influence of a scientific inspiration, his theory of Nature. I will not attempt the difficult task of condensing his propositions; to be apprehended they must be studied in his own terse and simple language; but in this we have a summary of that which he regards as fundamental: "The law which we call Gravity," he says, "exists on account of matter having been radiated, at its origin, atomically, into a limited sphere of space, from one, individual, unconditional, irrelative, and absolute Particle Proper, by the sole process in which it was possible to satisfy, at the same time, the two conditions, radiation and equable distribution throughout the sphere — that is to say, by a force varying in direct proportion with the squares of the distances between the radiated atoms, respectively, and the particular centre of radiation."

Poe was thoroughly persuaded that he had discovered the great secret; that the propositions of "Eureka" were true; and he was wont to talk of the subject with a sublime and electrical enthusiasm which they cannot have forgotten who were familiar with him at the period of its publication. He felt that an author known solely by his adventures in the lighter literature, throwing down the gauntlet to professors of science, could not expect absolute fairness, and he had no hope but in discussions led by wisdom and candor. Meeting me, he said, "Have you read *Eureka*?" I answered "Not yet: I have just glanced at the notice of it by Willis, who thinks it contains no more fact than fantasy, and I am sorry to see — sorry if it be true — suggests that it corresponds in tone with that gathering of sham and obsolete hypotheses addressed to fanciful tyros, the *Vestiges of Creation*;[3] and our good and really wise friend Bush, whom

---

[3] Robert Chambers. *Vestiges of the Natural History of Creation.* Published

<54>

you will admit to be of all the professors, in temper one of the most habitually just, thinks that while you may have guessed very shrewdly, it would not be difficult to suggest many difficulties in the way of your doctrine." "It is by no means ingenuous," he replied, "to hint that there are such difficulties, and yet to leave them unsuggested. I challenge the investigation of every point in the book. I deny that there are any difficulties which I have not met and overthrown. Injustice is done me by the application of this word 'guess:' I have assumed nothing and proved all." In his preface he wrote: "To the few who love me and whom I love; to those who feel rather than to those who think; to the dreamers and those who put faith in dreams as in the only realities — I offer this book of truths, not in the character of Truth-Teller, but for the beauty that abounds in its truth: constituting it true. To these I present the composition as an Art-Product alone: — let us say as a Romance; or, if it be not urging too lofty a claim, as a Poem. What I here propound is true: therefore it cannot die: or if by any means it be now trodden down so that it die, it will rise again to the life everlasting."

When I read *Eureka* I could not help but think it immeasurably superior as an illustration of genius to the *Vestiges of Creation*; and as I admired the poem, (except the miserable attempt at humor in what purports to be a letter found in a bottle floating on the *Mare tenebrarum*,) so I regretted its pantheism, which is not necessary to its main design.
. . .

FROM THIS TIME Poe did not write much; he had quarreled with the conductors of the chief magazines for which he had previously written, and they no longer sought his assistance. . . . His name was now frequently associated with that of one of the most brilliant women of New England, and it was publicly announced that they were to be married. He had first seen her on his way from Boston, when he visited that city to deliver a poem before the Lyceum there. Restless, near the midnight, he wandered from his hotel near where she lived, until he saw her walking in a garden. He related the incident afterward in one of his most exquisite poems, ["To Helen"] worthy of himself, of her, and of the most exalted passion.

---

anonymously in London in 1844, this was a speculative work on natural history and philosophy, containing some ideas that anticipated the work of Charles Darwin. The work not only offended religious sensibilities, but was also rejected by many scientists. Although not rejecting the idea of a Creator, Chambers' work insists that life passed through many changes over a long period of time, including the extinction of species. The American edition prompted an April, 1845 review in *North American Review* by Francis Bowen. Poe's *Eureka* was published in 1848.

<55>

They were not married, and the breaking of the engagement affords a striking illustration of his character. He said to an acquaintance in New-York, who congratulated with him upon the prospect of his union with a person of so much genius and so many virtues — "It is a mistake: I am not going to be married." "Why, Mr. Poe, I understand that the banns have been published." "I cannot help what you have heard, my dear Madam: but mark me, I shall not marry her." He left town the same evening, and the next day was reeling through the streets of the city which was the lady's home, and in the evening — that should have been the evening before the bridal — in his drunkenness he committed at her house such outrages as made necessary a summons of the police. Here was no insanity leading to indulgence: he went from New-York with a determination thus to induce an ending of the engagement; and he succeeded.

Sometime in August, 1849, Mr. Poe left New-York for Virginia. In Philadelphia he encountered persons who had been his associates in dissipations while he lived there, and for several days he abandoned himself entirely to the control of his worst appetites. When his money was all spent, and the disorder of his dress evinced the extremity of his recent intoxication, he asked in charity means for the prosecution of his journey to Richmond. There, after a few days, he joined a temperance society, and his conduct showed the earnestness of his determination to reform his life. He delivered in some of the principal towns of Virginia two lectures, which were well attended, and renewing his acquaintance with a lady whom he had known in his youth, he was engaged to marry her, and wrote to his friends that he should pass the remainder of his days among the scenes endeared by all his pleasantest recollections of youth.

On Thursday, the fourth of October, he set out for New-York, to fulfil a literary engagement, and to prepare for his marriage. Arriving in Baltimore he gave his trunk to a porter, with directions to convey it to the cars which were to leave in an hour or two for Philadelphia, and went into a tavern to obtain some refreshment. Here he met acquaintances who invited him to drink; all his resolutions and duties were soon forgotten; in a few hours he was in such a state as is commonly induced only by long-continued intoxication; after a night of insanity and exposure, he was carried to a hospital; and there, on the evening of Sunday, the seventh of October, 1849, he died, at the age of thirty-eight years.

It is a melancholy history. No author of as much genius had ever in this country as much unhappiness; that Poe's unhappiness was in an unusual degree the result of infirmities of nature, or of voluntary faults in conduct. A writer who evidently knew him well, and who comes before

<56>

us in *The Southern Literary Messenger* as his defender, is "compelled to admit that the blemishes in his life were effects of character rather than of circumstances." How this character might have been modified by a judicious education of all his faculties I leave for the decision of others, but it will so evident to those who read this biography that the unchecked freedom of his earlier years was as unwise as its results were unfortunate. . . .

THE CHARACTER OF Mr. Poe's genius has been so recently and so admirably discussed by Mr. Lowell, with whose opinions on the subject I for the most part agree, that I shall say but little of it here, having already extended this notice beyond the limits at first designed. There is a singular harmony between his personal and his literary qualities. St. Pierre, who seemed to be without any nobility in his own nature, in his writings appeared to be moved only by the finest and highest impulses. Poe exhibits scarcely any virtue in either his life or his writings. Probably there is not another instance in the literature of our language in which so much has been accomplished without a recognition or a manifestation of conscience. Seated behind the intelligence, and directing it, according to its capacities, Conscience is the parent of whatever is absolutely and unquestionably beautiful in art as well as in conduct. It touches the creations of the mind and they have life; without it they have never, in the range of its just action, the truth and naturalness which are approved by universal taste or in enduring reputation. In Poe's works there is constantly displayed the most touching melancholy, the most extreme and terrible despair, but never reverence or remorse. . . .

One of the qualities upon which Poe prided himself was his humor, and he has left us a large number of compositions in this department, but except a few paragraphs in his "Marginalia," scarcely anything which it would not have been injurious to his reputation to republish. His realm was on the shadowy confines of human experience, among the abodes of crime, gloom, and horror, and there he delighted to surround himself with images of beauty and of terror, to raise his solemn palaces and towers and spires in a night upon which should rise no sun. His minuteness of detail, refinement of reasoning, and propriety and power of language — the perfect keeping (to borrow a phrase from another domain of art) and apparent good faith with which he managed the evocation and exhibition of his strange and spectral and revolting creations — gave him an astonishing mastery over his readers, so that his books were closed as one would lay aside the nightmare or the spells of opium. The analytical subtlety evinced in his works has frequently been overestimated, as I have before observed, because it has not been sufficiently considered that his mysteries were composed with the express design of being dissolved.

<57>

When Poe attempted the illustration of the profounder operations of the mind, as displayed in written reason or in real action, he frequently failed entirely.

In poetry, as in prose, he was eminently successful in the metaphysical treatment of the passions. His poems are constructed with wonderful ingenuity, and finished with consummate art. They display a sombre and weird imagination, and a taste almost faultless in the apprehension of that sort of beauty which was most agreeable to his temper. But they evince little genuine feeling, and less of that spontaneous ecstasy which gives its freedom, smoothness and naturalness to immortal verse. His own account of the composition of "The Raven," discloses his methods — the absence of all impulse, and the absolute control of calculation and mechanism. That curious analysis of the processes by which he wrought would be incredible if from another hand.

He was not remarkably original in invention. Indeed some of his plagiarisms are scarcely paralleled for their audacity in all literary history: For instance, in his tale of "The Pit and the Pendulum," the complicated machinery upon which the interest depends is borrowed from a story entitled "Vivenrio, or Italian Vengeance," by the author of "The First and Last Dinner," in *Blackwood's Magazine*.[4] And I remember having been shown by Mr. Longfellow, several years ago, a series of papers which constitute a demonstration that Mr. Poe was indebted to him for the idea of "The Haunted Palace," one of the most admirable of his poems, which he so pertinaciously asserted had been used by Mr. Longfellow in the production of his "Beleaguered City." Mr. Longfellow's poem was written two or three years before the first publication of that by Poe, and it was during a portion of this time in Poe's possession; but it was not printed, I believe, until a few weeks after the appearance of "The Haunted Palace." "It would be absurd," as Poe himself said many times, "to believe the similarity of these pieces entirely accidental." This was the first cause of all that malignant criticism which for so many years he carried on against Mr. Longfellow. In his "Marginalia" he borrowed largely especially from Coleridge, and I have omitted in the republication of these papers, numerous paragraphs which were rather compiled than borrowed from one of the profoundest and wisest of our own scholars.

In criticism, as Mr. Lowell justly remarks, Mr. Poe had "a scientific precision and coherence of logic;" he had remarkable dexterity in the dissection of sentences; but he rarely ascended from the particular to the general, from subjects to principles: he was familiar with the microscope but never looked through the telescope. His criticisms are of value to the degree in which they are demonstrative, but his unsupported assertions

---

[4] The author alluded to is William Mudford, but the story which Poe may have read and imitated is a different one, "The Iron Shroud."

<58>

and opinions were so apt to be influenced by friendship or enmity, by the desire to please or the fear to offend, or by his constant ambition to surprise, or produce a sensation, that they should be received in all cases with distrust of their fairness. . . .

AFTER HAVING, IN no ungenerous spirit, presented the chief facts in Mr. Poe's history, not designedly exaggerating his genius, which none held in higher admiration, not bringing into bolder relief than was just and necessary his infirmities, I am glad to offer a portraiture of some of his social qualities, equally beautiful, and — so changeable and inconsistent was the man — as for as it goes, truthful. Speaking of him one day soon after his death, with the late Mrs. Osgood, the beauty of whose character had made upon Poe's mind that impression which it never failed to produce upon minds capable of the apprehension of the finest traits in human nature, she said she did not doubt that my view of Mr Poe, which she knew indeed to be the common view, was perfectly just, as it regarded him in his relations with men; but to women he was different, and she would write for me some recollections of him to be placed beside my harsher judgments in any notice of his life that the acceptance of the appointment to be his literary executor might render it necessary for me to give to the world. She was an invalid — dying of that consumption by which in a few weeks she was removed to heaven, and calling for pillows to support her while she wrote, she drew this sketch:

> You ask me, my friend, to write for you my reminiscences of
> Edgar Poe. For you, who knew and understood my
> affectionate interest in him, and my frank acknowledgment of
> that interest to all who had a claim upon my confidence, for
> you, I will willingly do so. I think no one could know him —
> no one has known him personally — certainly no woman —
> without feeling the same interest. I can sincerely say, that
> although I have frequently heard of aberrations on his part
> from 'the straight and narrow path,' I have never seen him
> otherwise than gentle, generous, well-bred, and fastidiously
> refined. To a sensitive and delicately-nurtured woman, there
> was a peculiar and irresistible charm in the chivalric, graceful,
> and almost tender reverence with which he invariably
> approached all women who won his respect. It was this which
> first commanded and always retained my regard for him. . . .

<59>

The influence of Mr. Poe's aims and vicissitudes upon his literature, was more conspicuous in his later than in his earlier writings. Nearly all that be wrote in the last two or three years — including much of his best poetry, — was in some sense biographical; in draperies of his imagination, those who take the trouble to trace his steps, will perceive, but slightly concealed, the figure of himself. The lineaments here disclosed, I think, are not different from those displayed in this biography, which is but a filling up of the picture. . . .

IN PERSON HE was below the middle height, slenderly but compactly formed, and in his better moments he had in an eminent degree that air of gentlemanliness which men of a lower order seldom succeed in acquiring.

His conversation was at times almost supra-mortal in its eloquence. His voice was modulated with astonishing skill, and his large and variably expressive eyes looked repose or shot fiery tumult into theirs who listened, while his own face glowed, or was changeless in pallor, as his imagination quickened his blood or drew it back frozen to his heart. His imagery was from the worlds which no mortals can see but with the vision of genius. Suddenly starting from a proposition, exactly and sharply defined, in terms of utmost simplicity and clearness, he rejected the forms of customary logic, and by a crystalline process of accretion, built up his ocular demonstrations in forms of gloomiest and ghastliest grandeur, or in those of the most airy and delicious beauty — so minutely and distinctly, yet so rapidly, that the attention which was yielded to him was chained till it stood among his wonderful creations — till he himself dissolved the spell, and brought his hearers back to common and base existence, by vulgar fancies or exhibitions of the ignoblest passion.

He was at all times a dreamer — dwelling in ideal realms — in heaven or hell — peopled with the creatures and the accidents of his brain. He walked the streets, in madness or melancholy, with lips moving in indistinct curses, or with eyes upturned in passionate prayer, (never for himself, for he felt, or professed to feel, that he was already damned, but) for their happiness who at the moment were objects of his idolatry; — or, with his glances introverted to a heart gnawed with anguish, and with a face shrouded in gloom, he would brave the wildest storms; and all night, with drenched garments and arms beating the winds and rains, would speak as if to spirits that at such times only could be evoked by him from the Aidenn, close by whose portals his disturbed soul sought to forget the ills to which his constitution subjected him — close by the Aidenn where were those he loved — the Aidenn which he might never see, but ill fitful glimpses, as its gates opened to receive the less fiery and

<60>

more happy natures whose destiny to sin did not involve the doom of death.

He seemed, except when some fitful pursuit subjugated his will and engrossed his faculties, always to bear the memory of some controlling sorrow. The remarkable poem of "The Raven" was probably much more nearly than has been supposed, even by those who were very intimate with him, a reflection and an echo of his own history.

Every genuine author, in a greater or less degree, leaves in his works, whatever their design, traces of his personal character: elements of his immortal being, in which the individual survives the person. While we read the pages of the "Fall of the House of Usher," or of "Mesmeric Revelations," we see in the solemn and stately gloom which invests one, and in the subtle metaphysical analysis of both, indications of the idiosyncrasies — of what was most remarkable and peculiar — in the author's intellectual nature. But we see here only the better phases of his nature, only the symbols of his juster action, for his harsh experience had deprived him of all faith, in man or woman. He had made up his mind upon the numberless complexities of the social world, and the whole system with him was an imposture. This conviction gave a direction to his shrewd and naturally unamiable character. Still, though he regarded society as composed altogether of villains, the sharpness of his intellect was not of that kind which enabled him to cope with villainy, while it continually caused him by overshots to fail of the success of honesty. He was in many respects like Francis Vivian, in Bulwer's novel of *The Caxtons*. Passion, in him, comprehended many of the worst emotions which militate against human happiness. You could not contradict him, but you raised quick choler; you could not speak of wealth, but his cheek paled with gnawing envy. The astonishing natural advantages of this poor boy — his beauty, his readiness, the daring spirit that breathed around him like a fiery atmosphere — had raised his constitutional self-confidence into an arrogance that turned his very claims to admiration into prejudices against him. Irascible, envious — bad enough, but not the worst, for these salient angles were all varnished over with a cold repellant cynicism, his passions vented themselves in sneers. There seemed to him no moral susceptibility; and, what was more remarkable in a proud nature, little or nothing of the true point of honor. He had, to a morbid excess, that desire to rise which is vulgarly called ambition, but no wish for the esteem of the love of his species; only the hard wish to succeed — not shine, not serve — succeed, that he might have the right to despise a world which galled his self-conceit.

<61>

EDGAR POE
AND HIS CRITICS (1860)
by Sarah Helen Whitman

PREFACE

Dr. Griswold's Memoir of Edgar Poe has been extensively read and circulated; its perverted facts and baseless assumptions have been adopted into every subsequent memoir and notice of the poet, and have been translated into many languages. For ten years this great wrong to the dead has passed unchallenged and unrebuked.

It has been assumed by a recent English critic that "Edgar Poe had no friends." As an index to a more equitable and intelligible theory of the idiosyncrasies of his life, and as an earnest protest against the spirit of Dr. Griswold's unjust memoir, these pages are submitted to his more candid readers and critics by

ONE OF HIS FRIENDS.

THE AUTHOR OF the "Original Memoir" prefixed to the volume of Poe's *Illustrated Poems*, recently published by Redfield, says, "Of all the poets, whose lives have been a puzzle and a mystery to the world, there is not one more difficult to be understood than Edgar Allan Poe."[5] The Rev. George Gilfillan, in his very imaginative portraiture of the poet, admits that the moral anatomists who have met and wondered over his life, have given up all attempts at dissection and diagnosis, turning away with the solemnly whispered warning to the world, and especially to its more brilliant and gifted intellects, "Beware!"[6]

[5] *The Poetical Works of Edgar Allan Poe, With Original Memoir.* New York: J.S. Redfield. 1858. The unsigned "memoir," acknowledging and praising Griswold, is on pp. xvii-xxx. The article may be by Charles Frederick Briggs, founder of *The Broadway Journal,* who withdrew from the business, leaving it to its doom in the hands of his partner John Bisco, and their editor, Edgar Poe.
[6] George Gilfillan. *A Third Gallery of Portraits* (1854). Gilfillan's sketches of literary personalities were widely read, and he was a prolific editor of collections of British poets. His depiction of Poe was vicious: "Poets, as a tribe, have been rather a worthless, wicked set of people; and certainly Edgar A. Poe, instead of being an exception, was probably *the* most wicked and worthless of all his fraternity" (p. 326). "He was no more a gentleman than he was a saint. His heart was a rotten as his conduct was infamous" (p. 327). Gilfillan's article appeared first in *The Critic, London Literary Journal* in March 1854, and was also picked up in the United States by *The Southern Literary Messenger* and *Little's Living Age.*

<62>

He confesses that a history so strange as that of Edgar Poe should prompt us to new and more searching methods of critical as well as moral analysis.[7] But before such analysis can be instituted we must have fuller, more dispassionate, and more authentic records of the phenomena to be analyzed. The well written, but very brief memoir prefixed to the *Illustrated Poems,* and the various sketches that have from time to time appeared in the French and English periodicals, are all based on the narrative of Dr. Griswold, a narrative notoriously deficient in the great essentials of candor and authenticity. "It is a rare accomplishment," says one of our most original writers, "to hear a story as it is told; still rarer to remember it as heard, and rarest of all *to tell it as it is remembered.*"[8]

If Dr. Griswold's "Memoir of Edgar Poe" betrays the want of any or *all* of these accomplishments, if its remorseless violations of the trust confided to him are such as to make the unhallowed act of Trelawney towards the enshrouded form of the dead Byron seem guiltless in comparison, we must nevertheless endeavor to remember that the memorialist himself now claims from us that tender grace of charity that he was unwilling, or unable, to accord to the man who trusted him as a friend. [9]

It is not our purpose at present specially to review Dr. Griswold's numerous misrepresentations and misstatements. Some of the more injurious of these anecdotes were disproved, during the life of Dr. Griswold, in the *New-York Tribune*[10] and other leading journals, without

---

[7] Ibid, p. 331
[8] George Herbert: "In a few instances in which I have been able to compare versions adopted by society of some given incident with the literal facts, I have found that the statements of the nearest and most authentic parties gambolled absurdly from the truth. The most tenacious memories have a trick of substituting one circumstance for another in the histories confided to them, in a manner which leaves the individual wholly unconscious of the change. When a narrative has passed through two or three lips, it is generally as much modified by the process as the sounds which conveyed it. It is a rare accomplishment to hear a story as it is told; still rarer, to remember it as it is heard; and rarest of all, to tell it as it is remembered." Qtd in Horace Binney Wallace, *Literary Criticisms and Other Papers* (1856), p. 337.
[9] This paragraph alludes to the calamities leading up to Griswold's death in 1857, including a fire-injury, a divorce, the near-drowning of a daughter, a hellish hounding by Poe's nemesis Mrs. Ellett, and a lingering death from tuberculosis. Little was in Griswold's room but a portrait of Poe and another of the poet Mrs. Osgood; friends destroyed some unpublished manuscripts that maligned other writers. At the time Whitman wrote this, Griswold's body was in a receiving tomb in Brooklyn's Green-Wood Cemetery. He would not be interred in the ground until 1865, without a tombstone. All this may be some comfort to the shades of Griswold's victims.
[10] William J. Pabodie, a poet-friend of Mrs. Whitman, and a witness to the Poe-Whitman romance, refuted Griswold's account of the Poe-Whitman break-up in a letter to *The New York Tribune* on June 2, 1852. In a letter-exchange

<63>

eliciting from him any public statement in explanation or apology. Quite recently we have had, through the columns of the *Home Journal,* the refutation of another calumnious story, which for ten years has been going the rounds of the English and American periodicals. [11]

We have authority for stating that many of the disgraceful anecdotes, so industriously collected by Dr. Griswold, are utterly fabulous, while others are perversions of the truth, more injurious in their effects than unmitigated fiction. But, as we have said, it is not our purpose at present to revert to these. We propose simply to point out some unfounded critical estimates which have obtained currency among readers who have but a partial acquaintance with Mr. Poe's more imaginative writings, and to record our own impressions of the character and genius of the poet, as derived from personal observation, and from the testimony of those who knew him. Although he had been connected with some of the leading magazines of the day, and had edited for a time, with great ability, several successful periodicals, Mr. Poe's literary reputation at the North had been comparatively limited until his removal to New York, in the autumn of 1847, when he became personally known to a large circle of authors and literary people, whose interest in his writings was manifestly enhanced by the perplexing anomalies of his character, and by the singular magnetism of his presence. One who knew him at this period of his life says, "Everything about him distinguished him as a man of mark: his countenance, person, and gait, were alike characteristic. His features were regular, and decidedly handsome. His complexion was clear and dark; the colour of his fine eyes seemingly a dark gray, but on closer inspection they were seen to be of that neutral, violet tint which is so difficult to define. His forehead was, without exception, the finest, in proportion and expression, that we have ever seen. The perceptive organs were not deficient, but seemed pressed out of the way by causality, comparison, and constructiveness. Close to these rose the proud arches of ideality. The coronal region was very imperfect, wanting in reverence and conscientiousness, and presenting a key to many of his literary characteristics. The ideas of right and wrong are as feeble in his chains of thought as in the literature of ancient Greece."[12] We quote this

between Pabodie and Griswold that followed, Griswold called Mrs. Whitman "insane." These letters are detailed in Quinn's *Edgar Allan Poe: A Critical Biography.*
[11] Unsigned letter in *The Home Journal,* February 6, 1858. The controversy alluded to here is the charge that Poe plagiarized a natural history book, *The Conchologist's First Book* (1839), when in fact its British author, Thomas Wyatt, hoping for good U.S. sales, contracted with Poe to have Poe's name on the title-page. See Quinn (p. 275) for details of Poe's additional editorial work on this edition, which also included Poe's own translations of animal descriptions from the French of Cuvier.
[12] Somewhat paraphrased from John Moncure Daniel. "Edgar Allan Poe."

<64>

description for its general fidelity. Its estimate of literary characteristics conveyed in the closing sentence we shall revert to in another place.[13]

The engraved portraits of Mr. Poe have very little individuality; that prefixed to the volumes edited by Dr. Griswold suggests, at first view, something of the general contour of his face, but is utterly void of character and expression; it has no subsurface. The original painting, now in possession of the New-York Historical Society, has the same cold, automatic look that makes the engraving so valueless as a portrait to those who remember the unmatched glory of his face when roused from its habitually introverted and abstracted look by some favorite theme or profound emotion. Perhaps, from its peculiarly changeful and translucent character, any adequate transmission of its variable and subtle moods was impossible. By writers personally unacquainted with Mr. Poe this engraving has often been favorably noticed. Mr. Hannay, in a memoir prefixed to the first London edition of Poe's poems, calls it an interesting and characteristic portrait, "a fine, thoughtful face with lineaments of delicacy, such as belong only to genius or high blood. The forehead is grand and pale, the eyes dark, gleaming with sensibility and the light of soul. A face . . . that would inspire [women with sentiment,] men with interest and curiosity."[14]

There is a quiet drawing-room in ———— [Twentieth] Street,[15] New York — a sort of fragrant and delicious "clovernook" in the heart of the noisy city, where hung, some three years ago, the original painting from which this engraving is a copy.[16] Happening to meet there at the time a company of authors and poets, among whom were Mary Forrest, Alice and Phoebe Cary, the Stoddards, T. B. Aldrich, and others, we heard one of the party say, in speaking of the portrait, that its aspect was that of a beautiful and desolate shrine from which the Genius had departed, and that it recalled certain lines to one of the antique marbles:

Southern Literary Messenger, March 1850. This is a phrenological description of Poe's features, ascribing psychological or moral traits to the formation of face and skull. Nineteenth-century readers were regaled with phrenological character descriptions in the fiction of Balzac, the Brontës, Lytton, Cooper, Dickens, Elliot, Melville, Poe and Thackeray.

13 Poe may have helped write, or may have entirely written, the phrenological portions of the foregoing analysis, which first appeared in *Philadelphia Saturday Museum* in March 1843.

14 James Hannay. *The Poetical Works of Edgar Allan Poe.* 1852 (p. xxiv). I have edited this quotation to match the punctuation in Hannay's original. Whitman also omitted "A face of passion it is, and in the lower parts wants firmness."

15 The home of Alice Cary, poet and essayist, who ran a Sunday literary salon, visited by Whitman in 1856.

16 Portrait painting by Samuel S. Osgood, 1845. A reproduction of this painting was the frontispiece for the 1860 edition of Whitman's essay.

<65>

Oh melancholy eyes!
Oh empty eyes, from which the soul has gone
To see the far-off countries![17]

Near this luminous but impassive face, with its sad and soulless eyes, was a portrait of Poe's unrelenting biographist.[18] In a recess opposite hung a picture of the fascinating Mrs. ———— [Osgood],[19] whose genius both had so fervently admired, and for whose coveted praise and friendship both had been competitors. Looking at the beautiful portrait of this lady, — the face so full of enthusiasm, and dreamy, tropical sunshine, — remembering the eloquent words of her praise, as expressed in the prodigal and passionate exaggerations of her verse, one ceases to wonder at the rivalries and enmities enkindled within the hearts of those who admired her genius and her grace, — rivalries and enmities which the grave itself could not cancel or appease.

Of the portrait prefixed to the *Illustrated Poems*, recently published by Redfield, Mr. Willis says, "The reader who has the volume in his hand turns back musingly to look upon the features of the poet, in whom resided such inspiration. But, though well engraved and useful as recalling his features to those who knew them with the angel shining through, the picture is from a Daguerreotype, and gives no idea of the beauty of Edgar Poe. The exquisitely chiseled features, the habitual but intellectual melancholy, the clear pallor of the complexion, and the calm eye like the molten stillness of a slumbering volcano, composed a countenance of which this portrait is but the skeleton. After reading The Raven, Ulalume, Lenore, and Annabel Lee, the luxuriast in poetry will better conceive what his face might have been."[20]

It was soon after his removal to New York that Mr. Poe became acquainted with the editors of the *Mirror*, and was employed by them as a writer for that journal. Mr. Willis, in a recent notice of the *Illustrated Poems*, has paid an eloquent tribute to his memory, expressed in a spirit of rare kindliness and generosity. [21]

From March 1845, to January 1846, he was associated with Mr. C. F. Briggs in editing the *Broadway Journal*. In the autumn of 1845[22] he

[17] Edmund Ollier. His poem "Eleusina" first appeared anonymously in Charles Dickens' weekly magazine, *Household Words*, Vols 7-8, p. 349. It did not appear in book form until 1867.

[18] A portrait of Griswold by Charles L. Elliott.

[19] A portrait of Frances Sargent ("Fanny") Osgood by her husband, Samuel S. Osgood, who did not object to his wife's status as Muse or *femme fatale* for poets.

[20] Nathaniel P. Willis. "Letter About Edgar Poe." *Home Journal*, October 30, 1858.

[21] Whitman appears to be referring to the *Home Journal* article cited above.

[22] Whitman's dating is incorrect, since "The Raven" had two print appearances

<66>

was often seen at the brilliant literary circles in Waverley Place,[23] where weekly reunions of noted artists and men of letters, at the house of an accomplished poetess, attracted some of the best intellectual society of the city. At the request of his hostess, Mr. Poe one evening electrified the gay company assembled there by the recitation of the weird poem to whose sad, strange burden so many hearts have since echoed. This was a few weeks previous to the publication of "The Raven" in *The American Review*. Mrs. Browning, in a private letter, written a few weeks after its publication in England, says, "This vivid writing — this *power which is felt* — has produced a sensation here in England. Some of my friends are taken by the fear of it, and some by the music. I hear of persons who are haunted by the 'Nevermore,' and an acquaintance of mine who has the misfortune of possessing a bust of Pallas, cannot bear to look at it in the twilight.

[. . .] Then there is a tale [of yours] [. . .] going the round of the newspapers, about mesmerism, which is throwing us all into 'most admired disorder' and dreadful doubts as to whether 'it can be true,' as the children say of ghost stories. The certain thing [. . .] is the power of the writer."[24]

A woman of fine genius, who at this time made his acquaintance, says, in some recently published comments on his writings: "It was in the brilliant circles that assembled in the winter of 1845-6 at the houses of Dr. Dewey, Miss Anna C. Lynch, Mr. Lawson, and others, that we first met Edgar Poe. His manners were, at these reunions, refined and pleasing, and his style and scope of conversation that of a gentleman and a scholar. Whatever may have been his previous career, there was nothing in his appearance or manner to indicate his excesses. He delighted in the society of superior women, and had an exquisite perception of all graces of manner, and shades of expression. He was an admiring listener and an unobtrusive observer. We all recollect the interest felt at the time in everything emanating from his pen, — the relief it was from the dullness of ordinary writers, the certainty of something fresh and suggestive. His *critiques* were read with avidity; not that he convinced the judgment, but that people felt their ability and their courage. Right or wrong, he was

---

in January and February of 1845.

[23] The literary soirées of Anne C. Lynch at 116 Waverly Place, a favorite haunt of Poe and the New York literary elite.

[24] A letter from Elizabeth Barrett Browning to Edgar Allan Poe. April 1846. The full text can be found in "Poe in New York," by George Woodberry, *The Century Illustrated Monthly Magazine*, Vol. 48, 1894, p. 859. The "tale" referred to is "The Facts in the Case of M. Valdemar," which was widely regarded as a true account.

<67>

terribly in earnest."[25] Like De Quincey, he never *supposed* anything, he always *knew*.

The peculiar character of his intellect seemed without a prototype in literature. He had more than De Quincey's power of analysis, with a constructive unity and completeness of which the great English essayist has given no indication. His preeminence in constructive and analytical skill was beginning to be universally admitted, and the fame and prestige of his genius were rapidly increasing. But the dangerous censorship he soon after assumed, as the author of a series of sketches, some of which have been since published as the "Literati," exposed him to frequent indignant criticism, while, by his personal errors and indiscretions, he drew upon himself much social censure and *espionage*, and became the victim of dishonoring accusations, from which honor itself had forbidden him to exculpate himself.

It has been said, in allusion to the severity of his literary strictures, that a most fitting escutcheon for Mr. Poe might have been found in the crest of Walter Scott's puissant Templar, Bois Guilbert,[26] a raven in full flight, holding in its claws a skull, and bearing the motto, "*Gare le Corbeau.*"

Mr. Longfellow has very generously said, in a letter to the editor of the *Literary Messenger:* "The harshness of his criticism I have always attributed to the irritation of a sensitive nature chafed by some indefinite sense of wrong."[27]

A recent and not too lenient critic tells us that "it was his sensitiveness to artistic imperfections, rather than any malignity of feeling, that made his criticisms so severe, and procured him a host of enemies among persons towards whom he entertained no personal ill-will."

In evidence of the habitual courtesy and good nature noticeable to all who best knew him in domestic and social life, we remember an incident that occurred at one of the *soirées* to which we have alluded. A lady noted for her great lingual attainments, wishing to apply a whole-

---

[25] This unsigned article about Poe by Mrs. Elizabeth Oakes Smith, includes absorbing details about Poe's apparent frailty and susceptibility to alcohol, including anecdotes that people gave Poe wine in order to witness the almost instantaneous change of personality: "We have been told that it was an amusement in some quarters for persons to present Poe with wine for no purpose but to watch its effect on his sensitive nerves ... 'he ridiculed, satyrized, imitated and abused [his contemporaries]'" (p. 268). Mrs. Whitman's quote from the article elides sentences and phrases from p. 264, but not in the order written. It is possible the she is quoting from a hand-written draft provided to her by the author. "Edgar A. Poe." *United States Magazine,* Vol. 4 No. 3, March 1857, pp. 262-268.

[26] *Bois-Guilbert.* The principal villain in Water Scott's *Ivanhoe* (1820).

[27] Longfellow. Letter to John R. Thompson, editor of *Southern Literary Messenger,* November 1849.

<68>

some check to the vanity of a young author, proposed inviting him to translate for the company a difficult passage in Greek, of which language she knew him to be profoundly ignorant, although given to a rather pretentious display of Greek quotations in his published writings. Poe's earnest and persistent remonstrance against this piece of *méchanceté*[28] alone averted the embarrassing test.

Sometimes his fair young wife was seen with him at these weekly assemblages in Waverley Place. She seldom took part in the conversation; but the memory of her sweet and girlish face, always animated and vivacious, repels the assertion, afterwards so cruelly and recklessly made, that she died a victim to the neglect and unkindness of her husband, "who," as it has been said, "deliberately sought her death that he might embalm her memory in immortal dirges." An article in *Fraser's Magazine*, published some two years ago, repeats the assertion that Poe was the murderer of his wife, "causing her to die of starvation and a broken heart."[29] Gilfillan, ascribing to him "passions controlled by the presence of art until they resembled sculptured flame," tells us that he caused the death of his wife that he might have a fitting theme for "The Raven." A serious objection to this ingenious theory may perhaps be found in the "refractory fact" that the poem was published more than a year before the event which these persons assume it was intended to commemorate.

We might cite the testimony alike of friends and enemies to Poe's unvarying kindness towards his young wife and cousin, if other testimony were needed than that of the tender love still cherished for his memory by one whose life was made doubly desolate by his death — the sister of his father, and the mother of his Virginia.

It is well known to those acquainted with the parties that the young wife of Edgar Poe died of lingering consumption, which manifested itself even in her girlhood. All who have had opportunities for observation in the matter have noticed her husband's tender devotion to her during her prolonged illnesses. Even Dr. Griswold speaks of having visited him during a period of illness caused by protracted anxiety, and watching by the side of his sick wife. It is true, that, notwithstanding her vivacity and cheerfulness at the time we have alluded to, her health was even then rapidly sinking; and it was for her dear sake and for the recovery of that peace which had been so fatally periled amid the irritations and anxieties of his New-York life, that Poe left the city and removed to the little Dutch cottage in Fordham, where he passed the three remaining years of his life. It was to this quiet haven, in the beautiful spring of 1846, when the

---

[28] *Méchanceté*. Spitefulness.
[29] The actual quote is: "He starved his wife, and broke her heart." Article signed "K. P. I." *Fraser's Magazine*, Vol. 55, June 1857, p. 700. The author was Andrew Kennedy Hutchison Boyd (1825-1899), a Scottish minister and author of *Recreations of a Country Parson*.

<69>

fruit trees were all in bloom and the grass in its freshest verdure, that he brought his Virginia to die. Here he watched her failing breath in loneliness and privation through many solitary moons, until, on a desolate, dreary day of the ensuing winter, he saw her remains borne from beneath its lowly roof to a neighbouring cemetery. It was towards the close of the year following her death, his "most immemorial year"[30] — that he wrote the strange threnody of "Ulalume." This poem, perhaps the most original and weirdly suggestive of all his poems, resembles at first sight some of Turner's landscapes, being apparently "without form and void, and having darkness on the face of it."[31] It is, nevertheless, in its basis, although not in the precise correspondence of time, simply historical. Such was the poet's lonely midnight walk; such, amid the desolate memories and sceneries of the hour, was the new-born hope enkindled within his heart at sight of the morning star —

Astarte's bediamonded crescent —

coming up as the beautiful harbinger of love and happiness yet awaiting him in the untried future; and such the sudden transition of feeling, the boding dread, that supervened on discovering that which had at first been unnoted, that it shone, as if in mockery or in warning, directly over the sepulchre of the lost "Ulalume." A writer in *The London Critic,* after quoting the opening stanzas of "Ulalume," says, "These to many will appear only *words,* but what wondrous words! What a spell they wield! What a withered unity there is in them! The instant they are uttered a misty picture with a tarn dark as a murderer's eye below, and the thin yellow leaves of October fluttering above, — exponents of a misery which scorns the name of sorrow, — is hung up in the chambers of your soul forever."[32]

An English writer, now living in Paris, the author of some valuable contributions to our American periodicals, passed several weeks at the little cottage in Fordham, in the early autumn of 1847, and described to us, with a truly English appreciativeness, its unrivalled neatness and the quaint simplicity of its interior and surroundings. It was at the time bordered by a flower garden, whose clumps of rare dahlias and brilliant

[30] Poe. "Ulalume."
[31] William Hazlitt on Turner's paintings: "All is 'without form and void.' Someone said of his landscapes that they were *pictures of nothing and very like.*" Hazlitt may have derived this perception from Coleridge. "Without form and void" is from the Book of Genesis, and Hazlitt makes the allusion clear: "They are pictures of the elements of air, earth, and water. The artist delights to go back to the first chaos of the world, or to that state of things when the waters were separated from the dry land, and light from darkness." *The Morning Chronicle,* Feb 5, 1814.
[32] Gilfillan, pp. 337-338, where even a Poe-hater had to admit to being smitten.

<70>

beds of fall flowers showed, in the careful culture bestowed upon them, the fine floral taste of the inmates.

An American writer, who visited the cottage during the summer of the same year, described it as half buried in fruit trees, and as having a thick grove of pines in its immediate neighborhood.[33] The proximity of the railroad, and the increasing population of the little village, have since wrought great changes in the place. Round an old cherry tree, near the door, was a broad bank of greenest turf. The neighbouring beds of mignonette and heliotrope, and the pleasant shade above, made this a favorite seat. Rising at four o'clock in the morning for a walk to the magnificent Aqueduct bridge over Harlem River, our informant found the poet, with his mother, standing on the turf beneath the cherry tree, eagerly watching

Poe walking on High Bridge.

the movements of two beautiful birds that seemed contemplating a settlement in its branches. He had some rare tropical birds in cages, which he cherished and petted with assiduous care. Our English friend described him as giving to his birds and his flowers a delighted attention that seemed quite inconsistent with the gloomy and grotesque character of his writings. A favorite cat, too, enjoyed his friendly patronage, and often, when he was engaged in composition, it seated itself on his shoulder, purring as in complacent approval of the work proceeding under its supervision.

During Mr. Poe's residence at Fordham, a walk to High Bridge was one of his favorite and habitual recreations. The water of the Aqueduct is conveyed across the river on a range of lofty granite arches, which rise to the height of a hundred and forty-five feet above high-water level. On the top a turfed and grassy road, used only by foot passengers, and flanked on either side by a low parapet of granite, makes one of the finest promenades imaginable.

---

[33] It is possible that Whitman was in possession of some version of Mary Gove Nichols' "Reminiscences of Edgar Allan Poe," an account of a visit to the cottage at Fordham, and the source of the revelation that the sale of "Ulalume" was hastened in order to buy Poe a pair of shoes. Nichols' account did not see print, however, until its February, 1863 appearance in London's *Six Penny Magazine*.

<71>

High Bridge and Aqueduct, c. 1900.

The winding river and the high rocky shores at the western extremity of the bridge are seen to great advantage from this lofty avenue. In the last melancholy years of his life — "the lonesome latter years"[34] — Poe was accustomed to walk there at all times of the day and night; often pacing the then solitary pathway for hours without meeting a human being. A little to the east of the cottage rises a ledge of rocky ground, partly covered with pines and cedars, commanding a fine view of the surrounding country and of the picturesque college of St. John's, which had at that time in its neighborhood an avenue of venerable old trees. This rocky ledge was also one of the poet's favorite resorts. Here through long summer days and through solitary, star-lit nights he loved to sit, dreaming his gorgeous waking dreams, or pondering the deep problems of "The Universe"[35] — that grand "prose-poem" to which he devoted the last and maturest energies of his wonderful intellect. The abstracted enthusiasm with which he pursued his great quest into the cosmogony of the universe is an earnest of the passionate intellectual sincerity which we shall presently take occasion to illustrate.

Wanting in that supreme central force or faculty of the mind, whose function is a God-conscious and God-adoring faith, Edgar Poe sought earnestly and conscientiously for such solution of the great problems of thought as were alone attainable to an intellect hurled from its balance by the abnormal preponderance of the analytical and imaginative faculties. It was to this very disproportion that we are indebted for some of those marvelous intellectual creations, which, as we shall hope to prove, had an important significance and an especial adaptation to the time.

A very intolerant article on Mr. Poe has recently been republished in this country from *The Edinburgh Review* for April, 1858,[36] in which the most injurious anecdotes of Dr. Griswold's memoir have been patiently copied and italicised, and their enormities enhanced by the gratuitous suppositions and assumptions of the writer.

---

[34] Poe. "The Conqueror Worm."
[35] "The Universe," Poe's *Eureka*.
[36] Bryan W. Proctor. "Edgar Allan Poe." *Edinburgh Review*, April 1858.

<72>

As an instance of the inconsequent reasoning in which the reviewer sometimes indulges, we quote a single passage from the article in question. "It is," says *The Edinburgh* critic, "a curious example of Poe's superficial acquaintance with the literature of other lands, that in recapitulating the titles of a mysterious library of books in 'The House of Usher' he quotes among a list of cabalistical volumes Gresset's *'Vertvert,'*[37] evidently in complete ignorance of what he is talking about. Gresset's *'Vertvert'* is the antipodes of Poe's 'Raven,' though the comic interest of the former and the tragic interest of the latter turn alike on the reiteration of bird-language."[38]

The process of reasoning by which Mr. Poe's "superficial acquaintance with the literature of other lands" is deducible from the fact that "Gresset's 'Vertvert' is the antipodes of Poe's 'Raven,'" may be very apparent to the learned reviewer, but is certainly not quite clear to the common reader.

We are not aware that any of the works cited in this catalogue bear a resemblance to "The Raven." Mr. Poe must certainly be acquitted of intending to suggest such a resemblance, since "The Raven" was at the time unwritten. *The Edinburgh* critic, after admitting that Poe's "Raven" belongs to "that rare and remarkable class of productions that suffice, *singly*, to make a reputation," assumes, oddly enough, that "the originality apparent in Mr. Poe's writings is due rather to the deformity of his moral character than to the vigor or freshness of his intellect," and, finding himself "profoundly impressed by Poe's wonderful solutions of the most difficult problems," suspects that "it is after all, an easy thing for man to solve the riddles which he himself has fabricated."[39]

There is a prevalent impression among critics and readers who have never felt the magnetism of Poe's weird imagination, nor come into full rapport with his genius, that his intellectual creations were always the result of deliberate effort and artistic skill, that they were not genuine

---

[37] Jean-Baptiste-Louis Gresset. *Vert-Vert, Histoire d'un Perroquet de Nevers* (1734), a comical work in verse about the adventures of a parrot owned by a convent of nuns, that falls into bad company and acquires a shocking vocabulary. The poem was famed for its atmosphere and delicacy of style. The work also earned some opprobrium from the Jesuits for its mockery of religion. The author repudiated the work in his old age. By the time of Poe's story, the book had likely been banned.

[38] The text Whitman quotes is a footnote to a sentence reading, "His reading was doubtless curious rather than accurate, desultory rather than wide; and his genius grew rank in a half-cultivated soil." In the example cited, the critic might have been more concise had he said simply that Poe mistook a banned *comic* work for a banned cabalistic one. *The Edinburgh Review,* April 1858, p. 427.

[39] Ibid, p. 428.

<73>

outgrowths of the inward life but arbitrary creations of the will and the intellect.

This opinion, founded in part upon the subtlety and refinement of his analytical faculty, has been seemingly guaranteed by some of his own statements in regard to his methods of composition. A writer in *The North American* characterizes his poetry as "word-maneuvering,"[40] and one of his critics, sitting at the time in *Harper's* "Easy Chair," says, "Such curious and beautiful performances as Poe's 'Raven' and 'Sleigh-bells' are not poems; they are, simply, ingenious experiments upon the sound of words."[41] Were this grand lyric of "The Bells" simply a lyric of "Sleigh-bells" as the "Easy Chair" pleasantly calls it, when were Sleigh-bells ever heard to ring so merrily before? Listen!

> How they tinkle, tinkle, tinkle,
>   In the icy air of night!
> While the stars that oversprinkle
> All the heavens, seem to twinkle
>   With a crystalline delight;
> Keeping time, time, time,
> In a sort of Runic rhyme,
> To the tintinnabulation that so musically wells
>   From the bells, bells, bells, bells,
>   Bells, bells, bells —
> From the jingling and the tinkling of the bells.

It cannot indeed be denied that the mere artistic treatment of this poem is truly marvelous. The metallic ring and resonance, — the vibration and reverberation of the rhythm, — are such that one of its admirers says, "We can never read it without pausing after every verse to let the *peals of sound* die away on the 'bosom of the palpitating air,' that we may commence the succeeding stanza in silence." Another, who appreciates its ideal truth of conception not less than its high rhythmical art, says, "I was astonished one night in watching a conflagration, and repeating, amid the clash and clang of the alarm-bells, the third stanza of the poem, to find how marvelously the movement of the verse *timed* with the peals of sound, and how truly the poem reproduced the sense of danger which the sound of the bells, and the glare and mad ascension of the flames, and the pallor of the moonlight conveyed. All the poetry of a conflagration is in that stanza, both in sound and sense, and Dante himself could not have rendered it more truly."

[40] Unsigned article by E. Vale Smith, "Works of the Late Edgar Allan Poe." *North American Review,* October 1856.
[41] "Editor's Easy Chair." *Harper's New Monthly Magazine.* Vol. 13, No. 73. June 1856, p. 129.

<74>

So many faculties were brought into play in the expression of Poe's poetical compositions that readers in whom the critical intellect prevails over the imaginative often acknowledge the refined art, the tact, the subtlety, the faultless method, while the potent *magnetism* of his genius utterly escapes them. There are persons whom nature has made non-conductors to this sort of electricity.

The critic of *The North American* to whose strictures we have alluded, charges him with overlooking moral and spiritual ideas, and calls his works "rich and elaborate pieces of art," wanting in "the *vis vitae* which alone can make of words living things."[42] Bayne, on the other hand, in his fine essay on "Tennyson and his Teachers," alludes to "The Haunted Palace" of "the great American poet," and contrasts its wonderfully spiritual, subjective, and ideal character with the rich and accurate detail of Tennyson's "Palace of Art."[43] He classes the American poet with those who have scattered *imaginative spells* rather than finished elaborate imaginative pictures. A greater mistake in literary criticism could not well be made than that which is evinced in the frequent application of the word "sensuous" to the singularly ideal and subjective character of Poe's imaginative creations. We do not, of course, intend to include among these, his stories of a purely inventive or grotesque character.

It is not to be questioned that Poe was a consummate master of language; that he had sounded all the secrets of rhythm; that he understood and availed himself of all its resources, — the balance and poise of syllables, the alternations of emphasis and cadence, of vowel-sounds and consonants, and all the metrical sweetness of "phrase and metaphrase." Yet this consummate art was in him united with a rare simplicity. He was the most genuine of enthusiasts, as we think we shall presently show. His genius would follow no leadings but those of his own imperial intellect. With all his vast mental resources he could never write an occasional poem, or adapt himself to the taste of a popular audience. His graver narratives and fantasies are often related with an earnest simplicity, solemnity, and apparent fidelity, attributable, not so much to a deliberate artistic purpose, as to that power of vivid and intense conception that made his dreams realities, and his life a dream.

The strange fascination — the unmatched charm of his conversation — consisted in its *genuineness*. Even Dr. Griswold, who has studiously represented him as cold, passionless, perfidious, admits that his conversation was at times almost "supra-mortal in its eloquence"; that "his large and variably expressive eyes looked repose or shot fiery tumult into theirs

---

[42] "Edgar Allan Poe." *North American Review.* October 1856, p. 428.
[43] Peter Bayne. *Essays in Biography and Criticism.* First Series, 1857. Boston: Gould and Lincoln. 1867, pp. 84-86.

<75>

who listened, while his own face glowed, or was changeless in pallor, as his imagination quickened his blood or drew it back frozen to his heart."[44]

These traits are not the possible accompaniments of attributes which Dr. Griswold has elsewhere ascribed to him. As a conversationist we do not remember his equal. We have heard the veteran Landor (called by high authority the best talker in England) discuss with scathing sarcasm the popular writers of the day, convey his political animosities by fierce invectives on the "pretentious coxcomb Albert," and "the cunning knave, Napoleon," or describe, in words of strange depth and tenderness, the peerless charm of goodness and the naïve social graces in the beautiful mistress of Gore House, "the most gorgeous Lady Blessington." We have heard the Howadji[45] talk of the gardens of Damascus till the air seemed purpled and perfumed with its roses. We have listened to the trenchant and vivid talk of the Autocrat;[46] to the brilliant and exhaustless colloquial resources of John Neal,[47] and Margaret Fuller. We have heard the racy talk of Orestes Brownson[48] in the old days of his freedom and power, have listened to the serene wisdom of Alcott, and treasured up memorable sentences from the golden lips of Emerson. Unlike the conversational power evinced by any of these was the earnest, opulent, unpremeditated speech of Edgar Poe.

Like his writings, it presented a combination of qualities rarely met with in the same person, — a cool, decisive judgment, a wholly unconventional courtesy and sincere grace of manner, and an imperious enthusiasm, which brought all hearers within the circle of its influence.

J. M. Daniel, Esq., United States Minister at Turin,[49] who knew Poe well during the last years of his life, says of him, "His conversation was the very best we have ever listened to. We have never heard any so suggestive of thought, or any from which one gained so much. On literary subjects it was the essence of correct and profound criticism divested of all formal pedantries and introductory ideas, — the kernel clear of the shell. He was not a brilliant talker in the common, after-dinner sense of the word; he was not a maker of fine points, or a frequent sayer of funny things. What he said was prompted entirely by the moment, and seemed

[44] From Griswold's "Memoir."
[45] *Howadji.* A traveler or merchant. Probably refers to George William Curtis, author of *Nile Notes of a "Hoawdji", or, The American in Egypt* (1856).
[46] *Autocrat.* Oliver Wendell Holmes, author of *The Autocrat of the Breakfast-Table* (1858).
[47] John Neal (1793-1876). The first American author to use colloquial language instead of formal language in published writing. He was a prolific author of articles, poems, plays and novels.
[48] Orestes Brownson (1803-1876), Transcendentalist essayist and founder of *The Boston Quarterly Review.*
[49] John Moncure Daniel (1825-1865), editor of *The Richmond Examiner* and a patron of Poe.

<76>

uttered for the pleasure of uttering it. In his animated moods he talked with an abstracted earnestness, as if he were dictating to an amanuensis, and, if he spoke of individuals, his ideas ran upon their moral and intellectual qualities, rather than upon the idiosyncrasies of their active visible phenomena, or the peculiarities of their manner."[50]

We have said that the charm of his conversation consisted in its genuineness, its wonderful directness and sincerity. We believe, too, that in the artistic utterance of poetic emotion, he was at all times passionately genuine. His proud reserve, his profound melancholy, his unworldliness — may we not say his *unearthliness* of nature — made his character one very difficult of comprehension to the casual observer. The complexity of his intellect, its incalculable resources, and his masterly control of those resources when brought into requisition for the illustration of some favorite theme, or cherished creation, led to the current belief that its action was purely arbitrary — that he could write without emotion or earnestness at the deliberate dictation of the will. A certain class of his writings undeniably exhibits the faculties of ingenuity and invention in a prominent and distinctive light. But it must not be forgotten that there was another phase of his mind, one not less distinctive and characteristic of his genius, which manifested itself in creations of a totally different order and expression. It can hardly have escaped the notice of the most careless reader that certain ideas exercised over him the power of fascination. They return, again and again, in his stories and poems, and seem like the utterances of a mind possessed with thoughts, emotions, and images of which the will and the understanding take little cognizance. In the delineation of these, his language often acquires a power and pregnancy eluding all attempts at analysis. It is then that by a few miraculous words, he evokes emotional states, or commands pictorial effects, which live forever in the memory, and form a part of its eternal inheritance. No analysis can dissect, no criticism can disenchant, them.

As specimens of the class we have indicated read "Ligeia," "Morella," "Eleanora." Observe in them the prevailing and dominant thoughts of his inner life, — ideas of "fate and metaphysical aid" — of psychical and spiritual agencies, energies and potencies. See in them intimations of mysterious phenomena which, at the time when these fantasies were indited, were regarded as fables and dreams, but which have since (in their phenomenal aspect simply) been recognised as matters of popular experience and scientific research.

In "Ligeia," the sad and stately symmetry of the sentences, their rhythmical cadence, the Moresque sumptuousness of imagery with which the story is invested, and the weird metempsychosis which it records,

---

[50] J.M. Daniel. "Edgar Allan Poe." *Southern Literary Messenger.* Vol. 16 No. 3, March 1850, p. 182.

<77>

produce an effect on the reader altogether peculiar in character and, as we think, quite inexplicable without a reference to the supernatural inspiration which seems to pervade them. In the moods of mind and phases of passion which this story represents we have no labored artistic effects. We look into the haunted chambers of the poet's own mind and see, as through a veil, the strange experiences of his inner life; while, in the dusk magnificence of its imagery, we have the true heraldic blazonry of an imagination royally dowered and descended. In this, as in all that class of stories we have named, the author's mind seems struggling desperately and vainly with the awful mystery of Death.

In "Morella," as in "Ligeia," the parties are occupied with the same mystic philosophies — engrossed in the same recondite questions of "life and death and spiritual unity," questions of "that identity which, at death, is, or is not, lost forever." Each commemorates a psychical attraction which transcends the dissolution of the mortal body and oversweeps the grave; the passionate soul of the departed transfusing itself through the organism of another to manifest its deathless love. Who does not remember as a strain of Æonian melody, the story of "Eleanora"? Who does not lapse into a dream as he remembers the "River of Silence" and "The Valley of the Many-Colored Grass"?[51]

In this story the purport, though less apparent to the general reader, and differently interpreted by a writer in *The North American Review*,[52] is still the same as in the preceding. Read the closing sentences, so eloquent with a tender and mysterious meaning, which record, after the death of the beloved Eleanora, the appearance "from a far, far distant and unknown land" of the Seraph Ermengarde. Observe, too, in these closing lines the indication, so often manifest in Poe's poems and stories, of a lingering pity and sorrow for the dead, — an ever-recurring pang of remorse in the fear of having grieved them by some involuntary wrong of desertion or forgetfulness.

This haunting remembrance — this sad, remorseful pity for the departed, is everywhere a distinguishing feature in his prose and poetry.

The existence of such a feeling as a prevalent mood of his mind, of which we have abundant evidence, is altogether incompatible with that cold sensualism with which he has been so ignorantly charged. So far from being selfish or heartless his devotional fidelity to the memory of those he loved would by the world be regarded as fanatical. A characteristic incident of his boyhood will illustrate the passionate fidelity which we have ascribed to him. While at the academy in Richmond, which he entered in his twelfth year, he one day accompanied a schoolmate to his

[51] *River of Silence* and *Valley of the Many-Coloured Grass* are two fantastic place-names in Poe's tale "Eleanora."

[52] Unsigned article by E. Vale Smith, "Works of the Late Edgar Allan Poe." *North American Review*, October 1856.

<78>

home, where he saw for the first time Mrs. H — S — [53], the mother of his young friend. This lady, on entering the room, took his hand and spoke some gentle and gracious words of welcome, which so penetrated the sensitive heart of the orphan boy as to deprive him of the power of speech, and, for a time, almost of consciousness itself. He returned home in a dream, with but one thought, one hope in life — to hear again the sweet and gracious words that had made the desolate world so beautiful to him, and filled his lonely heart with the oppression of a new joy. This lady afterwards became the *confidante* of all his boyish sorrows, and hers was the one redeeming influence that saved and guided him in the earlier days of his turbulent and passionate youth. After the visitation of strange and peculiar sorrows, she died; and for months after her decease it was his habit to visit nightly the cemetery where the object of his boyish idolatry lay entombed. The thought of her sleeping there in her loneliness filled his heart with a profound, incommunicable sorrow. When the nights were very dreary and cold, when the autumnal rains fell, and the winds, wailed mournfully over the graves, he lingered longest and came away most regretfully.

It was the image of this lady, long and tenderly and sorrowfully cherished, that suggested the stanzas "To Helen," published among the poems written in his youth, which Russell Lowell says have in them a grace and symmetry of outline such as few poets ever attain, and which are valuable as displaying "what can only be expressed by the contradictory phrase of *innate experience*." [54]

As the lines do not appear in the latest editions of his poems we give them here:

> Helen, thy beauty is to me
>   Like those Nicean barks of yore,
> That gently, o'er a perfumed sea,
>   The weary, wayworn wanderer bore
>   To his own native shore.

> On desperate seas long wont to roam,
>   Thy hyacinth hair, thy classic face,
> Thy Naiad airs have brought me home,
>   To the glory that was Greece,
>   To the grandeur that was Rome.

---

[53] Mrs Jane Stanard, assigned the name "Helen" by the love-struck poet.
[54] Lowell, James Russell. "Edgar A. Poe." *Works of the Late Edgar Allan Poe. Volume 1: Tales* (1849), p. ix.

<79>

> Lo! in yon brilliant window niche,
> How statue-like I see thee stand,
> The agate lamp within thy hand!
> Ah, Psyche, from the regions which
> Are Holy land!

In a letter now before us, written within a twelve-month of his death, Edgar Poe speaks of the love which inspired these verses as "the one, idolatrous, and purely *ideal* love"[55] of his passionate boyhood. In one of the numbers of *Russell's Magazine* there is a transcript of the first published version of the exquisite poem entitled "Lenore," commencing

> Ah, broken is the golden bowl! the spirit flown forever,
> Let the bell toll! a saintly soul floats on the Stygian river.

It is remarkable that, in this earlier version, instead of LENORE we have the name of HELEN.[56] The lines were afterwards greatly altered and improved in structure and expression, and the name of LENORE was introduced, apparently for its adaptation to rhythmical effect. Whatever may be the meaning that underlies this strange funeral anthem, it will always be admired for the triumphant music of its sorrow and for its sombre pomp of words. We may trust that the "Sabbath Song" did indeed

> Go up to God so solemnly the dead could feel no wrong.[57]

The ideas which haunted the brain of the young poet during his watch in the lonely churchyard, the shapeless fears and phantasms,

> Flapping from out their Condor wings
> Invisible Woe![58]

were the same which overwhelmed De Quincey at the burial of his sweet sister and playmate, as described by him in the *Suspiria de profundis*[59] —

---

[55] Poe. *Last Letters*, p. 10. Poe wrote: "written, in my passionate boyhood, to the first purely ideal love of my soul."
[56] Oral Sumner Coad points out that in an earlier version of the poem, published in 1831, "the dead girl is nameless."
[57] Poe. "Lenore." The line concludes: "the dead may feel no wrong."
[58] Poe. "The Conqueror Worm."
[59] De Quincey's *Suspiria de profundis* (Sighs from the Depths) is a series of unconnected essays or prose poems published in 1845, including memories of childhood but also influenced by the author's opium addiction. Portions of it appeared in his collected works in 1854; other parts were published posthumously. Ticknor, in Boston, began publishing DeQuincey's works in 1851, so Whitman might have read De Quincey in *Blackwood's* or in these

<80>

ideas of terror and indescribable awe at the thought of that mysterious waking sleep, that powerless and dim vitality, in which "the dead" are presumed, according to our popular theology, to await "the general resurrection at the last day." What wonder that the phantoms of "Shadow" and "Silence," once evoked there, could never be exorcised! What wonder that "the fable which the Demon told in the shadow of the tomb" haunted him forever!

"Now there are strange tales in the volumes of the Magi — in the iron-bound, melancholy volumes of the Magi, — glorious histories of the heaven, and of the earth, and of the mighty sea — and of the genii that overruled the sea and the earth and the lofty heaven; there was much lore, too, in the sayings of the Sybils. And holy, holy things were heard of old by the dim leaves that trembled around Dodona — but, as Allah liveth, that fable which the Demon told me as he sat by my side in the shadow of the tomb, I hold to be the most wonderful of all! And as the Demon made an end of his story, he fell back within the cavity of the tomb and laughed. And I could not laugh with the Demon, and he cursed me because I could not laugh. And the lynx which dwelleth forever in the tomb, came out and sat at the feet of the Demon and looked him steadily in the face."[60]

These solitary churchyard vigils, with all their associated memories, present a key to much that seems strange and abnormal in the poet's afterlife. Questions which no human tongue could answer, no human knowledge satisfy or silence, then found an utterance in the vast and desolate chambers of his imagination, and their mournful echoes are heard again and again in the magic cadences of his verse. In the "Colloquy of Monos and Una" he has imagined all the phases of sentient life in the grave, and in the "Bridal Ballad" are stanzas which, as read by the author, were full of a wild, sad pathos not easily forgotten. We will instance only two of the stanzas although their rhythmical effect is injured by their separation from those which precede and accompany them.

> And my lord he loves me well;
>> But when fast he breathed his vow
> The words rang as a knell,
> And the voice seemed *his* who fell
> In the battle down the dell,
>> And who is happy now.

★ ★ ★ ★ ★

American volumes.
[60] Poe. "Silence (Siope): A Fable." *Tales of the Grotesque and Arabesque* (1840). Whitman's quote is imprecise, substituting "strange" for "fine," changing Poe's punctuation and eliding some passages.

<81>

Would God I could awaken!
For I dream I know not how,
And my soul is sorely shaken
Lest an evil step be taken
Lest the dead, who is forsaken,
May not be happy now.

The thought which informs so many of his tales and poems betrays its sad sincerity even in his critical writings, as, for instance, in a notice of "Undine" in the "Marginalia."[61] Yet it has been said of him that "he had no touch of human feeling or of human pity," that "he loved no one but himself" — that "he was an abnormal and monstrous creation," — "possessed by legions of devils." The most injurious epithets have been heaped upon his name and the most improbable and calumnious stories recorded as veritable histories. Ten years have passed since his death, and while the popular interest in his writings and the popular estimate of his genius increases from year to year, these acknowledged calumnies are still going the round of the foreign periodicals and are still being republished at home.

WE BELIEVE THAT with the exception of Mr. Willis's generous tributes to his memory, some candid and friendly articles by the Editor of the *Literary Messenger*, and an eloquent and vigorous article in *Russell's Magazine* by Mr. J. Wood Davidson,[62] of Columbia, S. C. (who has appreciated his genius and his sorrow more justly perhaps than any of his American critics) this great and acknowledged wrong to the dead has been permitted to pass without public rebuke or protest.

In the memoir prefixed to the *Illustrated Poems*, it is said of him that "his religion was a worship of the beautiful," which is emphatically true, and that "he knew no beauty but that which is purely sensuous,"[63] which is, as emphatically, untrue. We appeal from this last assertion to Mr. Poe's own exposition of his poetic theory. He recognizes the elements of poetic emotion — the emotion of the beautiful, "*in all noble thoughts, in all holy impulses, in all chivalrous, generous, and self-sacrificing deeds.*"[64] His "aes-

[61] A sensitive and favorable review that contrasted the innocent soul of the water nymph Undine with that of the transformed woman who now experiences love. "What can be more divine than the character of the soul-less Undine? — what more august than the transition into the soul-possessing wife?" *Democratic Review*, December 1844.
[62] James Wood Davison, "Edgar A Poe." *Russell's Magazine*, Nov. 1857.
[63] "Memoir," attributed to Briggs, in the 1853 *Illustrated Poems*, p. xix.
[64] From the prose-poetic penultimate paragraph of Poe's. "The Poetic

<82>

thetic religion," which has been so strangely misapprehended, was simply a recognition of the divine and inseparable harmonies of the supremely Beautiful and the supremely Good.

The author of the very able and systematic *critique* in *The North American Review* (which is, nevertheless, essentially false in all its estimates of intellectual and moral character) tells us that he "*repudiated moral uses* in his prose fictions, as in his poetry, and that if moral or spiritual truths are found in them, they must have got there accidentally, without the author's permission or knowledge."[65] This is very unjust. To prove its injustice we have only once more to quote the author's own words. "*Taste,*" the sense of the beautiful, "*holds intimate relations with the intellect and the moral sense:* from the moral sense it is separated by so faint a difference that Aristotle has not hesitated to place some of its operations among the virtues themselves." Again, "The poetic sense is strictly and simply the human aspiration for supernal beauty. It is no mere appreciation of the beauty before us, but a wild effort to reach the beauty above — a prescience of that loveliness whose very elements, perhaps, appertain to Eternity alone."[66]

The current strictures on Poe's sinful worship of Beauty remind us of the satirist, Shoppe, in Jean Paul's *Titan,* who says, "In one respect we Germans are far in advance of the Greeks and Italians. We never seek the Beautiful without looking for collateral advantages; our caryatides must uphold pulpits, and our angels bear baptismal fonts."[67]

We are ready to admit, with the severe critic of *The North American [Review]*, that a very large proportion of Poe's stories are filled with monstrous and appalling images — that many of them oppress the reader like frightful incubi, from whose influence he vainly tries to escape. Ruskin tells us, in his treatise on the grotesque, that it is the trembling

Principle."
[65] Unsigned book review by E. Vale Smith, in *The North American Review,* October 1856, p.437.
[66] Quoted, but not precisely, from "The Poetic Principle."
[67] The sprawling novel, *Titan,* by Jean-Paul Richter, is a kind of Mount Everest of German literature. Carlyle says of Richter, "Unite the sportfulness of Rabelais, and the best sensibility of Sterne, with the earnestness, and even, in slight portions, the sublimity of Milton; and let the mosaic brain of old Burton give forth the workings of this strange union, with the pen of Jeremy Bentham!" (Carlyle, "Jean Paul", p. 13). The text of *Titan* was not available in English when Whitman wrote her essay, so she may have been traversing this monumental work on her own. A fellow Rhode Islander, Charles Timothy Brooks, of Newport, was the same time endeavoring to issue his English translation, which was finally published in Boston in 1862. Since Brooks also produced several volumes of translations of German poetry, and was himself a poet, it is very likely that Whitman knew Brooks and might have seen some of his translations in manuscript. That said, the passage Whitman quotes does *not* appear in Brooks' two-volume translation of Richter's *Titan.*

<83>

of the human soul in the presence of Death which most of all disturbs the images on the intellectual mirror, investing them with the grotesque ghastliness of fitful dreams. "If the mind be not healthful and serene the wider the scope of its glance and the grander the truths of which it obtains an insight the more fantastic and fearful are these distorted images."

Yet, as out of mighty and terrific discords noblest harmonies are sometimes evolved, so through the purgatorial ministries of awe and terror, and through the haunting Nemesis of doubt, Poe's restless and unappeased soul was urged on to the fulfillment of its appointed work; groping out blindly towards the light, and marking the approach of great spiritual truths by the very depth of the shadow it projected against them.

IT WOULD SEEM that the true point of view from which his genius should be regarded has yet to be sought. We are not of those who believe that any order of genius is revealed to us in vain, nor do we believe that the age would have gained anything if the author of "The Raven" had proved another Wordsworth, or another Longfellow. These far-wandering comets, not less than "the regular, calm stars," obey a law and follow a pathway that has been marked out for them by infinite wisdom and essential love. That the genius of Poe had its peculiar mission and significance in relation to the age we cannot doubt. Every man of electric temperament and prophetic genius represents, or rather anticipates, with more or less of consciousness and direct volition, those latent ideas which are about to unfold themselves in humanity. It is thus that Müller[68] accounts for the origin of the Greek Mythus, the simple invention of which he pronounces to be impossible, if by *invention* is meant a free and deliberate treatment of something known to be untrue. He regards the originators of the Greek Mythus merely as the more passive recipients and skilful exponents who first gave form and expression to those spiritual ideas which were tending to organic development at that particular stage of the world's progress — "the foci in which the scattered rays of spiritual consciousness were concentrating themselves to be radiated forth with new intensity."[69] When Poe's genius began to unfold itself the age was moving feverously and restlessly through processes of transition and development which seemed about to unsettle all things, yet gave no clear indication of whither they were leading us.

---

[68] Karl Ottfried Müller (1797-1840), professor at University of Göttingen, was the first German scholar to write a comprehensive history of Greek literature and culture. He placed Greek myth in its historical context. Some of his works translated into English and available to Whitman include *The History and Antiquities of the Doric Race* (1839), *Attica and Athens* (1842), and *History of the Literature of Ancient Greece to the Period of Isocrates* (1840).

[69] J.B. Stallo. *General Principles of the Philosophy of Nature* (1848), p. 175.

<84>

In our own country, Mr. Emerson's assertion of the transcendental side of the ever-recurring question between idealism and materialism marked the reaction of intellectual and spiritual tendencies against the materialism and literalism of the churches. Through him the fine idealism of the German mystics penetrated our literature and spiritualized our philosophies. His novel statements of truth had in them a strange force and directness, startling the sleepers like the *naïve* cadences of a child's voice heard amid the falsetto tones of the conventicle or the theatre. What a sovran grace of sincerity in his chapter on Experience. What noble ethics in his statement of spiritual laws. Yet, if we turn to the pages of Emerson and look for the evidences of his belief in the soul's individual immortality, we shall find that the words he has uttered on the subject express, for the most part, either a purely Oriental indifference or an aimless and anxious questioning. In his lecture to the divinity students of Cambridge, protesting against the formalism and famine of the churches, he told them that the faith of the Puritans was dying out, and none arising in its stead; that the eye of youth was not lighted by the hope of other worlds; that literature had become frivolous and science cold. In his "Lecture on The Times"[70] he says, "We drift like white sail across the wide ocean, now bright on the wave, now darkling in the trough of the sea. But from what port did we sail? Who knows? Or to what port are we bound? Who knows? There is no one to tell us, but such poor, weather-tossed mariners as ourselves, whom we speak as we pass, or who have hoisted some signal from afar, or floated to us some letter in a bottle. But what know they more than we?" In another of his essays he says, "I cannot tell if these wonderful qualities which now house together in this mortal frame shall ever reassemble in equal activity in a similar frame, but this one thing I know, that the *law* which clothes us with humanity remains new. We are immortal with the immortality of this law."[71]

These expressions indicate the pervading skepticism of the time. Coming, as they do, from a man who had been educated as a clergyman, a man for whose large culture and liberal faith in humanity the pulpits of the existing church seemed to offer no sufficient platform, they have an emphasis which no added word could heighten.

The negation of Carlyle, and the boundless affirmation of Emerson, served but to stimulate without satisfying the intellect. The liberal ethics of Fourier, with his elaborate social economies and systems of petrified harmony, were leading his disciples through forlorn enterprises to hopeless failures. A "divine dissatisfaction" was everywhere apparent. De Quincey saw something fearful and portentous in the vast accessions to

[70] Emerson, "Lecture on the Times." Read at the Masonic Temple, Boston. December 2, 1841.
[71] Emerson, "The Method of Nature." Read at the Society of the Adelphi, Waterville College, ME, August 11, 1841.

<85>

man's physical resources that marked the time, unaccompanied by any improvement in psychical and spiritual knowledge. Goethe had made his great dramatic poem an expression of the soul's craving for a knowledge of spiritual existences:

> O gibt es geister in der luft
> Die zwischen Erd' und Himmel [herrschen] weben,
> So steiget nieder aus dem goldnen Duft,
>   Und führt mich weg zu neuem buntem Leben![72]

> [If there be spirits in the air
> That hold their sway between the earth and sky,
> Descend out of the golden vapor there
> And sweep me into iridescent life!][73]

Wordsworth, in his finest imaginative poem, "Laodamia," represents and half reproves this longing. Byron iterates it with a proud and passionate vehemence in *Manfred*. Shelley's sad heart of unbelief, finding refuge in a despair too deep for aspiration, stands apart, as Elizabeth Browning has so finely sculptured him,

> —— In his white ideal
> All statue-blind, [74]

while Keats lies sleeping, like his own Endymion, lost in dreams of the "dead past." Then, sadder, and lonelier, and more unbelieving than any of these, Edgar Poe came to sound the very depths of the abyss. The unrest and faithlessness of the age culminated in him. Nothing so solitary, nothing so hopeless, nothing so desolate as his spirit in its darker moods has been instanced in the literary history of the nineteenth century.

IT HAS BEEN said that his theory, as expressed in *Eureka*, of the universal diffusion of Deity in and through all things, is identical with the Brahminical faith as expressed in the Bagvat Gita.[75] But those who will patiently follow the vast reaches of his thought in this sublime poem of "The Universe" will find that he arrives at a form of unbelief

---

[72] From a dialogue between Faust and Wagner in Goethe's *Faust, Part 1*, ll. 1118-1121.

[73] Whitman provided no translation. This interpolation is from the Walter Kaufmann translation, p. 145.

[74] Elizabeth Barrett Browning. "A Vision of Poets" (1844).

[75] Charles Wilkins' 1785 translation of the Baghavad-Gita was the first to make this work available to English readers. Whitman may have seen this, or a widely-distributed edition created for missionary use in 1849.

<86>

far more appalling than that expressed in the gloomy pantheism of India, since it assumes that the central, creative Soul is, alternately, not *diffused* only, but merged and *lost* in the universe, and the universe in it, — "a new universe swelling into existence or subsiding into nothingness at every throb of the heart divine."[76] The creative energy, therefore, "*now* exists solely in the diffused matter and spirit, of the existing universe."[77] The author assumes, moreover, that each individual soul retains in its youth a dim consciousness of vast dooms and destinies far distant in the bygone time, and infinitely awful, from which inherent consciousness the conventional "world-reason" at last awakens it as from a dream. "It says you live, and the time was when you lived not. You have been created. An intelligence exists greater than your own, and it is only through this intelligence that you live at all."[78] "These things," he says, "*we struggle to comprehend and cannot,* — cannot, because being untrue, they are of necessity incomprehensible.

"No thinking man lives who, at some luminous point of his life [of thought], has not felt himself lost amid the surges of futile efforts at understanding[,] or believing that anything exists *greater than his own soul.* [. . .] [T]he intense, overwhelming dissatisfaction and rebellion at the thought, together with the omniprevalent aspirations at perfection, are but the spiritual, coincident with the material, struggles towards the original Unity. [. . .] The material *and* spiritual God *now* exists solely in the diffused Matter and Spirit of the Universe, and the regathering of this diffused matter and spirit will be but the reconstitution of the *purely* Spiritual and Individual God."[79]

In a copy of the original edition of *Eureka,* purchased at the recent sale of Dr. Griswold's library, the following note was found inscribed in the handwriting of the author on the half-blank page at the end of the volume. It is singularly ingenious and characteristic.

> *Note.* — The pain of the consideration that we shall lose our individual identity, ceases at once when we further reflect that the process, as above described, is neither more nor less than that of the absorption by each individual intelligence, of all other intelligences (that is of the Universe) into its own. That God may be all in all, *each* must become God.

---

[76] *Eureka*, p. 139
[77] Ibid, p. 141
[78] Ibid, p. 141. I have added ellipsis indicating phrases omitted and changed capitalization to conform with Poe's first edition. Whitman omits two references to "no soul being inferior to another."
[79] Ibid, p. 141

<87>

This proud self-assertion betrays a mysterious isolation from the "heart divine" which fills us with sadness and awe.

We confess to a half faith in the old superstition of the significance of anagrams when we find, in the transposed letters of Edgar Poe's name, the words "a God-peer;" words which, taken in connection with his daring speculations, seem to have in them a mocking and malign import "which is not man's nor angel's."[80]

Yet, while the author of *Eureka*, like Lucretius,

> ——— dropped his plummet down the broad,
> Deep Universe and found no God,[81]

his works are, as if unconsciously, filled with an overwhelming sense of the power and majesty of Deity: they are even dark with reverential awe. His proud intellectual assumption of the supremacy of the individual soul was but an expression of its imperious longings for immortality and its recoil from the haunting phantasms of death and annihilation; while the theme of all his more imaginative writings is, as we have said, a love that survives the dissolution of the mortal body and oversweeps the grave. His mental and temperamental idiosyncrasies fitted him to come readily into rapport with psychical and spiritual influences. Many of his strange narratives had a degree of truth in them which he was unwilling to avow. In one of this class he makes the narrator say, "I cannot even now regard these experiences as a dream, yet it is difficult to say how otherwise they should be termed. *Let us suppose only that the soul of man, to-day, is on the brink of stupendous psychical discoveries.*"[82]

Dante tells us that

> ——— minds dreaming near the dawn
> Are of the truth presageful.[83]

Edgar Poe's dreams were assuredly often presageful and significant; and while he but dimly apprehended through the higher reason the truths which they foreshadowed, he riveted public attention upon them by the

[80] Elizabeth Barrett Browning, "A Drama of Exile."
[81] Elizabeth Barrett Browning, "Vision of Poets." Browning's lines read: "Lucretius, nobler than his mood,/Who dropped his plummet down the broad/ Deep universe, and said "No God."
[82] Poe. "A Tale of the Ragged Mountains." "And not now, even for an instant, can I compel my understanding to regard it as a dream." "Nor was it," said Templeton, with an air of deep solemnity, "yet it would be difficult to say how otherwise it should be termed. Let us suppose only, that the soul of the man of to-day is upon the verge of some stupendous psychical discoveries" (p. 520).
[83] Dante relates three dreams in his *Purgatorio,* each of which occurs before dawn.

<88>

strange fascination of his style, the fine analytical temper of his intellect, and, above all, by the weird splendors of his imagination, compelling men to read and to accredit as *possible truths* his most marvelous conceptions. He often spoke of the imageries and incidents of his inner life as more vivid and veritable than those of his outer experience. We find in some penciled notes appended to a manuscript copy of one of his later poems, the words, "All that I have here expressed was actually present to me. Remember the mental condition which gave rise to 'Ligeia' — recall the passage of which I spoke, and observe the coincidence." With all the fine alchymy of his subtle intellect he sought to analyze the character and conditions of this introverted life. "I regard these visions," he says, "even as they arise, with an awe which in some measure moderates or tranquillizes the ecstasy: I so regard them through a conviction that this ecstasy, in itself, is of a character supernal to the human nature — *is a glimpse of the spirit's outer world.*" He had that constitutional determination to reverie which, according to De Quincey, alone enables a man to dream magnificently, and which, as we have said, made his dreams realities, and his life a dream. His mind was indeed a "Haunted Palace," echoing to the footfalls of angels and demons. "No man," he says, "has recorded, no man has dared to record, the wonders of his inner life."

Is there, then, no significance in this "supernatural soliciting"?[84] Is there no evidence of a wise purpose, an epochal fitness, in the appearance, at this precise era, of a mind so rarely gifted, and accessible from peculiarities of psychical and physical organization to the subtle vibrations of an ethereal medium conveying but feeble impressions to the senses of ordinary persons; a mind which, "following darkness like a dream,"[85] wandered forever with insatiate curiosity on the confines of that

— wild, weird clime, that lieth sublime
Out of Space, out of Time! [. . .]
By each spot the most unholy,
In each nook most melancholy, [86]

seeking to solve the problem of that phantasmal shadow-land, which, through a class of phenomena unprecedented in the world's history, was about to attest itself as an actual plane of conscious and progressive life,[87] the mode and measure of whose relations with our own are already recognised as legitimate objects of scientific research by the most candid

---

[84] *Supernatural soliciting.* Shakespeare. *Macbeth* I:iii:134.
[85] Shakespeare. *A Midsummer Night's Dream.* V:i, 386.
[86] Poe. "Dream-Land."
[87] *A class of phenomena* … Refers to the arrival of the Spiritualist phenomena after 1848.

<89>

and competent thinkers of our time? We assume that, in the abnormal manifestations of a genius so imperative and so controlling, this epochal significance is most strikingly apparent. Jean Paul says truly that "there is more poetic fitness, more method, a more intelligible purpose in the biographies which God Almighty writes, than in all the inventions of poets and novelists."

THE PECULIARITIES OF Edgar Poe's organization and temperament doubtless exposed him to peculiar infirmities. We need not discuss them here. They have been already too elaborately and painfully illustrated elsewhere to need further comment. How fearfully he expiated them, only those who best knew and loved him can ever know. We are told that ideas of right and wrong are wholly ignored by him — that "no recognitions of conscience or remorse are to be found on his pages."[88] If not *there*, where, then, shall we look for them? In "William Wilson," in "The Man of the Crowd," and in "The Tell-Tale Heart," the retributions of conscience are portrayed with a terrible fidelity. In yet another of his stories, which we will not name, the fearful fatality of crime — the dreadful fascination consequent on the indulgence of a perverse will is portrayed with a relentless and awful reality.[89] May none ever read it who do not need the fearful lesson which it brands on the memory in characters of fire! In the relation of this remarkable story we recognize the power of a genius like that which sustains us in traversing the lowest depths of Dante's *Inferno*. The rapid descent in crime which it delineates, and which becomes at last involuntary, reminds us of the subterranean staircase by which Vathek and Nouronihar reached the Hall of Eblis, where, as they descended, they felt their steps frightfully accelerated, till they seemed falling from a precipice.[90]

Poe's private letters to his friends offer abundant evidence that he was not insensible to the keenest pangs of remorse. Again and again did he say to the Demon that tracked his path, "Anathema Maranatha!" but again and again did it return to torture and subdue. He saw the handwriting on the wall, but had no power to avert the impending doom.

In relation to this, the fatal temptation of his life, he says, in a letter written within a year of his death, "The agonies which I have lately endured have passed my soul through fire: henceforth I am strong. This those who love me shall know, as well as those who have so relentlessly sought to ruin me. . . . I have absolutely *no* pleasure in the stimulants in which I sometimes so madly indulge. It has not been in the pursuit of

[88] In a similar vein, Griswold, in the 1850 Memoir, wrote: "In Poe's works there is constantly displayed the most touching melancholy, the most extreme and terrible despair, but never reverence or remorse."
[89] Probably "The Black Cat."
[90] *Vathek, An Arabian Tale,* by William Beckford, published in 1786.

<90>

pleasure that I have perilled life and reputation and reason: it has been in the desperate attempt to escape from torturing memories, — memories of wrong and injustice and imputed dishonor, — from a sense of insupportable loneliness and a dread of some strange impending doom."[91] We believe these statements to have been sincerely uttered, and we would record here the testimony of a gentleman who, having for years known him intimately and having been near him in his states of utter mental desolation and insanity, assured us that he had never heard from his lips a word that would have disgraced his heart or brought reproach upon his honor.

Could we believe that any plea we may have urged in extenuation of Edgar Poe's infirmities and errors would make the fatal path he trod less abhorrent to others, such would never have been proffered. No human sympathy, no human charity could avert the penalties of that erring life. One clear glance into its mournful corridors — its "halls of tragedy and chambers of retribution,"[92] would appall the boldest heart.

Theodore Parker has nobly said that "every man of genius has to hew out for himself, from the hard marbles of life, the white statue of Tranquility."[93] Those who have best succeeded in this sublime work will best know how to look with pity and reverent awe upon the melancholy *torso* which alone remains to us of Edgar Poe's misguided efforts to achieve that beautiful and august statue of Peace.

THOSE WHO ARE curious in tracing the effects of country and lineage in the mental and constitutional peculiarities of men of genius may be interested in such facts as we have been enabled to gather in relation to the ancestry of the Poet. The awakening interest in genealogical researches will make them acceptable to many readers; and in their possible influence on a character so anomalous as that of Edgar Poe they are certainly worthy of note.

John Poe, the great-grandfather of Edgar Poe, left Ireland for America about the middle of the last century. He was of the old Norman family of Le Poer, a name conspicuous in Irish annals. Sir Roger le Poer went

---

[91] See *The Last Letters of Edgar Allan Poe to Sarah Helen Whitman*, p. 36. Although the 1909 edition of these letters was prepared from the original Poe manuscript letters, the quotation after the ellipsis does not appear in the letter. Whitman has apparently interposed a recollected conversation here: note that she calls the communication an "utterance."

[92] De Quincey, *Suspiria de Profundis*, "Memorial Suspiria," p. 711.

[93] Theodore Parker (1810-1860) was a radical Unitarian preacher and abolitionist. He may have used these phrases in more than one context. In *A Discourse of Matters Relating to Religion*, Parker writes: "Out of the hard marble of life, the deposition of a few joys and many sorrows, of birth and death, and smiles and grief, he hews him the beautiful statue of religious tranquility." The passage makes no mention of a "man of genius" (p. 131).

<91>

to Ireland, as marshal to Prince John, in the reign of Henry II, and became there the founder of a race connected with some of the most romantic and chivalrous incidents of Irish history. The heroic daring of Arnold le Poer, seneschal of Kilkenny Castle, who interposed, at the ultimate sacrifice of his liberty and his life, to save a noble lady from an ecclesiastical trial for witchcraft, the first ever instituted in the kingdom, was chronicled by Geraldus Cambrensis,[94] and has been commemorated by recent historians.

A transcript of the story, as told by Geraldus, may be found in *Ennemoser's Magic*[95] and in White's *History of Sorcery.*[96] The bitter feuds and troubled fortunes of the Anglo-Norman settlers in Ireland are well illustrated in a recent genealogical history of the Geraldines by the Marquis of Kildare, noticed in *The Edinburgh Quarterly* for October, 1858.[97] The disastrous civil war of 1327, in which all the great barons of the country were involved, was occasioned by a personal feud between Arnold le Poer and Maurice of Desmond, the former having offended the dignity of the Desmond by calling him a rhymer.[98]

The characteristics of the Le Poers were marked and distinctive. They were improvident, adventurous, and recklessly brave. They were deeply involved in the Irish troubles of 1641; and when Cromwell invaded Ireland, he pursued them with a special and relentless animosity. Their families were dispersed, their estates ravaged, and their lands forfeited. Of the three leading branches of the family at the time of Cromwell's invasion, Kilmaedon, Don Isle, and Curraghmore, the last only escaped his vengeance. The present representative of Curraghmore is the Marquis of Waterford. Cromwell's siege of the sea-girt castle and fortress of Don

---

[94] *Giraldus Cambrensis,* Gerald of Wales (c. 1146-c. 1223), archdeacon and historian.

[95] Joseph Ennemoser. *The History of Magic* (1854), pp. 464-474. The cited text is not by Ennemoser, but is part of a long appendix compiled by Mary Howitt, who extracted the narrative from Thomas Wright's 1851 *Narratives of Sorcery and Magic.* The valiant le Poer, after his rescue of the accused witch suffered this fate: "[T]he bishop now accused him of heresy, had him excommunicated, and obtained a writ by which he was committed prisoner to the castle of Dublin. Here he remained in 1328, when Roger Outlawe was made Lord Justice of Ireland, who attempted to mitigate his sufferings ... Arnold le Poer himself would probably have been declared innocent and liberated from confinement, but before the end of the investigation he died in prison, and his body, lying under sentence of excommunication, remained long unburied" (p. 474).

[96] A search did not turn up any book by this title. Whitman may have been referring the *Narratives of Sorcery* by Wright, which had an American edition in 1852.

[97] Kildare, Marquis. *The Earls of Kildare and Their Ancestors, from 1057 to 1773.* Dublin, 1858.

[98] Kildrea, p. 30.

<92>

Isle, which was heroically defended by a female descendant of Nicholas le Poer, Baron of Don Isle, is, as represented by Sir Bernard Burke in his *Romance of the Aristocracy*,[99] full of legendary interest. The beautiful domain of Powerscourt took its name from the Le Poers, and was for centuries in the possession of the family. Lady Blessington, through her father, Edmund Power, claimed descent from the same old Norman family. The fact is not mentioned in Madden's memoir of the Countess,[100] but is stated in a notice of her death published in *The London Illustrated News* for June 9th, 1849. The family of the Le Poers, like that of the Geraldines and other Anglo-Norman settlers in Ireland, passed from Italy into the north of France, and from France through England and Wales into Ireland, where, from their isolated position and other causes, they retained for a long period their hereditary traits with far less modification from intermarriage and consociation with other races than did their English compeers. Meantime the name underwent various changes in accent and orthography. A few branches of the family still bore in Ireland the old Italian name of De la Poe.

John Poe, the great-grandfather of Edgar Poe, married a daughter of Admiral McBride, distinguished for his naval achievements and connected with some of the most illustrious families of England.[101] From genealogical records transmitted by him to his son, David Poe, the grandfather of the poet, who was but two years of age when his parents left Ireland, it appears that different modes of spelling the name were adopted by different members of the same family. David Poe was accustomed to speak of the Chevalier le Poer, a friend of the Marquis de Grammont, as having been of his father's family. The grandfather of Edgar Poe was an officer in the Maryland line during the war of the Revolution, and, as Dr. Griswold has told us, the intimate friend of Lafayette. He married a lady of Pennsylvania, by the name of Cairnes, who is still remembered as having been a woman of singular beauty. The father of Edgar Poe, while a law student in the office of William Gwynn, Esq., of Baltimore, married, at the age of eighteen, Elizabeth Arnold, a young English actress, who was herself but a child. He first saw her at Norfolk, where he was sent on professional business, and in a few months they were married. Indignant at so imprudent a union, his parents refused their countenance to the marriage, and it was only after the birth of a

---

[99] J. Bernard Burke. *Anecdotes of the Aristocracy, and Episodes in Ancestral Story.* Vol. 1 (1849), pp. 92-100.

[100] R.A. Madden. *The Literary Life and Correspondence of The Countess Blessington.* London, 1855.

[101] John McBride (c. 1735-1800) had a long British naval military career including the Seven Years War, the war for American independence, and the war against Revolutionary France. He annexed the Falkland Islands for Britain and was later the MP for Plymouth.

<93>

child that he was forgiven and received back into the paternal mansion. During the period of his estrangement from his family he had joined his wife in a theatrical engagement. Edgar Poe was the offspring of this romantic and improvident union.

HAVING RECORDED OUR earnest protest against the misapprehension of his critics and the misstatements of his biographists, we leave the subject for the present, in the belief that a more impartial memoir of the poet will yet be given to the world, and the story of his sad strange life, when contemplated from a new point of view, be found — like the shield of bronze whose color was so long contested by the knights of fable — to present, at least, a silver lining.

THE END.

<94>

POE, CRITIC, AND HOBBY:
A REPLY TO MR. FAIRFIELD
by S.H.W. (Sarah Helen Whitman)

SIR: Mr. F. G. Fairfield, a gentleman who has had the temerity to pass "ten years among spiritual mediums" in the cause of science, having demonstrated that they are all more or less afflicted with epileptic mania, has recently turned his attention to poets and men of inspirational genius, and finds that they, too, from Ezekiel to Æschylus, from Æschylus to Coleridge, are all as mad as March hares. If there is method in their madness, there is also madness in their method. He frankly confesses in his book of mediums that he has himself had personal experience of the malady. He has studied it in all its phases. He intimates that "habitual lying" is one of its most trustworthy exponents. I by no means wish to undervalue Mr. Fairfield's researches in the nebulous atmosphere of peripheral nerve-auras. They are valuable and interesting, but does not his theory threaten to cover too much ground?

In the October number of *Scribner's* this gentleman has an article entitled "A Mad Man of Letters,"[102] in which he selects the author of "The Raven" as a favorable specimen of the epileptic type. Assuming chronic lying as symptomatic of the disease, he gravely quotes the following story in evidence of Poe's habitual mendacity. A single instance, he says, may suffice to prove the many. Here is the instance: A gentleman who professed to have received the "facts" from Mrs. Clemm told him that Poe, once on a time, after walking all the way from New-York to Fordham, swallowed up a cup of tea, sat down to his writing-desk, and dashed off "The Raven" substantially as it is now printed, and submitted it to Mrs. Clemm as the result of his evening's incubation! Unmindful of the fact that Poe did not reside in Fordham until long after "The Raven" was printed and published, Mr. Fairfield naively accepts this story as a choice bit of veritable history, illustrative of Poe's epileptic tendency to habitual lying. For how could "The Raven" have been composed at a single sitting, when Mr. Fairfield assures us that he has the evidence of Poe's literary contemporaries on this matter—gentlemen who were in the habit of meeting him at midday for a cozy chat in Sandy Welch's cellar. And did not these gentlemen assure him that the poem was produced line by line, stanza by stanza, and submitted by Poe, piecemeal, to the criticism and emendation of the Ann-St. Clique? — gentlemen who doubtless "know a hawk from a handsaw when the wind was southerly,"[103] and who suggested many valuable alterations and substitu-

---

[102] Francis Gerry Fairfield. "A Mad Man of Letters." *Scribner's*, October 1875.

<95>

tions. One of these gentlemen, says Mr. Fairfield, has even pointed out to me particular instances of phrases that were incorporated at his own suggestion, "showing that 'The Raven' was a kind of joint-stock operation in which many minds held small shares of intellectual property." After this we may not hope that the gentlemen who assisted at the incubation of this remarkable fowl in Sandy Welch's cellar will come forward in a body to claim their respective shares in this piece of joint-stock property, thus setting at rest forever all questions as to "Who wrote 'The Raven'?" "Was 'The Raven' a Persian fowl?" "Whence came the manuscript found in Mr. Shaver's barn?" and other interrogations of like import which have from time to time agitated the purlieus of Parnassus.

Having disposed of "The Raven," Mr. Fairfield applies his scalpel to Poe's wonderful poem of "Ulalume," calling it, in his haphazard way, "his last poem — a mere rigmarole in rhyme, exhibiting in its elaborate emptiness the last stages of mental decrepitude and decay." "Thus sang he, then died," exclaims this careful and conscientious commentator. On the contrary, "thus sang he," then wrote "Eureka," "The Bells," "Annabel Lee," and other of his most memorable poems. But when an "alienist"—I believe that is the correct word — mounts his hobby and rides rough-shod in pursuit of an epileptic subject to illustrate a favorite theory, he cannot be expected to pay much attention to such hard facts as happen to lie in his way.

The critic does not, in this instance, accuse the unhappy author of plagiarism; does not even remotely insinuate that the poem has been slicked up in Sandy Welch's cellar. It was altogether too rough a specimen for the contemporaries to have taken stock in. If Mr. Fairfield, who is not without poetic insight, had thought less of his theory and more of his subject, he might have better apprehended what he is pleased to call the geist of the poem; might have seen that it was not the "low-hanging moon," but Venus "Astarte"—the crescent star of hope and love, that, after a night of horror, was seen in the Constellation Leo:

> Coming through the lair of the Lion
> As the star-dials hinted of morn.

He might have seen the forlorn heart hailing it as a harbinger of happiness yet to be, hoping against hope, until, when the planet was seen to be rising over the tomb of a lost love, hope itself was rejected as a cruel mockery, and the dark angel conquered. He might have also discerned in this "empty rigmarole of rhyme" something of that ethical quality which an eloquent interpreter of Poe's genius, in the July number of *The*

---

[103] From *Hamlet*, II:2, lines in which Hamlet suggests that he is only a little mad, when it suits his interests. The "handsaw" is likely "heronshaw," a heron.

<96>

British Quarterly, finds in this strange and splendid phantasy.[104] Like the Episychidian of Shelley[105], it is a poem for poets, and will not readily give up "the heart of the mystery" to aliens and "alienists."[106]

When I compare the disparaging tone of this article with a paragraph from the same writer which appeared in *The Boston Radical* for April, 1871, I am perplexed to account for the discrepancy. " 'The Raven,' 'The Ancient Mariner,' and 'Queen Mab,' in their ghostly energy and magnificence of beauty, in their subtle etheriality of imagery, in the weird burst of moaning minor of their cadences, are among the most powerful creations of the imagination, and are, in ratio to their power, remarkable for a certain sublimation of the subjective, and dependent upon it for their effect." And again: "In the fiction of Brontë, Hugo, Poe, Hawthorne, Dickens, and other masters of the century, we find an intense subjectivity." How happens it that one of the masters of the century is now labeled, "A Mad Man of Letters." His "sublimation of the subjective" is now "epileptic egotism." "He was an egotist to the core." "In his 'Eureka' there is scarcely an original thought. Poe did not think, he was simply a dreamer." "Sent to college, he found his work interfering with his dreams. Hence he ran away (!) and afterward tried to atone for his lack of mental culture by cunning devices and feats of the solve-a-puzzle kind. He was incapable of honest work."

If this piece of amateur surgery is a specimen of "honest work," one must needs borrow Æsop's lantern to find out its honesty.

— September 29, 1875
Providence, Rhode Island
Published in *The New York Daily Tribune,* October 13, 1875

---

[104] "Edgar Allan Poe." Unsigned review of *The Works of Edgar Allan Poe,* edited by John Ingram. *British Quarterly Review.* Vol. 62, July 1875, pp. 212-213.

[105] "Episychidian," an 1821 poem by Shelley. Its title means "about a little soul." Its subject is a young woman sent against her will to a convent, and Shelley called it "an idealized history of my life and feelings."

[106] Ironically, Fairfield published, in the same year, several poems directly imitative of Poe, including "Dream Life and Day Life," which echoes Poe's "Ulalume." Fairfield *et al,* pp. 167-68.

<97>

INTRODUCTORY LETTER
The Life and Poems of Edgar Allan Poe
by Sarah Helen Whitman (1876)

Mr. Eugene L. Didier:

Dear Sir : — I am gratified to know that one who so sincerely admires the genius of Edgar Poe, and who must have access to many hitherto unexplored sources of information as to his early history and associates, is preparing to publish the result of his investigations in relation to a period concerning which we still know so little. I doubt not that whatever you may have to say on the subject will be of permanent value in the elucidation of a story whose facts are so singularly evasive and uncertain.

To translate that mysterious, shadowy, poetic life of his, with its elusive details and mythical traditions, into the fixed facts and clear outlines of authentic narrative, must, I fear, prove a difficult task to the most conscientious annalist.

In your letter of June 26, you say: "N. P. Willis speaks of Poe as living at Fordham while he was employed upon the *Mirror*, which was in the autumn of 1844 and early winter of 1845." I have no certain knowledge of the time when Poe was employed on the *Mirror*, but I have a very definite and decided knowledge as to the fact that during the whole of the winter 1845-6, he was residing in the city of New York — I think in Amity Street. He was, at that time, a frequent visitor and ever-welcome guest at the houses of many persons with whom I have long been intimately acquainted — among others, the Hon. John R. Bartlett, then of the firm of Bartlett & Welford, and Miss Anne C. Lynch, now Mrs. Botta — who were accustomed to receive informally at their houses, on stated evenings, the best intellectual society of the city. To reinforce my memory on the subject, I have just referred to letters received from various correspondents in New York, during the winters 1845 and 1846, in all of which the name of the poet frequently occurs.

In one of these letters, dated January 20, 1846, the writer says: "Speaking of our receptions, I must tell you what a pleasant one we had on Saturday evening, in Waverley Place; or rather I will tell you the names of some of the company, and you will know, among others, that of Cassius Clay; Mr. Hart, the sculptor, who is doing Henry Clay in marble; Halleck; Locke (the Man in the Moon); Hunt, of the Merchant's Magazine; Hudson; Mr. Bellows; Poe; Headley; Miss Sedgwick; Mrs. Kirkland; Mrs.

<98>

Osgood; Mrs. Seba Smith; Mrs. Ellet; and many others, more or less distinguished."

One of these letters, in which the date of the year is wanting, alludes to a controversy, which took place at one of the soirées, between Margaret Fuller (Ossoli) and Poe, about some writer whom, in her lofty, autocratic way, the lady had been annihilating. Miss Fuller was then writing critical papers for *The New York Tribune*. Poe, espousing the cause of the vanquished, with a few keen, incisive rejoinders, obtained such ascendency over the eloquent and oracular contessa, that somebody whispered, "The Raven has perched upon the casque of Pallas, and pulled all the feathers out of her cap."

In another letter, dated January 7, 1846, I find the following: "I meet Mr. Poe very often at the receptions. He is the observed of all observers. His stories are thought wonderful, and to hear him repeat the Raven, which he does very quietly, is an event in one's life. People seem to think there is something uncanny about him, and the strangest stories are told, and, what is more, believed, about his mesmeric experiences, at the mention of which he always smiles. His smile is captivating! . . . Everybody wants to know him; but only a very few people seem to get well acquainted with him."

This was in the spring of 1846, when Poe was at the very acme of his literary and social success among the literati of New York.

His wife's health, which had always been delicate, was now rapidly failing, and, hoping that she might be benefited by change of air, the family removed to Fordham. Mr. Poe first took his wife there on a house-hunting tour of inspection, when the fruit trees were in blossom, and the aspect of the little cottage temptingly beautiful to the invalid. Whether they engaged it and removed there at once, I do not know; but it is my impression that they did, and that Poe withdrew himself entirely from the literary circles where his presence had proved so attractive.

There had, moreover, arisen at this time, among Poe's friends and admirers, social as well as literary feuds and rivalries of an incredible bitterness, and an intense vitality — feuds and rivalries whose unappeased ghosts still "peep and mutter."

The malign paragraph, falsely attributed to Mrs. Elizabeth Oakes Smith, which recently went the rounds of the newspapers, was doubtless of this class. It was, apparently, an intentional perversion of a report stated by her in an able article, written for the *Home Journal*, which appeared early in March or April of the present year.[107]

[107] Elizabeth Oakes Smith. "Recollections of Poe." *Home Journal*, March 15, 1876. An earlier essay, part of Smith's never-completed autobiography, appeared in February 1867 in *Beadle's Monthly*. It has been suggested that the misattribution of negative comments about Poe to Mrs. Smith may come from the fact that another Mrs. Smith — E. Vale Smith — wrote the unsigned

<99>

I do not hesitate to say, without appealing to her on the subject, that the scandal so industriously circulated was neither written nor authorized by her. It is not only at variance with the whole tenor of the article in question, but with that of a private letter, written within the year, in which she says: "Mr. Poe was the last person to whom I should ever have attributed any grossness. . . . I saw women jealous in their admiration of him. I think he often found himself entangled by their plots and rivalries. I do not for a moment think he was false in his relations to them." [108]

Moncure Conway, too, who had reason to know something of Poe's habits, in this particular, from gentlemen of Richmond who had been intimately associated with him, says, in a cordial notice of Mr. Ingram's Memoir, prefixed to the Standard edition of Poe's works[109]: "Edgar Poe was exceptionally chivalrous in his relations with women," and he illustrates the remark by an anecdote corroborative of its truth. "The innumerable legends which accumulated round his life and name," says Mr. Conway, "were, in one sense, a tribute to his extraordinary powers. He is one of the few men who are represented by a mythology."[110]

The persistent enmity, which follows his fame like a shadow, is without a parallel in the literary history of our country. While many of the old slanders have lost their pungency, Poe's memory continues to be assailed on the most baseless and preposterous pretexts. Apparently society needs a typical Don Giovanni, a representative Mephistopheles, to frighten reprobates and refractory children, and to point a pious moral.

The Rev. Dr. Bartol, of Boston, a most exemplary and benignant gentleman, of progressive views and liberal tendencies, lately illustrated an eloquent specimen of pulpit oratory, by denouncing Poe as "the unhappy master, who recklessly carried the torch of his genius into the haunts of the drunkard and the debauchee, until he utterly extinguished it in his profligate poems!"[111] Evidently the good Doctor had not read

derogatory review of Poe's persona and works that appeared in *The North American Review* in 1856.

[108] Since the above was written, the following note from Mrs. Smith has been received:
Hollywood, Carteret Co., N. C.
Dear Mrs. Whitman:
I should be loth to think that any one who had ever known me could believe that I wrote the coarse, slanderous paragraph which you quote from the newspapers in your letter of the 12th instant. I never saw nor heard of it till now.
Mr. Poe was no such person as that would imply. Is it not strange that so much misrepresentation should still follow one so long in the grave? It is a tribute, but a cruel tribute, to the power of his marvelous genius.

[109] *The Works of Edgar Allan Poe.* John Ingram, ed. Edinburgh, 1874.

[110] I have not been able to track down this book review or notice. Whitman sent a copy of it to John Ingram in 1875, stating that it was published in Cincinnati. Conway was not in Cincinnati after 1862.

<100>

these "profligate poems" — poems to which the severest moralist accords "a matchless purity." At what shrine, then, was the torch of his clerical criticism lighted?

Probably he had been reading Mr. Francis Gerry Fairfield's "Mad Man of Letters,"[112] and vaguely associated with "the haunt of the drunkard," Sandy Welsh's cellar, the noonday glass of ale, the contemporaries, and the joint-stock company who got up the Raven! Out of such materials is the scroll of history replenished!

Mr. George Parsons Lathrop, in a note to his article on "Poe, Irving, and Hawthorne," as published in *Scribner's Monthly* for April, shows the heedless manner in which Mr. Fairfield cites his authorities.

"In his 'Mad Man of Letters,'" says Mr. Lathrop, "he quotes the testimony of Moreau de Tours as coincident with that of Maudsley in the assertion that the more original orders of genius are akin to madness." Mr. Lathrop says that Dr. Maudsley says nothing of the kind; that he admits that Poe's genius was akin to madness, but denies that it was genius of the highest kind. [113]

However this may be — and we think Dr. Maudsley is not always luminous and consistent with himself on this obscure question — it may not be uninteresting to cite here what the learned alienist said in a somewhat rhetorical article on Edgar Allan Poe, written for *The Journal of Mental Science*, April, 1860. The purport of the article was to show that, with a nature so rarely and sensitively organized, developed under circumstances so exceptionally perilous, Poe's strange and sorrowful career was not only natural, but inevitable.

"Strange," says Dr. Maudsley, "how far back lies the origin of any event in this world! Remembering the young law student, the father of the poet, sitting, with rapt countenance, in the pit of the Baltimore Theater, and absorbed in the enchanting actress upon whom every eye was turned in admiration, one cannot help reflecting that in this supreme moment lay the germ of things which were to occupy the world's attention, so long, it may be, as it existed: Edgar Poe, his poetry, and the amazement of mankind at his strange, lurid, and irregular existence."[114]

---

[111] Cyrus Augustus Bartol (1813-1900) was pastor of the West Church in Boston.

[112] Francis Gerry Fairfield. "A Mad Man of Letters." *Scribner's Monthly*, Oct. 1875. Fairfield published a lengthy two-part article in *Scribner's* in January and February of 1875 documenting the careers of numerous mediums and clairvoyants and attributing virtually all of their abilities to mental disorders. Although Fairfield acknowledges certain psychical phenomena such as telekinetic abilities or poltergeist-like physical mayhem, he asserts that psychics and mediums are suffering from mental disorders. Spiritualists would have found this article deeply offensive.

[113] George Parsons Lathrop. "Poe, Irving and Hawthorne." *Scribner's Monthly*, April 1876.

<101>

After this it matters little in what precise order or rank of the poetical hierarchy the Doctor accords him a place; his words are an involuntary tribute to a genius, "whose mere potency, dissociated from other elements," Mr. Lathrop admits to be "unrivaled and pre-eminent."

In connection with Dr. Maudsley's theory of antenatal influences, one of those strange coincidences which startled Macbeth as an intimation of "fate and metaphysical aid,"[115] happened to me yesterday.

Among a large collection of old plays and pamphlets, which, after lying *perdu* for half a century, I was just about to surrender to an importunate chiffonier, my eye fell upon one as worn and yellow as the priceless laces of a centennial belle. The title arrested me; it was *The Wood Daemon; or, the Clock has Struck!*, "a Grand, Romantic, Cabalistic Melodrama, in Three Acts, interspersed with Processions, Pageants, and Pantomimes [as performed at the Boston Theater with unbounded applause]. Boston, 1808."[116] I turned the page with a premonitory chill, and lo! among the list of performers, I found the name of "Mr. Poe."

In a curious preface, dated March 30, 1808, the *soi-disant* "author," admitting that he had taken the plot, etc., etc., from M. G. Lewis, "commits his *Wood Daemon*, with all its defects, to the fostering bosom of an indulgent public, in the trembling hope that, as the production of a native American, it may be found worthy of their cheering patronage."

Apparently the "gentle public" did not disappoint the trust reposed in it.

A note prefixed to Byron's unfinished drama, *The Deformed Transformed*, states that the plot was taken in part from the same romance which furnished M. G. Lewis with the plot of his *Wood Daemon*, and in part from the *Faust* of Goethe.[117]

Tales of the wild and wonderful were winging their way from Germany and from the Orient, to possess the minds of Scott and Coleridge, Shelley and Godwin, Moore and Southey, and Savage Landor, whose "Geher"[118] surpassed them all. A taste for melodrama, with its gorgeous pageants and grand spectacles, was beginning to take possession of the stage, until, as Mrs. Kemble has told us, in a recent chapter of her

---

[114] Henry Maudsley. "Edgar Allan Poe." *[Asylum] Journal of Mental Science*, 1860, p. 340.

[115] *Macbeth*, I:5.

[116] John D. Turnbull. *The Wood-Daemon. 1808*. Boston: D. True. David Poe is described as a principal dancer in the pageant.

[117] "This production is founded partly on the story of a Novel, called "The Three Brothers," published many years ago, from which M.G. Lewis's "Wood Demon" was also taken — and partly on the "Faust" of the great Goethe." Byron, p. 427.

[118] Possibly a reference to Landor's long poem, "Gebir," first published anonymously in 1798.

<102>

"Old Woman's Gossip," the splendid opera of *Der Freischutz* swept everything before it.

Sorcery and Necromancy, Wild Yagers and Wild Huntsmen, Wood Daemons and Specters and "Ghoul-haunted Woodlands" ruled the hour. The clock had struck; and, to judge from present appearances, the end is not yet.

When "The Daemon" made his first appearance in Boston, Dr. Maudsley's impressible young law student, then a husband and father, was seeking a precarious subsistence by playing, sorrowfully enough, we may well believe, his subsidiary part in the great pageant. To him, doubtless, "The play was the tragedy, Man/ And its hero, the Conqueror Worm."

What effect these dramatic antecedents and the influences of the hour may have had on the young poet, who made his first appearance on the stage of life within a year from that date, Dr. Maudsley may perhaps be able to determine.

Remembering these things, what a weird significance must ever henceforth attach to that wonderful poem, "Lo! 'tis a gala night."

SARAH HELEN WHITMAN.
Providence, R. I., July, 1876.

<103>

PERCY BYSSHE SHELLEY

CHARACTER AND WRITINGS OF SHELLEY
(1834)
by Egeria (Sarah Helen Whitman)

The poetry of Shelley has been but little read in this country, and is, indeed, of a nature too abstract and spiritual to become popular with the majority of readers in any country. Yet, Bulwer, in his late work on England, has attributed to it, a higher and more powerful influence than to that of any other poet of the present age, Wordsworth alone excepted. Those who have read the poems of Shelley with attention, will not be greatly surprised at this assertion. — They are formed to produce an impression on minds of a certain class, that may not be soon obliterated. His phraseology is remarkably rich, varied, and beautiful; and his imagination luxuriant and inventive: but the principal charm of his writings consists in that liberality of thought and of feeling, and in that enlarged philanthropy which inspires every line, and makes us the more deeply regret that with so much that is excellent and true, much also is blended that is pernicious and false.

Bulwer has drawn the following very just distinction between the writings of Shelley and of Wordsworth. "Wordsworth," he observes, "is the apostle and spiritualizer of things that are — Religion and her houses — Loyalty and her monuments — The tokens of the sanctity that overshadows the past. Shelley, on the other hand, in his more impetuous but equally intellectual and unearthly mind, is the spiritualizer of all who forsake the past and the present, and with lofty aim and a bold philanthropy, press forward to the future."[1]

From his earliest youth, Shelley appears to have discovered that ardor in the investigation of moral and metaphysical truth, that contempt for prejudice under all its modifications, that indifference to the opinion of the world, when opposed to the convictions of his own reason, and that independence of thought and of action, which characterised through life; drew upon him so much censure; and involved him in so many embarrassments. His acute and penetrating mind soon perceived with indignation and astonishment, the injustice and the wrongs that were perpetrated under the names of Religion and of Law: and untaught by experience to distinguish between the real and the apparent, the essential and the accidental, his hatred of oppression and hypocrisy led him into the opposite extremes of infidel and revolutionary principles.

How appropriately has Luther compared the human mind to a drunken peasant on horseback; who, when you prop him up on the one

---

[1] Bulwer-Lytton, *England and the English* (1833). Vol. 1, p. 99.

<107>

side, falls down on the other. Though expelled from the University of Oxford, for the publication of his skeptical opinions,[2] and suffering under the deep resentment of his father, incurred by his apostasy, Shelley still continued his pursuit of truth, with undiminished ardor; questioning religion and philosophy, the Christian and the pagan, the bigot and the infidel, for that concealed treasure which ever eluded his researches. The Bible was studied by him with deep interest and attention, and the character and percepts of the Saviour were held by him in high veneration. Generous and benevolent, as well by nature as from principle, he is said to have conformed his practice to the golden rule, in its most literal interpretation. It appears, however, that the Scriptures, considered as a divine revelation, presented obstacles to his subtle and speculative reason, which his faith was unhappily incapable of surmounting. It is to be regretted that Shelley's early errors of opinion had not been met by charitable forbearance and mild expostulation, the most effective weapons Christianity can employ in her holy warfare against skepticism and unbelief.

Perhaps it ought not to excite surprise, that a mind so peculiarly constituted as was that of Shelley, should be in its first eager but unenlightened survey of life, have been betrayed into inconsequent reasoning, and have arrived at false deductions, — that it should have been darkened by doubts, and perplexed by apparent inconsistencies.

It appears from the tenor of his writings, that his mind was often exercised in speculations on the origin and existence of Evil — that difficult problem — that dark enigma! over which, every reflecting being has at some period of his existence, mused, until thought grew dizzy, and the mind was lost in a labyrinth of contradictory and perplexing speculations. This, with the apparently partial distribution of happiness and of misery, appear to have been the principal obstacles to Shelley's faith. Yet he had an open mind to conviction; and had it not been confirmed in error by severity and intolerance; — had not his pride been interested in the support of those opinions for which he had incurred so much obloquy, he might, and doubtless *would*, have renounced them.

Reason and observation would have taught him the secrets of that divine alchymy by which apparent ills are transmuted into real blessings; and by which partial evils tend to the promotion of universal good. More enlightened views of the economy of nature[3] would have prepared his

---

[2] Shelley's pamphlet, "The Necessity of Atheism," was published in 1811. By 1813, Shelley had amended his hard atheist stance slightly by stating, "There Is No God. This negation must be understood solely to affect a creative Deity. The hypothesis of a pervading Spirit co-eternal with the universe remains unshaken" (*Queen Mab*, Canto VII, Note 13).

[3] *Economy of nature*. The idea of an overarching common good transcended the short-term ills experienced by individuals, as ordained by a Creator, occupied

<108>

mind for the reception of the divine truths of Revelation; he would have recognized unbounded benevolence and infinite wisdom.

Shelley was considered a profound metaphysician and an admirable classical scholar. He has clothed some of the beautiful speculations of the Grecian philosophers, in most exquisite verse; and has woven from their fine-drawn theories, a woof so brilliant and so beautiful, that its dazzling splendor almost blinds us to its fragility. His glowing fancies were richly nourished by the true naphtha[4] of true poetic inspiration: and his keen relish for the charms of nature, enabled him to discover many remote analogies and latent sources of beauty, in objects that would have been passed unnoticed by common observers. His description of a poet, in "Alastor, or the Spirit of Solitude," may well be applied to himself.

> By solemn vision, and bright silver dream,
> His infancy was nurtured — Every sight
> And sound, from the vast earth and ambient air,
> Sent to his heart its choicest impulses.
> The fountains of divine philosophy
> Fled not his thirsting lips — and all of great
> Or good, or lovely, which the sacred past
> In truth or fable consecrates, he felt
> And knew. [5]

Almost all his poems appear to have had for their object the illustration of some philosophical or moral truth. His philanthropy led him earnestly to desire the reformation of all those errors which custom and authority alone have sanctioned, in religion, laws, governments and social conventions. And his firm belief in the perfectibility of human nature, and in the final prevalence on earth of virtue and of happiness over vice and misery, served faintly to cheer those moments of dejection, when the pressure of existing and present evil, and fearful doubts of the soul's immortality, weighed upon his mind.

He is said to have practiced great self-denial in his mode of living; and to have been liberal, almost to a fault, in his charities. Emulation and ambition he appears to have considered as false principles of action. Revenge, and malice, and envy, found no place in his candid and gentle nature. — He condemned them as passions unfit to be harbored in the breast of a reflecting being. He constantly inculcated universal love and

---

philosophers such as Leibniz and Kant, and influenced natural science from the time of Aristotle through the work of Carolus Linnaeus. The work of Darwin and the consideration of catastrophism would shatter that idea.

[4] *Naphtha*. A flammable oil distilled from coal or petroleum.

[5] "Alastor," lines 67-75. Corrected to match the 1824 *Posthumous Poems*.

<109>

unbounded charity; and his writings are replete with passages like the following:

——— Justice is the light
Of love, and not revenge, and terror and despite.[6]

———We should
Own all sympathies, and outrage none;
And live as if to love and live, were one.[7]

In his preface to the tragedy of *The Cenci*, observing on the mistaken idea entertained by Beatrice, in supposing that the crime of any individual could reflect dishonor on the innocent victim of that crime; he says: "No person can truly be dishonored by the guilt of another; and the fit return to make to the most enormous injuries, is kindness and forbearance, and an endeavor to convert the injurer from his dark passions, to truth and love." Who can contemplate such sentiments, without regretting that a heart so gentle, a soul so generous, should pass through life's weary pilgrimage, without the consolations of religion, the hope of immortality? Dangerous indeed is the gift of intellect, when it tempts it possessor to daring speculations and unhallowed researches: and too often does the unchastened desire of knowledge lead to errors more fatal than could have been encountered in the repose of unquestioning ignorance.

Montaigne has well expressed this truth, in one of his essays; though we might in vain seek to transfuse the peculiar force and expressiveness of his quaint and nervous diction, into an English translation, "Genius," he observes, "is a hazardous possession. It is seldom found united with circumspection and order. In my own time, I have observed all who were possessed of any rare excellence or extraordinary vivacity of intellect, indulge in some license of opinion or of morals. Intellect is a piercing sword; dangerous even to its possessor, unless he knows how to arm himself with it discreetly and soberly. It is curious and eager: we may in vain seek to bridle and restrain it: we shall still find it escaping by its volatility, from the restraints of customs and of laws, of religions and of precepts, of penalties and of rewards."[8] Shelley's intellectual history is a striking exemplification that "the tree of knowledge is not that of life:"[9] of that first great truth taught in the garden of Eden, — that truth which had it been received on the word of God without a reference to stern experience, might have saved the human race from its inheritance of sorrow.

[6] Shelley. *The Revolt of Islam.* V:xxxiv.
[7] Ibid, VIII:xii.
[8] From Montaigne's essay, "On Presumption." Book II, No. 17.
[9] Byron. *Manfred*, I:i, 13

<110>

Early in life, Shelley married a very young and exquisitely beautiful woman: — but a dissimilarity of tastes, habits, and dispositions rendered their union unhappy; and they separated. Mrs. Shelley subsequently committed suicide; and their two children were removed from their father's care, by the Lord Chancellor Eldon,[10] on the plea of his incapacity to educate them in the truths of Christianity. These unhappy events preyed upon his feelings, and gave a blow to his constitution, from which it never entirely recovered. Before he was twenty-one years of age, he was again married to Mary Godwin, the daughter of William Godwin and of Mary Wollstonecraft. In her, were united with great kindness of heart and gentleness of disposition, all that power of intellect which she inherited as a birth-right from her celebrated parents. Shelley's affection for her, seems to have continued unabated during the remainder of his life; and forms the subject of some of his most sweet and touching verses.

Soon after their marriage, they resided for some time in Switzerland, near the lake of Geneva. Byron, who passed several months in their vicinity, has given a delightful description of those evenings of literary and social intercourse which he passed in their society. They afterwards repaired to Italy; and it was in that land of inspiration, that Shelley composed most of his poems. The last two months of his life were spent in tranquil happiness, on the borders of the Bay of Spezia, near those beautiful waters that were soon to helm him in their treacherous bosom. But the closing scene of his life has been so touchingly described by Mrs. Shelley, in her beautiful preface to the posthumous edition of his poems,[11] that it were doing her an injustice, to relate it in any but her own affecting words.

> In the wild but beautiful Bay of Spezia, the winds and waves which he loved became his playmates. His days were chiefly spent on the water; the management of his boat, its alterations and improvements, were his principal occupation. At night, when the unclouded moon shone on the calm sea, he often went alone in his little shallop to the rocky caves that bordered it, and sitting beneath their shelter wrote "The Triumph of Life," the last of his productions. The beauty but strangeness of this lonely place, the refined pleasure which he felt in the companionship of a few selected friends, our entire sequestration from the rest of the world, all contributed to render this period of his life one of continued enjoyment. I am

[10] John Scott, First Earl of Eldon, held the office of Lord Chancellor of Great Britain for two terms, from 1801 to 1827. In *The Masque of Anarchy*, Shelley wrote lines mocking Eldon in his "ermined gown."
[11] Shelley, Percy Bysshe. *Posthumous Poems.* 1824. London: John and Henry L. Hunt.

<111>

convinced that the two months we passed there were the happiest he had ever known; his health even rapidly improved, and he was never better than when I last saw him, full of spirits and joy, embark for Leghorn, that he might there welcome LEIGH HUNT to Italy. I was to have accompanied him, but illness confined me to my room, and thus put the seal on my misfortune. His vessel bore out of sight with a favorable wind, and I remained awaiting his return by the breakers of that sea which was about to engulf him.

He spent a week at Pisa, employed in kind offices toward his friend, and enjoying with keen delight the renewal of their intercourse. He then embarked with Mr. WILLIAMS, the chosen and beloved sharer of his pleasures and of his fate, to return to us. We waited for them in vain; the sea by its restless moaning seemed to desire to inform us of what we would not learn: — but a veil may well be drawn over such misery. The real anguish of these moments transcended all the fictions that the most glowing imagination every portrayed: our seclusion, the savage nature of the inhabitants of the surrounding villages, and our immediate vicinity to the troubled sea, combined to embue with strange horror our days of uncertainty. The truth was at last known, — a truth that made our loved and lovely Italy appear a tomb, its sky a pall. Every heart echoed the deep lament, and my only consolation was in the praise and earnest love that each voice bestowed and each countenance demonstrated for him we had lost, — not, I fondly hope, for ever: his unearthly and elevated nature is a pledge of the continuation of his being, although in an altered form. Rome received his ashes; they are deposited beneath its weed-grown wall, and "the world's sole monument"[12] is enriched by his remains. [13]

---

[12] Edmund Spenser. "The Ruins of Rome."
[13] Corrected to conform with the text and punctuation from Shelley's *Posthumous Poems* (1824), preface by Mary Shelley. Either Whitman, or the typesetter for *The Literary Journal*, omitted several sentences and radically altered Mary Shelley's punctuation.

<112>

WHAT IS GENIUS?

ON THE CHARACTER
AND ATTRIBUTES OF GENIUS (1835)
by Egeria (Sarah Helen Whitman)

◇———————————————————————◇

A MONG THE VARIOUS opinions respecting the essential nature and attributes of genius, there are few that are not liable to exceptions, either in consequence of the indefiniteness of language, or from the difficulty accompanying every attempt to reduce, under general distinctions, the innumerable varieties and combinations of the human mind.

It is the opinion of many eminent writers of the present day, and among others, of the Rev. Mr. Dewey,[1] that genius is exclusively derived from the faculty of attention; while on the other hand, it has as often been asserted that it is the especial concomitant of habits of abstraction

---

[1] Orville Dewey (1794-1882), Unitarian minister at New Bedford, later New York City. He had been assistant to William Ellery Channing in Boston. He was a controversial lecturer whose ideas bore a skeptical tint.

<114>

and internal concentration of thought. I think it is Gibbon who says that "solitude is the nurse of Genius, while society develops wit and talent."[2] Again, it has been contended that genius is an innate and independent power of the soul. This we are ready to admit, to a certain extent, and under certain limitations. Doubtless the germ from which it is derived, exists independently of education or circumstance; yet we cannot agree with some of the German metaphysicians, in the belief that any mind, however gifted, could originate or give birth to conceptions of power and beauty, though cut off from all impressions of the external world; on the contrary, we believe that the creative power of genius is immediately derived from a certain delicacy of organization, which renders the mind in a peculiar degree susceptible to external impressions, and that without these it would be as blank as the finest mirror, before light and form have been reflected from its polished surface. Yet we would not be understood to imply by this admission that genius emanates from the faculty of *attention* or *observation*. Attention, according to Spurzheim,[3] implies "*effort proceeding from a desire for information;*" while the vivid impressions of genius are, we think, derived from an intuitive feeling of whatever feeling of whatever is elevated and beautiful, rather than acquired by an effort of the will.

The faculty of attention is seldom found united with that meditative, impassioned and imaginative cast of character, which, as was before remarked, is nursed amid solitude and seclusion. The mind of Shakespeare, it must be allowed, presents a marked exception to this theory, exhibiting a wonderful combination of accuracy of observation, profundity of thought, and splendor of imagination; but in most cases, we are inclined to think, the above remark will be found to correspond with the testimony of experience. Everyone conversant with the writings of Coleridge must perceive that he is but little indebted to the observation of external objects for his powerful productions. His "Christabel" and

---

[2] Gibbon wrote, "Conversation enriches the understanding, but solitude is the school of genius." *The Decline and Fall of the Roman Empire.* Vol. 2, p. 80. Various writers up to Whitman's time used the phrase "Nurse of Genius" in association with such diverse causes as poverty, poetry, the Press, Liberty, and Italy.

[3] Enter phrenology. Johann Spurzheim (1776-1832) was a German physician who lectured extensively on phrenology, the pseudo-science of mind and personality based on the analysis of cranial shape and lumps. Spurzheim had local fame in Boston as he died there in 1832 while on a lecture tour. He was interred in Cambridge's Mt. Auburn Cemetery, and his internal organs were preserved in alcohol and displayed to his followers. Spurzheim's theories were published in London in 1815, and debunked in a notorious review in *The Edinburgh Review* in June of that year (see Gordon). Writers would continue to use phrenological terminology to describe and analyze personality for decades after Spurzheim's death.

<115>

his "Ancient Mariner" are original creations drawn from the abundant treasures of a fertile imagination. Reflection and fancy predominate in all his works, while they are deficient in those various portraitures of manner and character which are derived from acuteness of observation. These remarks are perhaps equally applicable to Wordsworth.

THE VERSATILE POWERS of Scott, on the other hand, are evidently formed on a close attention to life and manners, and he has himself avowed that his characters were, for the most part, copies from nature; many of them being individual pictures but slightly altered from their originals. Excellence in this style of writing would seem to require merely that species of talent which rendered the Dutch and Flemish artists so deservedly celebrated. But Scott has done more than this; around these faithful portraits his brilliant imagination has thrown a rich and fanciful drapery, which imparts to them a highly-romantic and picturesque effect, without in the least detracting from the *vraisemblance*[4] of the delineation.

To question Sir Walter's claim to the very highest order of genius, would, perhaps, be deemed by many one of the worst forms of literary heresy. Yet we must confess that we have often doubted whether its success was not the result of accuracy of observation, and habits of close attention respecting the *external* peculiarities of man, and of the material creation, rather than of great native powers of thought and imagination.

We hear much of the egotism of Rousseau, Byron and De Stael, while Scott is commended for never obtruding his own individual sentiments and feelings on his readers, nor delineating his own character under the mask of a fictitious personage. Yet what can be more interesting to beings loving, suffering, and erring, than to learn how others have loved and suffered — how they have borne with he various doubts and difficulties, trials and temptations of life.

How often, in the midst of our admiration for the brilliant narrative and gorgeous scenery of these splendid fictions, have we felt the want of that intimate communion with our author — that confiding revelation of his inmost thoughts and feelings, which constitute for us a writer's highest charms! Their power to interest and amuse is unrivalled; we are rapt into entire forgetfulness of ourselves and our author, and living only amid the creations of his fancy, are borne from adventure to adventure, with magical celerity and skill; but, after all, these are not the works which a man of thought and feeling loves and lingers over, and makes his bosom companions; nor do they, like some of our favorite authors, give that powerful impulse to the mind which forces us to lay down the volume in order to follow out the thronging thoughts which it inspires.

---

[4] *Vraisemblance*. Likelihood, verisimilitude.

<116>

Passing lightly over these causes and events that control the development of character, and influence the destiny of men, the author of *Waverly* expatiates almost to weariness, on the cut and color of a garment, the contour and complexion of a limb; describing every thing with an elaborateness of detail that has suffered no variety of form or gradation of matter to escape. He presents in bold relief, the most prominent and romantic features hat give an individual character to different ages and nations. He delights us with splendid pageants and glowing pictures, in which all the figures are picturesquely grouped and represented in striking and appropriate costume. But we have no nice and just analysis of character — no tracing of effects to causes — no deep insight into the human heart. It is essentially a description of *manners* and *actions,* as opposed to one of *motives* and *feelings.* We may look in vain for these comprehensive views of man's nature and destiny, which distinguish the German novels and Goethe and Wieland[5] — for the sweet pathos of Mackenzie[6] and St. Pierre,[7] or the impassioned eloquence of Godwin[8] and De Stael.[9]

ANOTHER DEFINITION OF genius — not less popular than that which describes it as the faculty of attention — comprises it under the term "inventive power" — an explanation obviously liable to objection, since many persons exhibit this power who deserve no higher epithet than that of cleverness or ingenuity. It depends upon the nature of the thing invented, whether the power which produced it can claim the name of genius. The power of invention enters into the dramas of Shakespeare, and the construction of a patent cooking apparatus. Yet sure it would be incongruous to apply the hallowed name of genius in common to their originators.

Neither inventive power, therefore, nor the faculty of attention correspond with our own views of the nature of genius. We have always

[5] Christoph Martin Wieland (1733-1813), German poet and author of the first *Bildungsroman* (coming-of-age story), *The History of Agathon.* By 1835, his works already comprised 53 volumes.
[6] Henry Mackenzie (1745-1831), Scottish novelist, author of *The Man of Feeling* (1771), and *The Man of the World* (1773).
[7] Jacques-Henri Bernardin de Saint-Pierre (1737-1814), botanist, engineer, and novelist, best-remembered for his 1788 novel, *Paul et Virginie.* He was an early advocate of ethical vegetarianism.
[8] William Godwin (1756-1836) was a radical political philosopher, publisher, and innovative novelist. His forthright biography of his late wife, the equally radical Mary Wollstonecraft, shocked many, as did his friendship with Percy Shelley, who married his daughter Mary. In his novel *Leon,* Godwin posited the ideas of life extension, and physical immortality, in a perfected society.
[9] Anne Louise Germaine De Staël-Holstein was a formidable salonist, novelist, travel writer, and historian, probably the most significant European literary woman of her time.

<117>

been of opinion that genius *originates* in that peculiar species of organization which renders a person exquisitely susceptible to whatever is beautiful or sublime in the material or moral world, and that it *manifests* itself in the power it possesses of embodying these exquisite impressions in the rare creations of art. Yet we are inclined to believe that the native elements of genius exist in many individuals, unaccompanied by the faculty of execution which would enable them to impart to others a faint reflection of their own glorious inspirations — although in most cases we believe the mind is oppressed by its own keen and thrilling conceptions of beauty, until they are breathed forth into the eloquent arts of poetry, painting, sculpture, or music, as into a natural language, by which is expressed those intense and vivid impressions, which, if unrevealed, produce a morbid excitement of the imagination, and cause the mind to consume and pine away amid the lustre of its own fires — or, to use an expression of Byron's, "render it diseased with its own beauty."[10]

In asserting that we consider genius as originating or consisting in an exquisite susceptibility to beauty, we use the word in its most comprehensive sense, as including all that Burke or Alison comprised in their definitions of the sublime and beautiful. A more limited interpretation of the word would lead to a misconception of our true meaning. For instance, we were lately asked was *beauty* was discoverable in Shakespeare's admirable delineations of the jealousy of Othello or the madness of Lear. Yet in the sense in which we use the words beauty and sublimity, they are equally applicable to the moral and physical world, and who will deny that there is more sublimity and power in the representation of Othello's noble mind, struggling in the insidious coils of jealous passion, or in the strong grasp of remorse, than there is in the far-famed Laocoön writhing in the folds of the serpent.[11] Or can those emotions of sublimity with which we contemplate a stately ship, foundering amid storm and tempest on the shoreless ocean, rival those with which we behold the old heart-broken Lear, tossed on the wild waves of passion and grief, and finally whelmmed beneath their billows just as the dawn had begun to break on his long night of mental darkness and despair? It is to these and similar impressions of power, and beauty, and sublimity — whether in the moral or material world — that the mind of the man of genius is, as I have said, exquisitely susceptible, and which his pen or his pencil so vividly portrays.

---

[10] "Of its own beauty is the mind diseased" from Byron, "Childe Harold's Pilgrimage."

[11] The unearthing of the horror-statuary depicting Laocoön and his sons being devoured by sea snakes in 1506, shocked Renaissance sensibilities. It was also the subject of Lessing's 1766 book *Laocoön,* which upset the idea that poetry should imitate the seeming self-restraint of visual art, and laid some of the groundwork for ideas of the romantic and the sublime.

<118>

I T HAS OFTEN been argued that there are many species of genius —
that the eminent mathematician, moralist, historian, and statesman,
all and each display various orders of genius. Yet excellence in these
pursuits should, we think, be attributed rather to a discriminating and
powerful intellect than to that peculiar character of mind which consti-
tutes genius.

Talent, again, though often miscalled genius, has, we think, a
signification differing essentially in its original nature, yet often blended
and united with that power. Talent, we conceive to be that peculiar faculty
in execution, which belongs to many individuals who possess neither
profound intellect nor powerful genius.

We are aware that we dissent from the popular opinion in instancing
Pope as an example of powerful talent, independent of any of the peculiar
attributes of genius. The two productions which have been lately cited
by an eloquent writer as vindicating his claims to this high, and we had
almost said, holy endowment, are the "Essay on Man," and the "Letter
of Eloise" — the latter a literal, though unacknowledged translation from
the French,[12] while the ideas and arrangement of the former were
furnished, as it has been said, by Bolingbroke, which, if correct, leaves
the author, as far as respects these two poems, no other merit than that
of harmonious and polished versification. With the exception of these —
of which one, it appears, is a translation, and the other suspected of being
a mere paraphrase — where shall we look among his writings for
evidences of true genius? His *Dunciad* and *Rape of the Lock* are highly-
polished and brilliant satires, evincing, it is true, admirable talents of a
certain order — great subtlety of intellect — a shrewd and sarcastic wit,
and a keen perception of the follies and frailties of human nature. Yet
what do we find in them to awaken those intense and fervid aspirations
after perfection and beauty — after purity and truth, which elevate us
above the sordid cares and earth-born interests of life, and inspire the
soul with a lofty and refining sense of its sacred attributes and high
destination?

It is by a test like this that we would estimate an author's claims to
genius. It is divine in its essence, purifying and elevating in its effects. It
recalls us to a sense of the glory of our nature, and of those whose high
capacities of happiness with which we are endowed.

The old aphorism, "Poeta nascitur non fit" — "Poets are *born*, and
not *made*," notwithstanding the wisdom and talent that have been
exercised in denouncing it, is not yet disproved. Attention may command
information, and lead to the acquisition of wisdom, taste, and talent; but

[12] The editor of *The Pearl* offered an editorial note suggesting another source:
"[T]he original source will probably be found in Ovid's *Dido Aeneae*, published
entire, with an excellent poetical translation . . . in *The Pearl*, Volume 4 No. 8",
The Boston Pearl, Vol. 5, p. 111.

<119>

genius is a portion of the soul's individual essence, an endowment of Heaven, possessed in holy trust for the elevation and solace of the human race. Though often perverted and united with evil, it is in itself pure and holy, allied to all religious faith, to all exalted enthusiasm, to all unfeigned love of goodness, beauty, and truth.

Heraclitus has said that what men call genius is a demon[13]. *We* believe it a ray from the divinity, throwing a halo around all objects within the sphere of its influence; illuminating every thing that it touches, with a portion of its own glory, and, like the alembic of the alchymist, converting all common metals into gold.

---

[13] *Demon,* from *daemon,* meaning a kind of companion or guardian spirit. The *daemon* in this pagan sense is not associated with evil. Heraclitus does not appear to have said this. His Fragment 119, Stobaeus Anth. IV, 40, 23, (p. 112) reads: "Man's character is his daemon," which would suggest that Heraclitus is debunking the idea of a separate spiritual entity.

<120>

JOHANN WOLFGANG VON GOETHE

CONVERSATIONS WITH GOETHE (1840)
by Sarah Helen Whitman

A Review of *Conversations with Goethe, In the Last Years of His Life. Translated from the German of Eckermann* by S. M. Fuller. Boston. 1839.

THIS VOLUME HAS added another valuable link to the extensive, yet fragmentary chain of memorials which the public already possess in relation to Goethe, and one which may perhaps assist us toward the better interpretation of a character which is, as yet, more talked of than understood among us. Yet, the number of works on the subject, which have been published since his death, would seem to furnish ample materials for the construction of a clue to guide us through all its intricacies. Writers are every day coming forward to present us with the result of their researches in this rich field of investigation. Some few have returned with information, that it is but a dry and parched land, in which there is no water. Others, again, have found there everflowing, exhaustless springs, at which they have drunken freely, and felt their spirits quickened and refreshed. There has been much sincere, heartfelt eulogium, much decided, unmitigated condemnation. Mr. Dwight, in his notes to the songs and lyrics of Goethe, has proved himself so eloquent an interpreter of the Oracle, that we cannot but regret he had not written more fully on the subject.[1] In Miss Fuller's preface to this volume, there is much just and comprehensive thought expressed in few words. Here is neither affected humility, nor arrogant dictation. She tells us distinctly and simply, what Goethe has been to her own mind, and she does this with so much calmness and candor — she discovers so fine an insight into his modes of thinking, so true a sympathy with his character and genius, that we look forward with increased interest to the more complete delineation of them which we have been led to expect from her.

It is interesting to compare these several transcripts of the same individual, represented under such different lights, and from such various points of observation. From the volume which Miss Fuller has so admirably translated, we derive much information respecting Goethe,

---

[1] John S. Dwight, in *Select Minor Poems Translated from the German of Goethe and Schiller* (1839), praises "that perfectly transparent style of Goethe's, which makes him the master in style, beyond dispute, of all the moderns" (p. xiv), and "It seems to have been his mission, like Wordsworth's, to reveal to us the poetry of this very world around us, and to present us with fresh flowers of poetry, of no hot-house growth, but from the true soil of Nature, our common inheritance" (p. 365).

<123>

which could have been obtained in no other way. Eckermann here portrays him to us in a new attitude, and under new relations. From the true and pure heart of this young disciple, we may behold his mighty spirit reflected, like some high and remote star, seen as mirrored in the calm and transparent bosom of a placid lake. Yet we should not neglect to make due allowance for the refraction which the rays of light must necessarily undergo in their transmission through even so pure a medium.

We have been warned against trusting to the verisimilitude of this delineation of Goethe's mind, on the ground of its having been drawn by the hand of one who loved him, and have been told that we must maintain towards the individual, whom we would fully understand and appreciate, an entire neutrality of feeling, — a maxim in which we have little faith. We believe, on the contrary, that no character reveals itself to us in all its completeness and beauty, until it is viewed by the full, clear, and mellow light of love; that no mirror reflects so faithfully, as the loving heart. Not only do a thousand delicate, evanescent shades of character, a thousand latent traits of goodness and beauty reveal themselves to the keenly apprehensive, and ever watchful eye of love, which would have escaped an indifferent observer; but is it not also true, in another and far higher sense, that love is the true interpreter of Humanity? May we not venture to hope that those qualities in the character of an individual, which excite our love and veneration, are indeed its inherent and essential elements, while the faults and blemishes, which seem so prominent to cavilers and critics, are but its accidental and adventitious accessories, depending on the circumstances and influences of the moment. There is a passage in Mr. Emerson's address to the Divinity Students of Cambridge, which has more than once been pointed out to us, as one to which it is difficult, if not impossible, to attach any definite meaning, but which to us seems radiant with a divine significance. The passage is simply this, — "Good is positive, evil only privative, not absolute."[2] Do not these words express a profound truth? Nay, do they not even furnish an adequate solution of the one great problem, the existence and origin of evil, — since they teach that evil is but imperfection, the absence and negation of good, (in a greater or less degree the necessary condition of all created beings,) even as in the natural world cold is the absence of heat, and darkness of light? What should we think of a naturalist, who, instead of seeking to observe the phenomena, and analyze the elements of light and heat, should turn all his attention to the study and contemplation of their opposites? Carlyle says, "of even unwise admira-

[2] "Good is positive. Evil is merely privative, not absolute. It is like cold, which is the privation of heat." Emerson. *An Address Delivered Before the Senior Class in Divinity College, Cambridge, Sunday Evening, July 15, 1838*, p. 7.

<124>

tion, much may be hoped, for much good is really in it; but unwise contempt is itself a negation. Nothing can come of it, for it is nothing."[3]

We will not, then, refuse to learn what we can of a great man, because it comes to us, as in the present instance, through the mediation of a devoted disciple, but thankfully receive what, with so much simplicity and good faith, Eckermann has here confided to us.

To trace the progress of a life like Goethe's, through all the bright stages of its culmination and decline, from the rich but misty light of its dawn, to the calm, serene, golden glories of its setting, would be a study of profound interest to every thoughtful observer.

The life of a man of genius is ever a life of conflict; ever is it exposed to trials and temptations, of which obtuser and calmer natures do not even dream. Montaigne says truly of the dangerous gift of genius, that "it is a sharp sword, which, if its possessor knows not how to arm himself with it discreetly and soberly, will pierce him to the heart."[4] The man of "time-serving mediocrity," molded and manufactured after safe conventional rules and formulas, treads the broad high-ways, and beaten paths of life, with a mechanical, unquestioning conformity, looking neither to the right nor the left, neither before nor after, and asking only, "what shall he eat, what shall he drink, and wherewithal shall he be clothed." Occupied with the immediate and the palpable, he heeds not the sad changes, the fearful contrasts, and all the mysterious, contradictory phenomena of human life. He feels no heart-sickening discrepancy between the wants of the spirit, and the actual condition of the external world. No bright vision of beauty and love exists within his own mind, to pale the splendor of the outward, and make him dissatisfied with reality. He knows nothing of those weary struggles, by which energetic and sensitive spirits exhaust themselves in a ceaseless conflict with the actual.

The Promethean ardor of genius, chained to the hard and sterile rock of reality, feels itself preyed upon by the vulture of unsatisfied desires, which pant after the ideal. Byron, Burns, Cowper, Shelley, Tasso, and Rousseau, — what a succession of shining beacons are here, to warn the beholder of those peculiar dangers to which minds, thus highly gifted and finely organized, are exposed! Too often, while sitting at the feast of life, like the stranger guest at the Egyptian banquet, their eyes are turned sadly upon the veiled memorial of mortality, where, from beneath its embroidered pall, the hollow visage of death seems to mock them with

[3] Thomas Carlyle. "State of German Literature." An unsigned article in *Edinburgh Review*, No. 92, 1827, included in Carlyle's *Critical and Miscellaneous Essays*, 1838, p. 50.
[4] From Montaigne's essay, "On Presumption." Book II, No. 17.

<125>

its ghastly and spectral gaze. Too often neglectful of the cheering intercourse, and all the kindly, familiar charities of social life, they stand solitary and apart in a wild and visionary world, brooding in misanthropic gloom over the perplexing mysteries of life, questioning the past and the future, and sending forth their proud thoughts to "wander through eternity."[5] We turn away with a sigh from the story of their lives, and are almost tempted to believe that there is some fatal and necessary connexion between genius, error, and suffering.

When we see the noble and the gifted, who went forth in the morning of life with loving hearts, and eager, expectant spirits, in search of knowledge and happiness, returning ere midday from their fruitless quest, with energies prematurely wasted, with blanched cheek and blighted hope; sick at heart and sullied, perhaps, in fame; then a deep oppression seizes us; we no longer trust ourselves to think; we would fain cease to feel; but nature, kind and friendly nature, will not leave us to nourish our sick fancies. She wins us out of these dark moods, for the most part, whether we will or not. And she does this most successfully, she most effectually cheers and strengthens us, by showing us examples of great men, who have borne unblanching the heat and burden of the day; men who have passed from hope to faith through the fiery trial of doubt. And even such an one to us is Goethe.

The history of a mind thus highly dowered, — of a soul penetrated with the bright ideal of goodness and truth — keenly sensitive to praise and blame — to pain and pleasure, to beauty and deformity. Alive to all the manifold and conflicting influences of the outward world, yet gathering strength and power from all — profiting alike by its failures and successes, and at last rising superior to evil through the force of an energetic will and a sincere integrity of soul. Such a delineation, affording materials for the solution of the highest psychological problems, and presenting a theme of all others the most fruitful in interest and instruction, is presented us in that long and ever active life, to whose serene close Eckermann has here so devoutly conducted us.

A ND WHAT A glorious privilege is this which he has accorded us! To commune with this great man in the privacy and quiet of his own home, — to mark the tranquil routine of his daily life, — to sit beside him in friendly converse, — to walk with him up and down the hushed and secluded apartments, hearkening to his rich, unpremeditated discourse, and receiving from him wise counsel and friendly caution. All this is to us a source of unwonted pleasure.

In the fine mornings of Spring, we may walk out with him through his grounds and gardens, — listen with him to the earliest notes of the

---

[5] "Those thoughts that wander through eternity." Milton. *Paradise Lost*, II:148.

<126>

blackbird and the thrush, — watch the opening beaks of the hyacinth, and welcome the palmy glories of the crown imperial. Sometimes, we find him still there in the dusk of evening, sitting with his little grandson beside him, beneath the lindens which were planted by his own hand forty years before. If he has been reading, he lays down the volume to impart to us some of the wealth of his full mind. We may ride out with him in the bright afternoons, when the orchards are white with blossoms and the birches in full leaf. Then may we see how closely he observes all the varying aspects of nature, all beautiful effects of light and shade, all rich hues and waving outlines; and learn in what school it was, and under whose teaching, that he acquired his fine appreciation of art. On our return we see him gazing thoughtfully at the setting sun; but he turns cheerfully and says, "At the age of seventy-five, one must often think on death, but the thought causes me no uneasiness, I am so fully convinced that the soul is indestructible and that its activity will continue through eternity. It is like the sun which seems to our earthly eyes to set in night, but is in reality gone to diffuse its light elsewhere." Sometimes we visit him at his country-house, which commands a view of rich meadows with the Sale meandering through the valley. On the east are wooded hills, where we may watch the retreating showers or behold the rising sun. In this beautiful retreat Goethe tells us, that he enjoys day and night equally. "Often," says he, "I awake before dawn and lie down by the open windows to enjoy the splendor of the three planets, which are at present to be seen together, and the gradual irradiation of the clouds. I pass almost the whole day in the open air, and hold spiritual communion with the tendrils of the vine, which say many good things to me, and of which I could tell you wonders."[6]

In Weimar we meet at his house celebrated men, and listen to his conversation with them; though in such assemblies, he loves best to be a listener. With him we look at pictures and engravings from the best Italian and Flemish masters. We hear him speak of great writers of the past and present time, — of Voltaire and Moliere, — of Cousin and Guizot, — of De la Vigne and Béranger, — of Manzoni, Byron and Scott, and of all with a noble, sincere enthusiasm which might put to the blush the lukewarm, reluctant commendation of self-mindful, cautious critics, who would fain manifest their penetration by discovering nothing but faults. Yet this is the man of whom Heine has somewhere said, that his approbation is a "brevet of mediocrity."[7] The true key to this is, not that

---

[6] Eckermann. *Conversations with Goethe*, p. 108.
[7] Heinrich Heine. *The Romantic School* (1833), originally published in French. Heine unkindly asserts that "Goethe feared every writer of independence and originality, but glorified and praised all the petty authorlings. He carried this so far that to be praised by Goethe came at last to be considered a brevet of mediocrity" (p. 51).

<127>

Goethe was in any way insensible to the merits of writers of established reputation, but that, his mind being open to every manifestation of excellence, he frequently discovered much good in the writings of young and obscure authors, whose laurels were yet unreaped, which men, more fearful of risking their own reputation by premature praise, would not have ventured to notice.

EVERYWHERE IN THIS book, do we see indications of Goethe's self-relying, self-sufficing spirit, which unfolded itself tranquilly without a reference to the opinions and prejudices of the world. Thus, when Eckermann says, "[I]f Faust could be represented as you have designed it, the public would sit astonished and would not know how to comprehend it;" he replies, "Go, — leave your public, of which I would not willingly hear anything. The only thing for me is to write it, — let the public receive it as it may, and use it as far as it can."[8] Goethe had not a particle of restless vanity, nor any petty pride in his works. He considered everything that he had done as a means rather than an end. He was ever striving forward, and when he had completed a work, he laid it aside and thought of it no more.

We also find here many evidences of that which we most admire and reverence in him, — his entire and genuine honesty of spirit, — his fearless confidence in truth and nature. Falk says of him, "I might almost affirm, that a faulty and vigorous character, if it had any native qualities as its basis, was regarded by him with more indulgence and respect, than one which at no moment of its existence is genuine, — which is incessantly under restraint. 'Oh,' said Goethe, sighing, 'if these people had but the heart to commit some indiscretion, there would be hope of them, — they would at least be restored to their own natural soil, free from all hypocrisy and acting; and wherever that is the case one may entertain the hope, that something will spring from the germ of good which nature has implanted in every individual; but on the ground they are now upon nothing can grow.' "[9]

His clear and penetrating intellect, — his abhorrence of all hollow shows and solemn mockeries, — his determined opposition to everything false and factitious, led him to eschew those officious *soi disant* friends of religion, who pride themselves on their superior sanctity in opposing

---

[8] *Conversations with Goethe,* p. 328.
[9] Johannes Daniel Falk. "Goethe, Portrayed from Familiar Personal Intercourse," in Sarah Austin's *Characteristics of Goethe* (1833), p. 29. Whitman substitutes "indiscretion" for "absurdity." In Eckermann's *Conversations with Goethe* will be found a fine entry from March 12, 1828, which Fuller does not include, about "sunken-chested" young German scholars, "completely wrapped up in ideas" and ending with the lament "if a man is not young when he is twenty, how can he be young when he is forty!" (O'Brien trans, p. 131).

<128>

all the genial impulses of nature; nay, who start and recoil at the very word, as if it were some strange cabalistic sound, pregnant with monstrous heresy.

At this folly, he has, in the second part of *Faust*, aimed one of those sharp and sure arrows which always go straight to the mark; a sapient cardinal says, in reply to Mephistopheles, who asks, "What may not be done by one gifted with man's nature and spiritual energies,"

> Natur und Geist, — so spricht man nicht zu Christen.
> Dehalb verbrennt man Atheisten,
> Weil solche Reden höchst gefährlich sind,
> Natur ist Sünde, Geist ist Teufel;
> Sic hegen zwischen sich den zweifel &c. — p. 15.[10]

> Nature and Spirit!
> Why these are words to make a Christian quake, —
> For such have atheists perished at the stake.
> Such words are perilous, — full fraught with evil,
> Nature is Sin, and Spirit is the Devil,
> And between both they nurse the monster doubt &c.

GOETHE'S FAITH WAS manifested by a mild pervading spirit of goodness, — a benignant charity, — a genial, steadfast trust. Eckermann was one day interested by the parental love of a hedge-sparrow, which could in no way be induced to forsake its young. Such affection, he says, superior to danger and imprisonment, moved me deeply, and I expressed my admiration to Goethe. "Simple man," he replied, with a smile, "if you believed in God you would not wonder. If God did not inspire the bird with this all-powerful love for its young, and did not similar influences pervade all animate nature, the world could not subsist. Even so is the divine energy everywhere diffused, and the divine love everywhere active."[11] Goethe's opponents are constantly talking of his Pantheism; but if this be Pantheism, it seems in no way inferior to our orthodoxy. Eckermann says, "Goethe has been accused of having no faith, simply because the common faith was too narrow for him."[12] And after all, what confession of faith can equal that of a life at once thoughtful and serene?

This book is invaluable to us for adding confirmation to our faith in the integrity of Goethe's character. Dark hints have been thrown out from time to time, as if all was not as it should be in his life. Yet we hear

[10] *Faust, Part 2.* Whitman cites the page number for the original German edition of 1832, so the translation is doubtless her own.
[11] *Conversations with Goethe,* p. 405.
[12] *Conversations with Goethe,* p. 377-378.

<129>

of no definite charges. Heine, who was once most bitter against him, has publicly avowed since his death, that his opposition sprung from envy. Yet Heine never attacked him as an author, but only as a man. Some writers, sincere friends of Goethe too, tell us "that with this we have nothing to do, that we should look at him and all other authors merely as artists, and enjoy their works apart from any feelings of partiality or dislike to them as individuals." But this we cannot consent to do. We seek in a work of genius first of all to acquaint ourselves with the mind of its author, — to understand and enter into his character. Above all, is the knowledge we have acquired of Goethe's mind most precious to us. We would sooner part with all his works, could we attain an adequate knowledge of his character through any other medium, than to lose that higher satisfaction which we derive from the consciousness that such a man has lived; and we joy to find, notwithstanding all which has been said of him as a "mere artist," that in these conversations, he repeatedly speaks of the want of character in a writer, as one which can be supplied by no mechanical skill; that for an author to write nobly he must first be noble, and above all does be insist upon the indispensable element of love.

GOETHE WAS A great man and a true. Yet his was not a character that he who runs may read, — not every superficial observer and cold formalist can enter into the springs of such a mind; or understand how its complex and diverse elements blend and assimilate into a consistent and harmonious whole. The symmetrical unity, the classic, statue-like repose that characterized him, have been denounced by many as the dictation of a cold, selfish, apathetic nature. To form a candid estimate of these later manifestations, we must go back to the earliest characteristic developments of his mind, as they are exhibited in his *Dichtung und Wahrheit.*[13] We may there observe its nature and inherent traits, and ascertain in what manner they were modified and tempered by the circumstances and discipline of life. We may look quite through the crystal transparency of his young, unshrouded spirit, and watch the gradual expansion of all those noble elements, which were afterwards matured and expanded under judicious culture into full and rare perfection. The striking contrast, which the earlier characteristics of his mind present to those exhibited toward its close, is an interesting and important feature in his history. In his youth, Goethe seemed possessed as it were by his Genius, — in after life, it might be said of him most emphatically that he possessed and ruled it. In youth he exhibited all the passionate fervor and morbid sensibility, the impetuous energies and

---

[13] *Aus meinem Leben: Dichtung und Wahrheit (From My Life: Poetry and Truth),* Goethe's autobiography, published in parts from 1811 to 1833.

<130>

strong volitions peculiar to the poetic temperament. He seemed ruled by a spirit mightier than himself, and uttered oracles of whose high import he was himself unconscious; but in his maturity he had acquired a calm supremacy, a serene, self-possessed control over the plastic powers and obedient energies of his mighty intellect. Over all the subject faculties of his mind, his will seemed to preside as a sovereign.

To our thinking, never was criticism more false than that which a writer in the *Edinburgh Review* pronounced, when he said of Goethe, that "his mind wandered without distinct aim or object, given to quarrel with all those who possessed a firmer faith or a more practical will than himself." On the contrary, notwithstanding the objective character of his later writings, his mind was eminently and intently self-conscious. He thoroughly knew and understood himself. He had ranged over a wide field of mental action and passion, he had had extensive experience of life under its various forms of being, doing, and suffering, and he made a wise and enlightened use of that experience. He profoundly analyzed and justly estimated the capacities of his nature; he chose his path deliberately, and went rejoicing on his way.

That the man who had written *Werther* and *Faust*, which, as he acknowledges, are for the most part confessions of his own moods of mind and habits of thought, should have been able manfully to struggle through those darker periods of conflict and doubt, and to win for himself a tranquil and serene region, where he possessed his soul in peace, and wrought diligently in the career of science, literature, and art, which he had marked out for himself, — this surely was no trivial achievement, no unworthy example. The powers of his mind recovered from their morbid excitability, and now in full and healthy action, expanded so freely and matured so rapidly, that Schiller, himself no laggard in this glorious pathway, found himself, according to his own confession, "completely distanced in the course." An expression, however, which Goethe has reciprocated in the following noble testimony to the genius of his friend. "If," said he, "I was a week without seeing Schiller, when we met I was astonished and knew not where to lay hold of him, I found him so much further advanced."[14] This mutual tribute of these great minds affords the strongest evidence of their intellectual excellence. Yet amidst all the healthy activity and calm serenity of his maturity, Goethe's imagination was still excitable, and his feelings sensitive to a degree seldom witnessed, except in the first freshness and bloom of existence. We have a singular proof of this, in the intensity of his impressions with regard to Italy. His desire to behold the land, where "through dark bowers the golden orange

[14] *Conversations with Goethe*, p. 133. This appears to be Whitman's own translation or paraphrase. Fuller translates, a little awkwardly, "Every eight days became he other and greater than before; each time that I saw him, he seemed to me to have gone forward in knowledge and judgment."

<131>

glows," amounted to a passion, insomuch, that for many years he dared not look into any Latin writer, or contemplate anything which renewed the idea of Italy in his mind. Herder, he says, used to taunt him with learning all his Latin out of Spinoza, for he had observed, that this was the only Latin book that he studied. "He did not know," continues Goethe, "how sedulously I was obliged to guard myself from the ancients, — how I sought a refuge from the very fever of my spirits in these abstruse generalities."[15] This is a characteristic trait, and speaks volumes in refutation of his indifference. It shows, that his calm serenity of spirit, far from being the result of constitutional coldness, or acquired, time-taught apathy, was the fruit of that noble self-restraint which he so sedulously cultivated. Instead of sinking, like less energetic natures, under the trials and disappointments that crossed his path, or turning aside from them to seek relief in exhausting factitious excitements, he only applied at such periods with increased assiduity to the noblest exercises of the intellect. Whenever he had suffered from excess of emotion, he sought to still the fever of the passions by intense and persevering application, taking refuge from the haunting recollections and corroding cares of life, in the investigation of the abstract principles of science, or exercising his powers in some rare creation of art. His genius was a gem that paled not, like the opal, when sorrow and clanger threatened its possessor, but flashed forth at such moments an intenser and keener radiance.

WE HEAR MUCH of Goethe's indifference to the great political interests and exciting public movements of his time. While he has been denounced as heartless and selfish, if not soulless and sensual, for not more actively forwarding the various philanthropic efforts for the amelioration of social wrong; but to us it seems not unworthy of commendation, in an age when all are seeking to teach, to guide, and to elevate their fellows, that one among the many should manifest through the contented activity, the calm serenity, and mild practical wisdom of his life, that he had at least acquired something worthy of being imparted. We would refer those, who condemn him for his political neutrality, to his own beautiful defence of the course he had adopted, given by him in his conversations with Eckermann.

"If a poet would work politically," says he, "he must give himself up to a party, and so soon as he does that, he is lost as a poet; he must bid farewell to his freedom of spirit, and draw over his ears the cap of bigotry

---

[15] Goethe knew his classics well, but during his Latin studies with Herder, he was frequently the victim of his teacher's sarcasm over his favorite reading matter. In *Truth and Poetry*, Goethe writes, "He had destroyed my enjoyment of so much that I had loved before, and had especially blamed me in the strongest manner for the pleasure I took in Ovid's *Metamorphoses*." (Vol. 2, p. 356).

<132>

and blind hatred. The poet may as a man and a citizen love his native land, but the native land of his poetic energies and poetic action is the good, noble, and beautiful, which is confined to no province nor country; which he is to seize upon and body forth wherever he finds it. And what then is meant by love of one's country? What is meant by patriotic deeds? If the poet has employed a life in battling with pernicious prejudices in setting aside narrow views, in enlightening the intellects, purifying the tastes, ennobling the feeling and thoughts of his countrymen, what better could he have done, how shown himself more truly a patriot?"[16] "Also," Eckermann tell us, "he blamed the political course, so much praised by others, of Uhland." "Watch well," said he, "and you will see the politician devour the poet. To be a member of the estates, and live among perpetual jostlings and excitements, is not the life for a poet. His song will soon cease. Swabia has plenty of men sufficiently well educated, well meaning, able and fluent of tongue, to be members of the estates; but only one poet of Uhland's class."[17]

Goethe, moreover, believed with Dr. Johnson, that our happiness is comparatively but little influenced by the form of government under which we live. It was his conviction, that far less could be done for a man from *without* than from *within*. There is an expression to this effect in the Helena.

Lass der Sonne Glanz verschwinden,
Wenn es in der Seele tagt,
W er in eignen herzen finden
Was die ganze welt versagt.[18]

Let the Sun's light fade away,
If within the soul 't is day, —
The heart's deep fountain shall supply
What all the world doth still deny.

But why should we ask of the poet, that he should be also a politician, that he should mingle in the stormy and conflicting interests of public life, thereby to endanger perhaps the universality of his sympathies and the comprehensiveness of his vision? Should we not rather look upon him as the great high priest of Humanity, — as one of a consecrated race, set apart to minister to the wants of the spirit, — to illustrate the eternal laws of Beauty, — to feed with the pure naphtha of genius that divine flame of enthusiasm, which burns with more or less intensity in every

[16] *Conversations with Goethe*, pp. 411-412.
[17] Ibid, p. 413.
[18] *Faust* 2, III Arkadien. Chorus in dialogue with Phorykos, Euphorion and Helena.

<133>

bosom, that love of the ideal and the spiritual, which warms and elevates at times even the coldest and dullest heart? The poet should be for us the interpreter of the dream of life, — he should reveal to us the secret treasures that lie within the depths of our own spirits, — he should show us all the beauty, the harmony, and the glory of existence, — he should be for us, at once, the expounder of the past, the prophet of the future, the idealizer of the present.

Novalis says finely, "that the greater part of our humanity yet sleeps a deep sleep."[19] Thus it seems to us, in some natures do those faculties, which belong to the ideal, still seem buried in a profound slumber. This portion of our being it is which the poet divines for us, — he reveals to us a foretaste of those higher instincts, which are hereafter to be more fully developed within us. When the ideal is born within us, then do we wake to a new existence, and take possession of a princely heritage, a celestial and imperishable kingdom.

Perhaps no man has ever more nobly conceived, and assuredly none has more eloquently described the poet's high vocation, than Goethe has done in his *Wilhelm Meister*. Had he written but this one thing, it would amply attest the splendor of his genius. The words seem to trace themselves upon the memory in characters of light. Among other things, he says, "He, who is fashioned like a bird to soar over the world, to nestle upon high cliffs, and to draw his nourishment from the flowers and fruits, exchanging lightly one bough with another; he cannot accustom himself to draw the plough like the steer, or guard the household like the mastiff."[20]

Those persons, who refuse to see anything admirable in Goethe, because to all his own rare and varied excellence he did not also unite the active benevolence of a Howard,[21] with the Christian zeal and political disinterestedness of a Wilberforce,[22] remind us of those insidious advisers,

[19] Novalis (Friedrich von Hardenberg) (1772-1801). An aphorism from the 1802 *Novalis Schriften* (Novalis's Writings), edited by Ludwig Tieck and Friedrich Schlegel. Carlyle, in his 1829 review of the book's fourth edition in *The Foreign Review* in 1829, translates the aphorism as, "The greater part of our Body, of our Humanity itself, yet sleeps a deep sleep." Carlyle, *Essays*, p. 181.

[20] Goethe. *Wilhelm Meister, Book II, Chapter 2,* p. 80. This appears to be Whitman's paraphrase of a more elaborate passage, translated thus by Carlyle in 1839: "What! thou wouldst have him descend from his height to some paltry occupation! He who is fashioned like the bird to hover round the world, to nestle on the lofty summits, to feed on buds and fruits, exchanging gayly one bough for another; *he* ought also to work at the plough like an ox; like a dog to train himself to the harness and draught; or perhaps tied up in a chain, to guard a farmyard by his barking!"

[21] John Howard (1726-1790), British philanthropist and prison reformer.

[22] William Wilberforce (1759-1790), British philanthropist, and leader of the movement against the slave trade.

<134>

who persuaded Aladdin, that his magnificent palace was incomplete and worthless, without the addition of the Roc's egg, the acquisition of which in some way involved the sacrifice of the whole fabric.

Granting, that his intellect was more active than his feelings, and that it thoroughly controlled and guided them, shall we therefore refuse to accord him aught of our sympathy and admiration? Feelings of greater impulsiveness and impetuosity, might probably have been associated with an intellect less comprehensive and discriminating, — more social and patriotic activity, with an inferior degree of artistic culture and a less catholic spirit. Let us take great men as we find them, as God and nature have moulded, as circumstances and their own efforts have modified them, and be thankful for the good, without dwelling captiously upon the evil. It is idle for men to attempt to say what Goethe would have been, if certain qualities had been abstracted from, and certain other qualities added to his nature. As it is, we find positive excellence of a high and rare order. Would it not be wiser to study this with a spirit of genial sympathy, than painfully to hunt after defects? A mind like his, apprehensive of all beauty, and ever watchful after truth, never slumbering, never tiring in its pursuit, cannot but have left treasures for those who will receive them, and a glorious example for all who will observe and profit by it.

THIS VOLUME OF Conversations will be cordially welcomed by some, if only for the light which it throws upon the enigmatical conclusion of *Faust*. Not a few of the many problems, contained in that strange phantasmagoria, are solved by Goethe in the various incidental allusions to it, thrown out in conversation while the work was in progress. The commencement of this wild poem was written at that stage of mental transition, when we are first rudely waked from the dreams of the imagination to all the sterner realities of life, — when Hope has thrown aside her radiant pencil, and no longer paints on the dark curtain, that conceals from us the future, her bright enchanting story. When we look around despairingly on a world that seems destitute of interest, harmony, or design, and begin to ask ourselves those strange and agitating questions, which, when they have once suggested themselves to the understanding, cannot be silenced by any wisdom which is of this world.

Fontenelle tells us, that "when we discover the utter vanity and worthlessness of all that occupies and surrounds us in life, we become too wise, we tear from nature the heart of her mystery, and ceasing to act, we do nothing but think." "While nature," he says, "revenges herself upon us for thus seeking to penetrate her secrets, by the sadness reflection

<135>

causes us." The acute Frenchman with all his wisdom never got beyond this![23]

Voltaire too, at the very close of his long and brilliant life, writes from Ferney to Madame du Deffand in the same spirit. "Let us wholly resign ourselves to our fate, which only laughs at our endeavors to escape from it. Let us live as long as we can and how we can, we shall never be as happy as fools are; yet let us endeavor to be so in our own way. Death of itself is nothing, but thinking of it makes us melancholy. Let us therefore banish it from our minds, and live from hand to mouth. Let us say, when we rise, 'what shall I do to-day for the benefit of my health and for my amusement?' That is all we ought to think of at our age. Life is a baby which must be rocked till it falls asleep." And again, "All our trifling consolations are only so many plasters applied to that wound our existence." Alas! for the sage of Ferney, with his rocking-cradle and his plasters![24]

This stage our German had now reached, but it was one in which no true German could rest, least of all Goethe. He felt its desolation too keenly to abide in it, — he could not pitch his tent there, — he knows that he must get beyond that barren wilderness, or perish in it. But let us hear how he describes this weary period of his "apprenticeship."

> In the popular drama of which Faust is the hero, I found more
> than one tone which vibrated through my soul. 1 also had
> passed through the circle of the sciences, and had early
> convinced myself of their vanity. All my endeavors to find
> felicity in life had hitherto proved fruitless. I shared to excess
> in that restlessness of spirits, that leads the contemplative man
> to dwell on internal disquietudes, which have but a transitory
> existence in unreflecting minds. I was already acquainted with
> the miseries of social life, — my adventure with Margaret, and
> the consequences of that connexion, had opened my eyes to

[23] Bernard Le Bovier de Fontenelle (1657-1757), French Enlightenment writer and scientist, wrote and published prolifically, and unlike his contemporary Voltaire, his works were never banned. The passages here, from *Dialogues of the Dead*, appear to be Whitman's translation. Whitman is not entirely just in attributing the thought expressed to Fontenelle himself, since the text is an imaginary dialogue between the ancients Theocritus and Parmenides, the latter being the speaker. In the John Hughes translation, the second passage reads: "By what appears 'tis not Nature's intention that we should think too refinedly, because she sells these thoughts at so dear a rate! You are for making reflections, says she; but beware! — I'll have my Revenge, by the Sadness they shall give you."

[24] Probably Whitman's own translation. The letters from Voltaire were available in *Correspondence Général*, the 61st volume of Beaumarchais' 1784 edition of Voltaire. Deffand's letters to Voltaire were published separately in 1810 in London.

<136>

the strange irregularities that are to be found in the bosom of civil society, where the polished smoothness of the surface is strangely contrasted by the internal convulsions, caused by passions whose influence is more fatal, in consequence of those restraints which oppose their outward development. When we consider the effect produced by these internal conflicts on an ardent temperament, — when we reflect on the seductions of the imagination and the continual agitation of life, we cannot wonder at the impatience, which man often evinces, to free himself from the burden of existence. There are also many individuals, who, unable to find an object on which to exercise their activity, and led astray by extravagant desires, become disgusted with an existence which to them seems too monotonous and peaceful. Such was at one time the peculiar disposition of my own mind, and I well remember how much pain I suffered, and how many efforts I made to effect a cure.[25]

Thus has he eloquently described that state of feeling, to which all susceptible natures are necessarily exposed, at a certain period of their progress. With that prompt and keen apprehensiveness of excellence, which belonged to his nature, Goethe at once seized upon what was still vital and genuine in this old legend of Faust, the growth of an ignorant and superstitious age; and concentrating upon it the light of his genius, the simple germ expanded and unfolded into a plant of rare and surpassing beauty, putting forth leaf after leaf, and producing gradually the fairest flowers and the richest fruits, — its roots striking far down into the earth, and its branches waving freely in the blue depths of ether. Its seeds have been wafted abroad over far lands, and have sprung up again in power and beauty from many a foreign soil. Byron's *Manfred*, perhaps the *chef-d'oeuvre* of his genius, is evidently a scion of this noble plant. Coleridge gives manifold proofs of having been quickened and stimulated by its influence,[26] and Mrs. Hemans has not hesitated to pluck now and then a fair flower from its branches. We remember few things more perfect of their kind than her "[A] Spirit's Return." Yet one of its finest touches seems to us a beautiful, though perhaps unconscious appropriation of an expression in Goethe's *Helena*. In her wonderful and awe-inspiring description of a being, recalled by the passionate adjuration of love from the spirit land, Mrs. Hemans says,

---

[25] Here Whitman has combined selected passages from Goethe's *Memoir*.
[26] It was not known until quite recently that Coleridge was the anonymous translator of an early edition of excerpts from *Faust* in 1834, titled *Faustus*.

<137>

Before me there
He, the departed stood! Oh, for strong words
To bring conviction o'er thy thought, —
Aye, face to face, *so near, — yet O how far!*[27]

The words in italics are precisely the same which Goethe has put into the mouth of Helena, who when invoked from the lands of departed spirits, says to Faust, with a perplexed half-consciousness of her newly awakened existence, "*Ich fuhle mich so fern, und doch so nah.*" We might instance other examples, for they occur very frequently in the latter poems. Goethe justifies this "culling of sweets," and commends Lord Byron for the sagacity which he evinced in discovering and adopting the best thoughts of the best writers. For ourselves, we would rather see the flowers growing on their native stem, unless indeed they are fairly incorporated and engrafted into the foreign plant and not merely fastened upon it as ornaments.

FIFTY YEARS HAD elapsed after the publication of this first part of *Faust*, before the second was fully completed and given to the world. In this long interval, great and important changes had taken place in the mind of its author. He was no longer a lonely exile on earth, — he had reconciled himself to existence, and brought his finely tempered spirit into perfect harmony with itself and the external world. In Experience he had found a rude, yet not unfriendly teacher, in Nature the gentlest mother and the kindest nurse, and within his own heart a tranquil, happy home. He no longer shared in that satiety of spirit that wrung from Israel's luxurious monarch the despairing anathema on life, which the world-weary heart of humanity has echoed for so many thousand years, — "All is vanity!" But while he too sorrowed and suffered and felt at times the weariness of existence, he knew and felt in his inmost heart, that that sorrow and that weariness would in some way become the ministers of good. In his mouth the fruit of the tree of knowledge, for from turning to "bitterness and ashes," yielded a bland and sweet nourishment, maturing and strengthening all the powers of his soul. He had too now learned that great truth, the discovery of which forms so important an era in the life of every thinking man, that

We receive but what we give,
In our life alone doth nature live.[28]

---

[27] Felicia Hemans (1793-1845). This poem does not appear in the 1840 *Works*, but is in an undated edition, The Poetical Works, pp. 368-372, where the poem is dated 1830. Whitman has re-arranged the order of Hemans' lines. Hemans' poem begins with an epigraph from Byron's *Manfred*.
[28] Coleridge. "Dejection: An Ode," ll. 47-48.

<138>

He appears to have attained that conviction, so contradictory to the simple suggestions of the understanding, that, even as in the natural world the diurnal changes from light to darkness are produced by our globe's revolving on its own axis, so also is it in the spiritual. That not the revolution of any foreign object, any external source of light and heat, makes the soul's night and day, — its morning and evening; but while external things remain comparatively unchanged in their relations to us, it is but the rotations and transitions of our own spirits that causes our sun to rise and set, — that creates for us the serene radiance of the dawn, or involves us in the gloom and darkness of midnight.

On these great truths his mind was nourished, and from them it acquired freedom, serenity, and power. The eye of his understanding became keener, the wing of his imagination bolder. His writings had now entirely lost their subjective character. His high artistic culture, his practised eye, and above all his confirmed faith, that the divine spirit reveals itself equally in every manifestation of being, — had won him from that exclusive contemplation of his own spirit, which marked some of his earlier writings, into a wider range of observation, and prepared him for a more varied delineation of life.

The change, of which we speak, is vividly indicated in two engraved heads of Goethe, which are now lying before us. The one a beautiful outline in profile, taken we should suppose from a bust, and accompanying the London edition of the Correspondence with Bettina Brentano. The other a fine engraving by Weber prefixed to a copy of *Faust*.

How eloquent are they both, yet how different is the language they utter. The former, representing him in his youth, seems the very incarnation and embodiment of poetic thought. The attitude of the head is one of exceeding beauty, and in itself full of character, so lofty is it, so expressive of the triumphant consciousness of power, so graceful, fearless, and free. The far-glancing eye looks neither to heaven nor earth, but forward into a purely ideal region, while it seems to dilate and kindle as with the thought of its proud inheritance. The countenance expresses a mingled sweetness and fervor, gentleness and pride; and though a shade of sadness lingers around the rich curvature of the lip, in the whole we see tokens of a spirit, for which life has yet many stern lessons in store, many heavy, weary hours. This picture reminds us of a young race-horse eager to run his course, "standing with flowing mane, arching neck, and dilated nostrils, ready to leap all barriers and dash aside all obstacles that threaten to impede his progress." It recalls to us, also, the description which Jacobi gives of him in 1774. "Goethe was with us," says he in a letter to a friend, "a handsome youth of twenty-five; from the crown of his head to the sole of his foot all genius, power, and strength, — a spirit of fire with the wings of an eagle, '*qui ruit immensus ore profundo.*' The

<139>

more I think of him, the more intensely I feel the impossibility of writing to any one, who has not seen or heard him, anything comprehensible concerning this extraordinary creature of God. It requires to be only an hour in his company to find it in the highest degree preposterous, to desire him to think or act after any other fashion than his own."[29]

But now let us look at the other picture representing him at an advanced period of his existence, even as he might have looked, when Bettina Brentano first saw him, and thought upon what King David said, "Each man may be king over himself." Even so, perchance, looks he here as he then looked upon her, with that grave, serene, penetrating glance, whose light never afterwards faded from her young innocent heart. For let us not be deterred from trusting in the reality and purity of such affection as hers, by the doubtful smiles of the infidel worldling, — rare and evanescent as it is, the power of feeling and believing in such love is among those higher instincts, which redeem our nature from the curse of the serpent, condemned to grovel forever upon the earth.

In this picture the calm supremacy of the mature intellect, — the repose of the self-conquered spirit may be seen in the increased expansion of the marble brow, and in the full, serene eye, which seems to look quite through the object of its gaze, insomuch, that at a first glance, it appears to be fixed on vacancy, so far does it penetrate beyond the surface. The beautiful expression of the mouth which expresses refinement without fastidiousness, — the mild benignant lustre of the eye, — the steadfast majesty of the broad brow, — the tempered, chastened calm that pervades the whole, speak a mind and character to which life had richly ministered.

L ET US PAUSE a moment longer, — we are fond of looking at busts and portraits, — to compare this last with a wonderfully expressive head wrought in marble, which stands on yonder cabinet. It might pass for a representation of Mephistopheles, but it is not so, it is the head of a real personage, — a great man, one who has of late been often compared with Goethe, not unfrequently pronounced decidedly

---

[29] Here Whitman has elided two different descriptions of Goethe, that of Jacobi, and another admirer named Heinse. See Lewes, *Life and Works of Goethe*, pp. 287-288. Friedrich Heinrich Jacobi (1743-1819) was a German philosopher who accused the Enlightenment thinkers of encouraging nihilism. Young Jacobi's first meeting with Goethe inspired him to write two *sturm und drang* novels, and to study the philosophy of Spinoza. He promptly became an anti-Idealist, and attacked or quarreled with most of the philosophers of his time, including those close to Goethe. Despite this, Jacobi and Goethe remained on cordial terms until 1812. "We loved one another, without understanding one another," Goethe said. For a full account of the Goethe-Jacobi relationship, see George di Giovanni's Introduction to *Main Philosophical Writings*. Jacobi's admiration for Goethe was described by contemporaries as adulation, and is seen today as a romantic "crush."

<140>

his superior. Nay, we have been even assured by a writer in the a contemporary journal, that he had by far the more faith of the two, that he was by no means so rank an infidel, — perhaps a comparison of these heads might assist us in settling the question. Let us look at this last. Here, too, is precision, piercing sharpness, sagacity, shrewdness, discrimination, but no insight. Those eyes cannot even look you directly in the face, — far less can they penetrate beyond the surface into the core and marrow of being. They look on life with an oblique, cynical, side-long glance, — a cold, sneering, distrusting smile, which is full of world-wisdom, it is true; but is this the countenance of a man at peace with the world and with his own heart? If so, it is but a hollow compact, — a treaty in which there is no sure reliance, no steadfast feeling of security. Has he any true joy in the present, — any faith in the unseen and the spiritual? Goethe enjoyed life without fearing death; Voltaire, alas! (for it is his bust that we are contemplating,) was neither happy in life nor resigned to death. The *wound* still throbbed painfully, for there was no healing balm in the specifics that were applied to it. Nor could the vibratory motion of the infant's cradle charm away the fear of spectral dreams. Nevertheless, we trust that he now sleeps in peace; and having satisfactorily decided for ourselves the question above alluded to, we leave others to determine it at their leisure, and return to our subject of *Faust*.

We believe that the continuation of this poem is as yet but little known out of Germany. Eckermann tell us, that Goethe relied for its success upon the high point of culture to which his nation had arrived. It does not reflect life in its simplicity, — it is not calculated, like the works of Shakespeare, to please the learned and the unlearned, — the wise and the simple, — it is full of refinements and abstractions, — it deals in symbols and hieroglyphics. We have nothing in English literature, that at all resembles it, or approximates to it. The English critics, who have alluded to it, have for the most part condemned it unread. A writer in the *Edinburgh* tells us, that it is "a crude and revolting mass of absurdities."[30] Yet Eckermann says, that Goethe agreed with him in thinking, that a far richer world was here displayed than in the earlier portion. Goethe confessed, that ["]The first part was almost entirely subjective, proceeding from an oppressed, impassioned state of the individual character,["][31] while in the second, he says, "there was exhibited a higher, broader, clearer, and more passionless region, of which those, who have not lived and looked about them sometime, will hardly know what to think."[32]

[30] In an unsigned book review of Sarah Austin's *Characteristics of Goethe*, the reviewer calls Goethe's "Helena" sequel to *Faust* "an incoherent, revolting mass of unsubstantial contradictions." *Edinburgh Review*, July 1833, p. 379.
[31] This passage is verbatim from *Conversations with Goethe*, pp. 366-367.
[32] This passage is not the same as Fuller's on p. 367, so here Whitman is

<141>

The slighting and disparaging tone of remark, which has been adopted in relation to it by English critics, reminds us of a passage in this poem, where Mephistopheles is made to say, as if in anticipation of the manner in which it would be treated by this class of writers:

Daran erkenn' ich den *Gelehrter herrn!*
Was ihr nicht tastet steht euch meilen fern;
Was ihr nicht fasst, das fehlt euch ganz und gar;
Was ihr nicht rechnet, glaubt ihr sey nicht wahr;
Was ihr nicht wägt, bat für euch kein Gewicht;
Was ihr nicht münzt, das, meint ihr, gelte nihbt.

By this, I know what learned men ye are,
What ye can handle not, seems miles afar,
What ye can grasp not, is an empty shade,
What ye divine not, must all search evade,
That which yo have not poised of weight is stinted,
And no coin current, save what ye have minted.[33]

Yet it should not perhaps excite our surprise, that these "*Gelehrter herrn*" (learned gentlemen), cannot see, at one glance, all that is comprised in this rare production, the rich results of a life of contemplative observation and poetic insight.

Diderot tells us, "that there are a thousand learned men (*hommes instruits*), for one enlightened man, — a thousand enlightened men, for one man of fine insight and acute penetration, (*clair-voyant*), and a thousand clairvoyants for one man of genius." "The man of genius," he says, "creates things, — the clairvoyant deduces principles from them, — the enlightened man makes the application of those principles. The merely learned man is ignorant neither of the things which have been created, nor the laws which have been deduced from them, nor of the application which has been made of those laws, — he knows all, but he produces nothing and comprehends little."[34]

Many commentaries have been written upon this portion of *Faust*, — many theories invented respecting its object and design. Yet still, to the majority of readers, it remains as much an enigma as ever, — to a large proportion of the Germans even a "stumbling block," and to the English "foolishness." For ourselves, we read the work without an interpreter, and brooded over it in the silence of the spirit, — neither commentary nor analysis had found its way to our remote seclusion, — no friendly reader sympathized with our pleasure and perplexities, — no

substituting her own translation.
[33] *Faust 2*. Act 1: Throne Room Scene, ll. 10-15.
[34] Diderot. *Encyclopédie*. Vol. 11. Entry for "Eclaire, Clairvoyant," pp. 643-644.

<142>

critic intermeddled with our joys, — we groped our way in the darkness, and often came unawares upon rich treasures, — lumps of pure golden ore, and gems of rare lustre. It is true that, after its first perusal, we retained of it for a time only a confused and dream-like recollection, produced by the constant change of scene and strange blending of objects.

The quaint and merry songs of the masquers were ringing in our ears, blended with the carols of of sea-nymphs, and the silver-sweet chorus of angels and blessed spirits; the wild imagery and grotesque *dramatis personae* of the "Classical Walpurgis night," with the severe simplicity and antique contour of the "Helena." All these left at first a confused and disjointed impression on the mind, as of some rich and graceful but fantastic tracery of arabesque, viewed in faint and partially obliterated outline on the frieze of some ancient temple, — but as we continue to gaze, the finely carved tracery becomes fairer, and more sharply defined; centaurs and griffins are now seen at intervals amid the fantastic foliage, — laughing satyrs leer upon us from some vine-wreathed covert, — pensive caryatids are discovered supporting the rich entablature, their symmetrical figures shrouded in flowing drapery, and their thoughtful faces full of high symbolic meaning. What seemed at first but a confused and fragmentary delineation of objects, now unfolds a design of rich and rare significance. By degrees, the several groups assume more of prominence and distinctness, the lights and shades become stronger, — the outline bolder, till at last, they stand forth in all the rounded and finely molded perfection of Grecian art. The forms, it is true, are marble still, — still wanting in all the life-warm coloring and glowing freshness of nature, and still, as with all figures wrought in relievo, one side of the object only being delineated by the artist, it is left for the imagination of the beholder to supply the rest, and to give the figure its full completeness and finish.

We cannot hope to form a correct and candid estimate of such a work, by comparing it with the writings of other poets. We must not, like the author of an article in a late number of the *Foreign Quarterly*, expect to arrive at a just estimate of Goethe by measuring him with Shakespeare, or think to manifest our fairness by condemning him, because we can find no resemblance between the two. We must endeavor to forget all our favorite standards of excellence, — all the trodden and accustomed paths in which our fancy is wont to wander, and giving up our band into that of our strange guide, follow in child-like simplicity and confidence, wherever his genius may prompt him to lead us. If we do this, we shall not fail to find regions of rare and varied beauty, unfolding their treasures to us as we proceed, and everywhere the brilliant atmosphere, and mellow

<143>

golden light of a poetic imagination, hovering over and pervading the landscape.

We know of nothing, that approaches this work in exuberance and prodigality of genius, in the lavish expenditure that is exhibited of all the richest materials of poetry; neither are the closing scenes without a pure spiritual beauty, a divine glory which reflects back its mellow radiance, along the whole rich vista of the narrative, lined as it is with images of beauty and terror, magnificence and simplicity, grotesqueness and gloom.

In these concluding pages, every sentence, every line is full of meaning, yet are the thoughts expressed with so much conciseness and simplicity, that it is not often at a first reading, that we take in their entire significance. They are like those paintings of the old masters, where color is often laid upon color to produce the effect of entire transparency. How much, for instance, is implied in that reply of a happy spirit to the entreaty of Mephistopheles, that she would approach and bless him with her presence.

We approach e'en now, — wherefore dost thou recoil?
We come, — then stay thee if thou canst and meet us.[35]

But this he cannot do. How finely do these lines indicate that heaviest punishment of wickedness, the incapacity to draw near to, or even to bear the approach of goodness and purity, — not hatred, but love itself becomes their avenger, and, self-exiled, they shun the pure atmosphere of light and love, which to them seems an element of torture.

Ever in reading this poem are we discovering some new beauty, some fine and delicate meaning which had hitherto escaped the notice. There are, it is true, many things here which we do not understand, many which from our remote position can be seen into but dimly and imperfectly, — many indeed, which in our eyes are decided blemishes and defects. Yet we leave these last to those critics, who have already shown themselves so prompt in discovering the errors of this great man.

A RECENT NUMBER OF *Blackwood's Magazine* contains an article on Goethe,[36] expressing such extravagant and indiscriminate condemnation, exhibiting such determined opposition, and such a total want of candor, that we had supposed there could be but one

[35] Angelic voices mocking Mephistopheles in the final scene of *Faust Part 2*, ll. 11778-11779 (Kaufmann trans).
[36] "A Discourse on Goethe and the Germans," published in *Blackwood's Magazine*, Vol. 45, 1839, pp. 247-256. The piece is an informal tirade, a long run-on after-dinner speech in effect, most of it a long plot synopsis of Goethe's *Elective Affinities*. It is more comic than critical, but it does depict female readers of German poetry as shallow fools unversed in their own literature.

<144>

feeling in regard to it, among those who knew anything of the subject of all this invective. Yet not only has this article been highly commended by a writer in the *Foreign Quarterly*,[37] but the same extravagant and reckless hostility expressed with an increased degree of virulence. So utterly misplaced and unfounded do some of these observations appear, that they would almost lead a calm observer to believe, that the writer, having a talent for invective and denunciation, had exercised his gift indiscriminately on the first luckless victim that chanced to fall in his way, especially as no attempts have been made to substantiate these charges. After lavishing the most bitter opprobrium upon "elaborate infamies of which no maid, no wife, no woman could hear but the outline," the names of which "elaborate infamies" are not even once mentioned, lest perhaps these, too, might prove offensive to the fastidious reader, he at last ceases to war with shadows and says more definitely, "But we are reminded of *Faust*. In what does the marvel of this consist? In what is Goethe's claim borne out to the title of the German Shakespeare? Shakespeare ruled the heart and swayed the sympathies of mankind, — his thoughts lay open the intellectual world of man, his aspirations ennoble the mind. The most that Goethe does is to surprise: when he talks of feeling, it is to drone or to sneer, his powers are fantastical, his imaginations half cold," &c. &c. What must we think of such criticism as this, proceeding, too, from a work that affects to guide the tastes of the whole English nation in foreign literature!

"*In what does the marvel of Faust consist?*" since it in no way resembles the works of the great English dramatist. And again, "*when Goethe talks of feeling, it is to drone!*" Has this writer read the story of Margaret? — and does he call its profound heart-rending pathos, its touching simplicity and tenderness, "*droning?*" Has he read unmoved the eloquent appeal of "Clärchen?" Has he looked coldly on the desolate anguish of Tasso, — on the silent, life-consuming passion of Mignon? If so, it were in vain to remonstrate with him; we might as well talk of colors to the blind.

At length, after a series of quotations from *Faust*, whose excellence is faintly and reluctantly admitted, he comes at last to speak of that sublime chorus of the archangels, whose surpassing majesty has no parallel, save in the inspired writings of the prophets and bards of Israel. This noble chaunt differs essentially from all creations of the kind. Milton's "Address to Light," Coleridge's "Hymn to Mount Blanc," and Byron's "Thunder Storm amid the Alps," all, great and glorious as they are, seem still to be the efforts of a finite being, striving to raise itself to the conception of the infinite; but here there is no effort, no striving after sublimity. The calm, free, majestic movement of the verse seems like the

---

[37] The following quotes are all from "Histoire de la Litterature Allemande," *Foreign Review*, April 1839, pp. 75-76

<145>

unimpeded motion of the heavenly orbs through the vaults of space. It is indeed a song of the archangels. One would have thought that here, at least, the critic would have felt and owned the divine power of genius, and been awed for once into reverence and silence. But let us hear his comments upon this matchless poem. "This passage," he says, "is elaborately gorgeous; but if the wonders of creation were the theme, why confine it to the mere terrestrial phenomena? The opening would indicate the necessity of more, but it opens so only to disappoint us. The planetary and other systems were known fully at the time this was written, and yet they are not referred to. There is nothing here, like the grandeur of the cloud-capt towers and gorgeous palaces of Shakespeare's age, — far less of his genius."[38]

We are here forcibly reminded of a fanciful little story of Tieck's,[39] in which we are told how a worthy matter-of-fact sort of man, who was always questioning of the "*cui bono,*" having by chance strayed into the region of the ideal, — the "Garden of Poesy," found himself strangely at a loss, how to interpret the unaccustomed sights and sounds that greeted him on every side. He compared the appearances around with the most approved models, — tested them by the most unexceptionable standards, but could make nothing of them. The flowers were often larger than life, and presented many new combinations of color. They had, moreover, human voices, and conversed eloquently and fluently, a fact which he could in no way reconcile with the teachings of experience and common sense, — at length, chancing to meet with a joint stool, a table, and a sirloin of roast beef, he begins to feel himself quite *au-fait,* — these are tangible palpable realities; he knows at once their uses and ends, and promptly avails himself of them. Our translator has somewhere finely said, that "there are some people whom nature has made non-conductors to the electricity of genius."

In this article, Goethe is constantly spoken of as a mere artist, the word being used in that limited sense commonly assigned to it by English writers, and the term being very frequently confounded with *artificiality.* Goethe was in so far an artist, that he applied himself with a sincere devotion to the study and contemplation of the beautiful, but we may everywhere see, that he does this in the full faith, that there is an eternal connexion between beauty, — goodness, and truth, — and indeed, do not the good and the true necessarily evolve themselves from the beautiful, even as the fruit from the flower? Schiller has a beautiful passage to this effect in his "Artist."[40] The opening lines of which we

[38] Ibid, p. 78.
[39] Ludwig Tieck (1773-1853), German poet, critic, translator, and writer of fantasy fiction in the guise of literary fairy tales.
[40] Friedrich Schiller. "The Artists." These are not the opening lines, and Whitman has made a lovely paraphrase, more gracious than Bulwer Lytton's

<146>

venture to give from a perhaps imperfect recollection of the original, yet we are sure of the thought:

> Through Beauty's morning gate alone,
> We penetrate to wisdom's throne;
> Tempered by her auroral ray,
> The mind may brave Truth's noontide sway.

And Rousseau somewhere says, "*J'ai toujours cru que le bon n'etait que le beau mis en action.*"[41]

In the same spirit he has been condemned as cold and trifling, for being able to throw himself with such entire unreserve into the occupation of the moment, for that rare power of mental concentration, which enabled him to elicit from the subject of his contemplation, however trivial might be its nature, all the instruction and amusement it was capable of affording. He loved the finite not for itself, but that he saw in it ever a type and symbol of the infinite. He looked on nature with a microscopic eye, and a thousand secret treasures were revealed to his devout and earnest gaze. A flower, a mineral, or an insect, was to him a mine of exhaustless wealth. Thus, too, did he view the incidents and characters of every-day life. His spirit was so rich and comprehensive, that it often, as in some parts of *Wilhelm Meister*, imparted his own rich hues to the most common objects and incidents of this working-clay world, — like the golden atmosphere of a Claude,[42] diffused over and pervading the scenes of a Van Ostade[43] or a Teniers.[44]

GOETHE'S WRITINGS HAVE been often objected to, on the ground of their not teaching any definite and distinct moral. *Wilhelm Meister* is supposed to be deficient in this respect, — yet experience teaches us to perceive a moral in all the events of life. Why then may we not do this in a work of art? If the writer has drawn a faithful picture of life, why may we not find for ourselves the moral, without its being directly pointed out for us? Goethe says in his conversations with Eckermann, "that he had supposed, that a rich and manifold life brought close to the eye, might suffice without any distinct moral tendency." For 1844 translation.

[41] Jean-Jacques Rousseau. *Œuvres Complètes. La Nouvelle Héloise*. Part 1, Letter 12, p. 27. "I have always believed that the Good was the Beautiful brought to life."
[42] Claude Lorrain (d. 1682). French landscape painter, noted for introducing the sun and its bright rays into his paintings.
[43] Adriaen van Ostade (1610-1685). His late work, influenced by Rembrandt, employs lighting and chiaroscura effects.
[44] David Teniers the Younger (1610-1690), a prolific painter of landscapes and scenes from everyday life.

<147>

us *Wilhelm Meister* possesses a species of interest, which we might look for in vain in the works of most English novelists. The bright and polished mirror of Scott's genius, instead of reflecting the spirit and character of the present age, flashes back upon us again and again some picture of other days. The age of chivalry and adventure, of romantic daring and high achievement, is represented by him in all its imposing magnificence. But there are times when we turn away from the splendid panorama of crusades and tournaments, of courts and camps, warriors and princes, to brood over the complex situations and feelings excited by the existing relations of social life, and would fain see them delineated by a hand as free and powerful as that of this great master. Those English writers, who have hitherto attempted the representation of life in the nineteenth century, have for the most part seized only its most superficial and obvious characteristics, without penetrating below the exterior covering, which is in itself alike destitute of pictorial or poetic beauty. The individual peculiarities of character are far less prominent now than formerly, the events of life less imposing, but beneath this calmer aspect, the undercurrent of thought and passion rushes perhaps with greater intensity and force. This inner life of the spirit is one which Scott, with all his richness of invention and dramatic power, could not have depicted. Coleridge went so far as to say, "that Scott had never presented him with a single new idea." Yet in his own broad range, he was ever bold, masterly, and true. He has brought to the Temple of English literature the richest treasures, and adorned its proud walls with an embroidered tapestry wrought in rare and enduring colors. We honor him for what he has so nobly done, and ask not that he should have been other than he was. For one person, who reads such a work as *Wilhelm Meister*, we may find thousands who delight in the animated, pictorial scenes of Scott, and the school to which he has given rise. Many probably would throw aside *Wilhelm Meister* with distaste after reading a few pages, yet we venture to say, that few, who have read the book once, have read it *but* once. It is a work so suggestive to a thinking mind, it presents so rich and profound a study to the observer of human nature, that we find ourselves often returning to it, to compare the examples of life there depicted, with the results of our own experience and observation. No one knew better than Goethe, how to analyze the blended elements of social life, so as to produce at will new combinations and associations, alike true to individual nature and in harmony with the ideal world of art.

<148>

Margaret Fuller

WE WOULD SAY one word ere we close, on the manner in which the study of German literature is too frequently regarded by our countrymen. Goethe says, "that it is in the German nature, duly to honor everything produced by other nations." The Americans, on the contrary, seem in danger of becoming too exclusively national. We could wish that they had a little more of the German cosmopolitanism. Perhaps it is natural, that whenever any attempt is made by a portion of the community to lead the public mind to new trains of thought or modes of action, to introduce new theories, or point out new fields for exertion or enterprise, that an antagonist party should spring up, whose tendency it is to resist all innovation. Perhaps it is a wise provision of nature, that has thus furnished every age with its sentinels and warders, as well as with its bold and adventurous pioneers, — and provided they conduct themselves fairly and discreetly in their vocation, we have no desire to annul their office or deprive them of its rightful exercise. Let the sentinels give challenge to all new claimants, but let them not refuse admittance to any who can furnish a fair passport, and make out a clear title to be admitted within the guarded citadel of established and time-hallowed customs. Since the efforts which have recently been making, to introduce German literature among us, it is not unusual to hear the most unqualified, indiscriminate opposition expressed to the study of a language, rich in every department of its literature, and characterized by an originality and power of thought, which entitles it, in the opinion of the first European scholars, to an equal estimation with our own noble mother tongue. Yet we rejoice to discover, even in the bitterness of its opponents, an indication of the increasing interest with which the German is looked upon among us. We are in no way disturbed by the fear, that its subtleties, refinements, and abstractions, should have an evil influence on our national character, the individuality of which seems in no danger of being neutralized by such antagonist principles, though it may perchance be favorably modified by them. "The Germans have their faults," the author of this translation of Eckermann has somewhere told us, "but these faults

<149>

are as good as virtues to us, since being the exact opposites of our own, they may teach us most important lessons."[45]

The opposers of German literature are fond of advocating the claims of common sense over those of philosophy, of elevating the actual over the ideal. They talk much, and rather vaguely of Transcendentalism, — they tell us of the folly of believing in innate ideas, and triumphantly quote Locke and his "*tabula rasa.*" They are afraid of all vagueness and mysticism, and tremble like children at the shadowy appearances seen in the twilight. They will have nothing to do with that which they cannot handle, — they will receive nothing which they cannot fully comprehend, — they like to see all objects clearly and sharply defined in the broad light of day. Yet at night, in the darkness, we may see much that cannot be seen by day. The near glare of the sun conceals from us those far lights of heaven, that are forever burning in the vaults of space, even as the acute, shrill sounds of day, prevent us from hearing the deep voices of nature. The Shechinah, [46]which was by day only a cloud of smoke, became by night a pillar of fire.

In literature their favorite models are those writers who are most remarkable for clearness, polish and precision. They seem to prefer vigorous rather than comprehensive thinkers, — writers whose vision is clear but limited, — who deal manfully with facts and events, but care not to penetrate beyond the surface of being, showing us things as they are, without questioning of the how and the why. They love to "pace steadily and safely along with the smooth-tongued Addison, the gorgeous Johnson, and the sublime Burke," never deviating from the direct path, and looking upon all who go down in diving-bells, or mount up in balloons, as hair-brained tempters of fate.

They fear all new aspects of truth, and gravely tell us, that "it is better with our fallible natures and limited capacities, to rest with humble reliance upon certain ideas and opinions that have been received as plausible, rejecting all speculations upon subjects which can never be decided nor farther developed, while the soul remains in the thralls of flesh."

Supposing a reflective mind could bring itself to act upon this suggestion, or rather to cease from acting, for ourselves, we know of no opinions which have been universally received as "plausible," and did we know any such, we could not receive them as truths, until they had been submitted to the test of our own reason. Who shall tell us, that any man or class of men have monopolized the right of thought? What is truth to another is not truth to us, until our own understanding has verified it.

---

[45] Margaret Fuller. Review of Heinrich Heine's "Present State of German Literature." *American Monthly Magazine.* July 1836.

[46] Shechinah, Hebrew Shekinah, for "dwelling," or the resting place of God.

<150>

Whatever danger there may be in leaving every man to decide for himself, there is surely far less than in any attempt to restrict the individual right of opinion, through regard to expediency or respect for authority.

We could not, if we would, have every man a philosopher, and we think there need be little fear, that our countrymen will become infected by any undue fondness for abstract researches. The mind that has never tried to grasp the great problems of human life and destiny, — that has never sought to wrest a reluctant meaning from the hieroglyphic characters inscribed on the broad page of nature, needs no such restriction, — the mind that has done this, will hardly be checked in its onward impulse by the *cui bono* of the utilitarian. It sounds almost like mockery, to ask one who has ever caught a single ray of the warm, living light of the sun of truth, to satisfy himself with the frippery, gilt-paper toy of "plausibility."

These timid counselors remind us of Solomon's slothful man, who keeps housed and says, "there is a lion in the streets, if I go forth I shall be slain."[47] There are some who cannot be thus easily restrained, — they must "go forth," even at a worse peril, — they must meet the lion and wrestle with it as they may, — and often do they find, that when they look their formidable foe calmly in the face, he loses all his terrors and becomes at once harmless and tractable.

These people are constantly opposing Revelation to Nature, and Faith to Reason. We cannot agree with them in apprehending any danger to Christianity, from the investigation of calm, tolerant, philosophic spirits, who fear not to look at both sides of a question, lest they should meet with something opposed to established and time-hallowed opinions.

The timid faith that fears to question, cannot satisfy us, — such assent is far worse than honest denial. The only fatal skepticism, as it seems to us, is that of the man who wants faith in the human soul and fears to trust its promptings.

For ourselves, we rejoice in the increasing number of those, who are willing to follow truth wherever she may lead them, in the spirit of that child-like confidence and perfect love which casteth out fear. We look for the time when philosophy shall aid in reconciling reason and faith, — not by depressing faith but by elevating reason. When we shall be able to interpret in all its beautiful simplicity the word of him, who taught us to read the gospel of nature, — to observe the lilies of the field, — and to seek for the kingdom of heaven within our own hearts.

The enforcement of this self-reliance, this faith in the power of the individual to discover for himself truth, is one of the leading heresies of which the "New School" is accused. Yet highest stars of heaven may be

---

[47] Proverbs 26:13.

<151>

seen mirrored within the single drop of dew that trembles within the heart of the violet.

This faith in truth and nature, — this desire to free the mind from its slavery to creeds and conventialities, though the growth of no particular school, has, it is true, within the last twenty years been more profoundly felt, and more earnestly inculcated, than at any former period. It gives a tone to all the noblest literature of the day, and is slowly but surely working a change in the character of the times.

It is this which prompted the obnoxious declaration of Dr. Channing,[48] that "man is great as man, be he what and where he may." This is what was implied by Emerson, when he said, "Let a man plant himself on his instincts, and the whole world will come round to him," — or in other words, everything will work in harmony with him. It is this which illumines every page of Carlyle as with the glory of an inspired scroll, and imparts to the profound philosophy of Cousin[49] its vivifying power.

This doctrine which was taught by a few sincere and simple spirits, amid the darkest gloom of Jewish superstition and bigotry,[50] has caused one of the most true-hearted believers of our own day to assert, that the vital truths of Christianity are too deeply in-wrought into the very nature of the human soul, to be in any danger from a free and fearless examination into the true character of the Christian miracles. It is this growing conviction, which is beginning to render all persecution for opinion's sake as disgraceful as it ever was futile, — and this it is, above all, which is teaching the instructors and guardians of youth, that the great objects of education are not to be achieved by the exhibition of facts, or the inculcation of theories, but by developing and strengthening the powers of the mind for individual and independent action.

Much, though not all of this is, we think; attributable, more or less directly, to the Germans. Much, that in our own literature is but faintly

[48] William Ellery Channing. "Self-Culture." 1838 lecture. Its tone of elevating the masses ("the truly great are to be found everywhere") seems somehow to have offended Whitman. Perhaps the entire clan was disliked: his nephew William Henry Channing (1810-1884), was minister, editor of *The Present* (1843-44), and co-author of the *Memoirs of Margaret Fuller*. A Socialist, he rejected many of the individualist ideas of Emerson and Thoreau. W. H. Channing's 1843 Essay, "Oneness of God and Man" seems to damn Transcendentalists with faint praise as mere harbingers of a religious awakening.

[49] Victor Cousin (1792-1867), a French philosopher who tried to meld together German idealism and Scottish common-sense realism. He also helped introduce Prussian education methods into French schools, and his ideas on this subject were influential in the United States as well.

[50] *Jewish superstition* ... I take this to mean merely the theology of Old Testament literalism among hard-line Protestants, of which Whitman experienced plenty.

<152>

and dimly shadowed forth, is in theirs developing itself in free and luxurious growth. In the German literature, to use one of their own expressive phrases, "Man finds himself." — The "sweet, sad music of Humanity" pervades every department of it. In its deep, earnest, philosophic spirit; in its fearless, trusting, transparent simplicity; in the holy fervor of its poets, the serene, spiritual, far-reaching gaze of its theologians and moralists, we may find much which even the rich classical literature of England cannot supply.

To us Germany has ever been a bright land of promise, since first in early youth we listened, with kindling heart and eager sympathy, to the tidings which Madame De Stael had brought us of a people, who, in an age of artificiality, had dared to follow the suggestions of their own spirits, and to show us nature, as she had mirrored herself within their own hearts. And now, having possessed ourselves of the golden key, which is to unlock to us this rich world of thought, we cannot but glory in our new found treasures, and endeavor to win others to become partakers of our joy.

— Providence, August 15, 1839.
Boston Quarterly Review, January 1840

<153>

RALPH WALDO EMERSON

EMERSON'S ESSAYS (1845)
by A Disciple (Sarah Helen Whitman)

"The highest office of the intellect is the discovery of essential unity under the semblance of difference." — Coleridge.[1]

"Surprising, indeed, on whatever side we look is the revival of the individual consciousness of a living relation with the All Good. Our literature is very day more deeply tinged with a sense of the mysterious power which animates existence, and governs all events." — W. H. Channing.[2]

IT HAS BEEN SAID that "the office of criticism is to bridge over the waters that separate the prophet from the people — to compass the distance that divides the understanding in the auditor from the intuition of the utterer,"[3] — an office more easily indicated than fulfilled; and one which few persons have attempted to perform, for one of the most profound thinkers and inspired seers of our time: perhaps because the partition waters were too wide — the intervening gulf too deep.

Carlyle, who has lovingly unfolded to his countrymen the pure and cloistral genius of Novalis, the profound significance of Goethe and the intricate opulence of Jean Paul,[4] has, in presenting them with the evangel of our western prophet, left them to solve the problem as they may.

His preface to the English edition of the Essays, imports that the name of Ralph Waldo Emerson is not entirely unknown in England. Distinguished travelers, he says, "have carried thither tidings of such a man — fractions of his writings have found their way into the hands of the curious: fitful hints that there is, in New England, some spiritual notability, called Emerson, glide through Reviews and Magazines."[5] For himself, he finds that "the words of this man, such words as he finds it

---

[1] In his essay on *Othello*, Coleridge writes: "There are three powers: — Wit, which discovers partial likeness hidden in general diversity; subtlety, which discovers the diversity concealed in general apparent sameness; — and profundity, which discovers an essential unity under all the semblances of difference" (p. 185).
[2] William Henry Channing. "Call of the Present No 3 — Oneness of God and Man."
[3] Attributed to Charles Lane, from the first issue of *The Dial*. I do not find this text in the scanned Volume 1 of *The Dial*, nor anywhere online.
[4] Thomas Carlyle's reviews and articles on Novalis, Goethe, and Jean Paul Richter were republished in book form in *Critical and Miscellaneous Essays*.
[5] Carlyle, Thomas. "Preface." *Essays by R. W. Emerson*. 1841. London: James Fraser. p. vi.

<157>

good to speak, are worth attending to, and that by degrees, a small circle of living souls, eager to hear, are gathered."[6] And in these few words, he has, perhaps, said all that the critic can effectually say in his office as Mediator between the prophet and the people. He cannot induct his readers with the "*aura*" of an author's genius, he can only point them to the source from which it emanates. He may say much that will be received with delight by those who are already the participators or recipients of the new revelation, but he cannot construct any bridge or thoroughfare by which "understanding of the populace shall pass to the intuition of the Seer." No mechanical aids can avail us here.

Authority decides in the circle of the sciences, but intuition alone, a fine inner sense assumed by all, and possessed by few, judges of the true and the beautiful, of poetry and philosophy, the two foci in the intellectual ellipse. For the highest act of philosophy also, is a divination — an intuition and not an inference.

Bulwer, in his preface to the translations from Schiller, says that the chief aim of the poet, with that of the orator on the husting, should be to make himself intelligible to the multitude;[7] but Bulwer has little insight of the subject on which he writes; else would he know that the poet never troubles himself with thoughts like these. He sings as the bird sings,[8] because his soul is o'erburdened with love and beauty. He casts the fertilizing flower-dust of his heart to the winds of heaven, nor asks if they have borne it to a fitting receptacle.

The most profound thinker cannot defend his faith in the inner world, nor the poet his vision thereof from the vapid gain-saying of the scoffer. Not the Seer, but the Savant is honored of the world. Spinoza had not a single follower in the age in which he lived, and it has been said that there are not at any time ten men on the earth who read Plato.

The great philosopher and poet is he, who understands the spirit of his age. To do this, he must transcend the existing order of things, overlooking it from a point of view above the level of his contemporaries, and attainable as a common standpoint, only to succeeding generations; and just in proportion as he transcends the popular level, is his speech an enigma or a reproach to the multitude, who, regarding their own minds as the normal measure of human intelligence, oppose themselves with sullen determination to the new revelation, and groan, like the

---

[6] Ibid, ix.

[7] "Goethe says well of Schiller's style, — that it is best where he does not philosophise; where be does, indeed, he falls into almost the worst fault a poet's style can have — obscurity. A poet should always suppose his audience to be a multitude — a people; and obscurity is as inappropriate in him as in an orator on the hustings," Edward Bulwer-Lytton. "A Brief Sketch of the Life of Schiller." *The Poems and Ballads of Schiller.* 1843. London. Page c.

[8] *He sings as the bird sings.* From Goethe's *Wilhelm Meister.*

<158>

mandrake,[9] when a new idea threatens to uproot them from the soil in which they vegetate.

There is no paradox so absurd, no heresy so dangerous, that men will not sooner forgive it than a truth prematurely enunciated. And no man excites such pious horror, such unmitigated reprobation, as the promulgator of such truth. The effect of a resisting medium[10] becomes perceptible only as the planet approaches its perihelion.

The world, unwillingly aroused from its slumbers, thinks, like the silly housemaids in Aesop, by wringing the neck of poor Chanticleer to retard the dawn![11]

"Beware," says Emerson, "when the great God lets loose a thinker on this planet, then all things are at risk — the very hopes of man, the religion of nations, the manners and morals of mankind are all at the mercy of a new generalization. Generalization is always a new influx of the Divinity into the mind."[12] But to see things under this new law, they must be seen from the same level, and through the same medium. The results of the synthetic intellect cannot be reached through any critical or analytical process.

A man of Emerson's large faith and intuitive reason, who has drunk deep at the fontal truths of being, and sent his plummet to the ocean-depths of thought, cannot accommodate his free unchartered utterances to the limited apprehension of men who, engrossed by the narrow arts of detail, have no capacity for the wisdom of the complex. Yet perhaps so few persons could command the rapt attention of a popular audience, to thought so abstruse, expressed in language so delphic and poetic. The charm of his presence is pervasive, like music. He commands the attention of his audience, and constrains their sympathy by a power which they cannot analyze, by a spell that transcends their knowledge.

Severe truthfulness characterizes every look, tone, and gesture. He speaks from the commanding and regal attitude of one who reposes firmly on his convictions. Those earnest eyes seem to hold commune with *soul*, and regardless of the world's penalties and rewards, make their direct appeal to the inner tribunal of the conscience.

Their look of profound repose, or concentrate[d] thought deepening all times beneath a frown (severe, yet beautiful in its passionless rebuke)

---

[9] The mandrake, whose roots often resemble the human form, was assigned magical properties by sorcerers and witches.

[10] *Resisting medium . . . perihelion.* An allusion to the then-current theory that outer space was full of an invisible substance called *ether.* Astronomers sought evidence that planets might be restrained in their orbits by the resistance of this mysterious substance. A planet at perihelion is as its closest approach to the sun in its orbit.

[11] Aesop's fable of The Old Woman and Her Maids.

[12] Emerson. "Circles," From *Essays* (1841).

<159>

which can hardly fail to remind one of the austere majesty in the countenance of the angel sent to expel Heliodorus from the temple, one of the finest of Raphael's inimitable heads.[13] At such moments our prophet might, with Heraclitus, be compared to the Sybil, who "speaking with inspired mouth, inornate and severe, pierces through centuries by the power of the God."[14]

The spell of his immediate influence is felt and acknowledged by the most uncultivated audience, yet we hear a constant reference to his obscurity and vagueness. Men complain that no intelligible ideas have been gained, no definite notions acquired. They were charmed while they listened, but when they seek to explain and seize the charm, its secret escapes them. They cannot analyze it — they cannot appropriate it. It is a fairy gift that turns to dross in the handling. In return for their time and money, they have brought away nothing positive and available — nothing that can be weighed and measured and turned to useful account.

But what went ye forth for to see? A partisan? a polemic? an exponent of creeds and doctrines? a propounder of articles of faith, and theories of civil polity? Verily ye have sought in vain! Yet somewhat have ye heard that stirred your stagnant souls, but what, ye know not. A wild, mysterious music, as of the winds of paradise, murmuring afar off through the Tree of Life, an improvisation, as it were, of the central laws of being. The oracular enunciation of a mystic and sublime Theosophy. Ye hear the sound thereof, yet know not whence it cometh nor whither it goeth. It is as the heavenly manna which cannot be heaped or hoarded, but which refreshes the pilgrim on his weary life-path, and imparts new strength to bear the burthen of the way.

Emerson's speech is affirmative and oracular. We must be satisfied to receive from him the enunciation of the idea, we cannot hope to hear it demonstrated, or explained. We find no attempt at a formal, scientific statement of truth, but rather an oriental dogmatism, an apostolic yea and nay. His mind betrays a quick apprehension of logical sequence, yet he renders no account of the actual process by which he arrives at results. He attacks no creed, convinces no skeptic, but he gives adequate and beautiful expression to the most profound and cherished convictions — to the most earnest and devout aspirations of the age. To some of the loftiest minds and purest spirits of the nineteenth century, his voice is as "the voice of their own souls, heard in the calm of thought."[15]

---

[13] Raphael. *The Expulsion of Heliodorus from the Temple* (1511-1512). Fresco in Vatican Museum.
[14] *Speaking with inspired mouth* ... This passage, attributed to Heraclitus by Plutarch, was well-known in Whitman's time. Thoreau quotes it in the "Sunday" chapter of *A Week on the Concord and the Merrimack* (p. 109) and it is quoted in an review of Ritter's 1838 *History of Philosophy* (*Brownson's* 1855).
[15] Shelley, "Alastor, or The Spirit of Solitude."

<160>

His novel statements of the most familiar phenomena of life, have often a strange force and directness, and startle us by their simple verity, like the naïve cadences of a child's voice heard amid the falsetto tones of the conventicle or the theatre.

No man is better adapted than Emerson to comprehend the spirit of the age and to interpret its mission. His insight is marvelously clear, and though less conversant than many others with concrete, special instances, he yields to none in the synthetic grasp of his intellect, and in a comprehensive and generic classification of the facts of experience. He looks not so much at that aspect of things, often partial, trivial and grotesque, which they bear to time, as at that solemn anti serene, which faces eternity. The earth is to him not one of Gardiner's globes,[16] mapped off into petty divisions of province and empire, state and territory, but one of the more recent planets of our system, moving on its destined path through space and harmoniously fulfilling its part in the grand diapason of the universe. He sees not so much the things in which man differs from man as those grand features common to humanity.

Life is viewed by him from no parish belfry, but from an "exceeding high mountain, from whence he can behold all the kingdoms of the world and the glories thereof."[17] Seen from these serene altitudes, all conventional distinctions fade into insignificance, and Satan cannot tempt the soul even to a momentary deviation from its worship of essential truth and beauty.

With the same synthetic glance, he looks at inanimate nature; and, with Novalis, studies her not in her isolated phenomena, but in her essential unity. To him she is not the chance playmate of an hour, but the fair bride of the spirit, and its destined companion through eternity, — reflecting back from her loving and gentle eyes all that the soul hopes or fears, enjoys or suffers. He lives with her in sweet and intimate communion, as one who has won from her the "heart of her mystery,"[18] and

16 Boston was a center of globe-making, with several different manufacturers vying for sales to schools and private libraries. Alonzo Gardiner published a school-text titled, *How to Draw A Map*, which taught students how to draw maps using various projections from a globe. I did not find any references to a Gardiner as globe-maker, but the allusion may be to the textbook.

17 Matthew 4:8.

18 Nathaniel Hawthorne's *English Note-books* were not published in full until 1870, but is it possible that Whitman saw, in manuscript or in a magazine, Hawthorne's diary entry for "Scotland-Glasgow," where he matches this idea precisely: "But in truth, I doubt if anybody ever does really see a mountain, who goes for the set and sole purpose of seeing it. Nature will not let herself be seen in such cases. You must patiently bide her time; and by and by, at some unforeseen moment, she will quietly and suddenly unveil herself, and for a brief space allow you to look right into the heart of her mystery. But if you call out to her peremptorily, 'Nature! unveil yourself this very moment!' she only draws her veil the closer; and you may look with all your eyes, and imagine that

<161>

divined the last word of her secret, or rather as one who has learned that she has no "last word," but like the fair *raconteur* of the Arabian tale,[19] improvises from day to day, from year to year, from age to age, an interminable romance — a series of inventions, the last of which has still some mysterious connection with the first, elucidating and carrying forward but never ending her wondrous story. "To the intelligent[,] Nature converts herself into an infinite promise."[20]

Nor is this view of Nature, as the inseparable companion and counterpart of spirit, contradictory to the Berkeleyan idealism which frequently manifests itself in Emerson's writings, particularly in the earlier Essays. For in proportion as matter is divested of its rigid positiveness and substantial objectivity, do we the more readily conceive of it as a permanent mode of existence, capable of infinite adaptation to the wants of the spiritual intelligences that are associated with it. "The vast picture which God paints on the instant eternity of the soul."[21] The inferences of modern science in relation to this subject are pregnant with results of the highest importance to spiritual and mental philosophy. But while science is slowly collecting facts, inducting theories and reducing results, the poet, with a surer instinct, suggests the true idea of nature, divines her mission and indicates her method. His sentient and mobile being faithfully transmits all her influences. In all her aspects and changes, he perceives a significant beauty and a mysterious sympathy with humanity. In her presence he feels not weariness, nor fears satiety: he knows that her resources are inexhaustible, and that, elastic, ductile, and permeable to spirit, she reforms herself for ever in conformity with the soul's infinitely expanding ideal.

Like Gray, Emerson delights to hear the gnarled and hoary forest-trees droning out their old stories to the storm. He listens to the song of the winds in the pine-tree and

> Hears within their cadent pauses
> The charms of the ancient causes —
> Heeds the old oracles, — ponders the spells
> Song wakes in their pinnacles when the wind swells,[22]

and responds to these sylvan melodies in "wood-notes" not less wild and Orphic than their own.

---

you see all that she can show, and yet see nothing" (31-32).
[19] Scheherezade, the narrator of *The Thousand-and-One Nights*.
[20] Emerson, "Nature." *Essays, Second Series*, 1844.
[21] From Emerson's "Idealism": "as one vast picture, which God paints on the instant eternity, for the contemplation of the soul." *Nature*, p. 74.
[22] These lines are cobbled together from Emerson's "Woodnotes II" (1847) (*Early Poems*, 72, 73).

<162>

We find in him always that uniform repose and serenity of mind that affects us somewhat like the aspect of nature itself,

Calm pleasures there abide, majestic pains.[23]

There is an absence of that vivid sense of personality — that intense individualism which so often manifests itself in the morbid and jealous sensitiveness, peculiar to what is called the "temperament of genius." Instead of this, we find a cheerful, inflexible courage, an Oriental quietude. We might fancy him dreaming away his life with the Sacontala,[24] among the Lotus flowers that border the Ganges, or like the starry Magian evoking from night and silence their eternal mysteries. The words of Plotinus in relation to the supersensual portion of the triune soul, might aptly be applied to him — "Remaining free from all solicitude, not seeking to modify the world in accordance with the discursive reason, nor to transform anything in its own nature. but by the vision of that which is prior to itself informing the world with an infinite beauty."[25]

This severity has been termed by his critics, "a vice of temperament," "an undue preponderance of the intellectual faculty,"[26] "a want of harmonious development," of "generous sympathy with humanity."[27] I do not so understand it, nor can I assent to the criticism of a rare contemporary genius when, in speaking of these essays, he says — "They are truly noble, reporting a wisdom akin to that which the great and good of all time have lived and spoken; yet the author neither warms nor inspires me: he writes always from the intellect to the intellect, and hence some abatement from the depth of his insight, purchased always at the cost of vital integrity. But this is the tax on all pure intellect."

Can we then so separate the functions and faculties of our nature, as to believe that an intellect whose product is "a wisdom akin to that which the great and good of all times have lived and spoken," is developed at the cost of vital integrity? A sufficiency of life — a true vital integrity — would enable us to transcend these pernicious distinctions, and to see that love and wisdom are inseparable. Can the contemplation of eternal

---

[23] Wordsworth, "Laodamia."

[24] The seven-act Sanskrit drama, *Shakuntala*, by the 5th-century poet Kalidasa, was widely read in the 1789 English translation by Sir William Jones.

[25] Although this echoes ideas from Plotinus's *Fifth Ennead*, it does not appear to be a literal quotation. Whitman may be quoting an unspecified commentary.

[26] *Undue preponderance.* This may be a paraphrase from an unsigned review of Emerson's *Essays* in *The Athenaeum*, October 23, 1841.

[27] *Sympathy with humanity.* This may also be a paraphrase. A number of reviews chastised Emerson's "Self-Reliance" essay, with lack of sympathy for others listed as a consequence, such as a March 1840 review by "R.M.N." in *London and Westminster Review*, and an unsigned book review in April 1841 in *New York Review.*

<163>

verities leave the heart cold and void? Is not the holy energy of true love ever sagacious, far-sighted and prophetic? Truth is not isolated: it is not a part, but the whole. It is love, and beauty, and joy. The wise man does not believe and opine, but he knows and is the very truth which be utters. His thought is action: his knowledge is love.

It is very common to hear persons speak of the mind as if reason, imagination and sensibility constituted different and distinct portions of it, though the consciousness speaks, *ex cathedra*, of a living unity. This is in part attributable to the popular empirical psychology which bears the same relation to the true, as the Grecian Theology to the Mosaic. And as the Hellenic deities make war upon each other, so in the popular psychology the faculties are represented as antagonistic, as a profound intellect and a loving heart. Yet, all great philosophers and theosophists have been devout and good men — else were their theories as profitless as their lives. Do not the bard and the prophet offer sacrifice at the same altar? Must the laurel crown extinguish the pure flame of the saintly aureole? The greatest thinker of modern Europe, who united the poetic insight of Plato with the exact method of Aristotle, says, "Voluntas et intellectus unum idemque sunt."[28] Nay, more: that we know the right through the very attraction. which it possesses for us. "Quod quisque ex legibus naturae suae (rationalis) necessario appetit et adversatur id bonum vel malum hujus naturae est."[29]

This doctrine, that the soul, in its entire, unperverted action, instinctively seeks its highest good — a doctrine which lies at the foundation of all pure ethics — is held by Emerson with a cheerful, invincible faith, based on his knowledge of an infinite and divine life instant in the finite.

Of the *soul* he would say what Dr. Pusey[30] says of the *Church* — "Our duty is not to reform it, or take away from it, but to *obey* it."

"For to the soul, in her pure action, all the virtues are natural and not painfully acquired."[31] We want, then, not so much self-denial as self-knowledge and self-trust.

And as that friendship only is sweet to us which is won without any concession or compromise of our own individuality, so those virtues only are gracious and beautiful in which the whole nature transpires.

"People," says Emerson, "represent virtue as a struggle, and take to themselves great airs on their attainments, and the question is everywhere vexed, when a noble nature is commended, whether the man is not better

---

[28] Spinoza. Will and intellect are one and the same.
[29] Spinoza, *Ethics*, Part IV, Prop. 19: "Every man, by the laws of his nature, necessarily desires or shrinks from that which he deems to be good or bad."
[30] Edward Bouverie Pusey (1800-1880), Anglican clergyman and member of the Oxford Movement.
[31] Emerson. "The Over-Soul."

<164>

who strives with temptation?"[32] And here the most acute casuists are often at fault, and are fain to confess with honest Geoffrey Chaucer —

> For me, I cannot bolt it to the bran
> As can the holy Doctor Aúgustin.[33]

Carlyle, who, with all the dazzling lights and electric splendors of his cometic genius, seldom sees a truth with that calm and steadfast glance with which Emerson transfixes and holds it, in his review of Diderot loses himself in what he calls the "eternal ravelment" of the subject; asks if virtue is indeed synonymous with pleasure? — if Paul the apostle was not virtuous, and if virtue was its own reward when *his* approving conscience told him that he was the chief of sinners? — gets warm at the self-complacent tone in which the poor encyclopedist speaks of the delights of *"vertu, honnêteté, grandeur de l'ame," &c.*, and piously adjures him in the Devil['s] and his grandmother's name, to be virtuous and say no more about it: — predicts, nevertheless, that the ascetic system will not soon recover its exclusive dominancy, and admits that the close observer may discern filaments of a nobler system, wherein this of self-denial and duty may be included as one harmonious element. Yet again relapsing into his doubts, asks how tolerance for the wrong can co-exist with an ever-present conviction that the right stands related to it as a God to a Devil?"[34]

Here, then, lies the grand difficulty — the radical error of the popular creed — as of the Kantian ethics which closely approximate to it. Kant makes the highest morality to consist in the strength of a man's will — a power to conform his life to an idea of duty. Yet that which reason or conscience imposes as "the right" neither wins his credent love by its beauty, nor brings with it blessedness and joy. Its rewards are referred to a distant period and an exoteric source. Kant has been not unjustly charged with dislocating and subdividing the faculties of the human mind. He puts far apart knowledge and power, being and doing, wisdom and love. In like manner he divides the universe into antagonistic parts and principles, as matter and spirit, God and nature, good and evil, &c. Yet, not until men saw this opposition projected in a strong light, did they feel its inadequacy, and seek to restore the great idea of essential unity in a system adapted to the wants and culture of the age. Jacobi[35] was one of the first to call attention to the vital defects of the Kantian philosophy, which sees nothing in Christianity but a code of duties, and

---

[32] Emerson. "Spiritual Laws."
[33] Chaucer. "The Nun Priest's Tale." ll. 4430-4431. Can be translated as "For me, I cannot separate the wheat from the chaff, as can the Holy St. Augustine."
[34] Thomas Carlyle. "Diderot," p. 239.
[35] Friedrich Heinrich Jacobi (1743-1819), originator of the term "nihilism."

<165>

represents the Creator of the universe as a mere Supreme Being — *Deus extramundanus*[36] — apart from the creation and from man. In referring all action to a sense of obligation, in defining duty, as an antagonistic principle, Kant leaves the subject involved in that "eternal ravelment"[37] from which few men know how to disengage it.

But these difficulties lie not in Emerson's path. He dwells ever in that clear and serene region where neither Loke[38] nor Ahriman,[39] Typhon[40] nor Devil, interfere to divide with God the empire of the universe. With the great thinkers of all time, he sees that no evil is pure; that the principle of good enters into all things. "There is no pure lie, no pure malignity in nature — the belief in depravity is the last profligacy and profanation — there is no skepticism, no atheism but that."[41] The malevolent man is he who holds all things, as evil; and hence his destructive propensity. Sir Thomas Brown[e],[42] on the other hand, who was incapable of forming strong conceptions of evil, says, he could never bring himself heartily to hate the Devil. Emerson seems, with the Platonists, to regard evil as a defect, a privation, a deviation from subsistence. He sees that God imparts to all things good, and to each that quantity of good which it is qualified to obtain. This faith cannot subsist with any purely dualistic philosophy where wrong stands opposed to right, as a Devil to a God rather than as Negation to Being: but in proportion as we free ourselves more and more from a false, fragmentary and superficial life, the soul more distinctly articulates her gospel of peace

---

[36] *Deus extramundanus*. God outside the world, the central deist concept of god as "absentee landlord."

[37] Lessing, Kant and other philosophers labored over whether immortal souls have an infinity of time in which to achieve perfection, whether the perfection finally comes to all humans, and whether souls are re-born to work toward their perfection. The concepts of infinity and immortality were linked as a necessary connection.

[38] *Loke*. Loki, the Norse god of mischief, and a great evildoer in the final unraveling of the gods.

[39] Ahriman is the Zoroastrian destructive spirit.

[40] Typhon was the most dreaded of all the monsters and Titans banished to Tartarus. Zeus defeated him in a world-shaking battle.

[41] Emerson. "New England Reformers." *Essays, Second Series*.

[42] Sir Thomas Browne (1605-1682), polymath, brilliant writer, and coiner of hundreds of new words, said of the Devil: "For this do I honour my own profession and embrace the counsell even of the Devill himselfe: had he read such a Lecture in Paradise as he did at Delphos, we had better knowne our selves, nor had we stood in feare to know him. . . . Search where thou wilt, and let thy reason goe/ To ransome truth even to the Abysse below." (*Religio Medici*, Part 1, Section 13). Browne was more apt to internalize the personified evil, writing: "The heart of man is the place the devill dwels in; I feele somtimes a hell within my selfe, Lucifer keeps his court in my brest, Legion is revived in me" (*Religio Medici*, Part 1, Section 49).

<166>

and love; we then not only believe, but know, that all evil is relative, all being progressive, all life an emanation from the Divine.

It is this beautiful soul-trust, and not self-trust, as some would render it, that Emerson inculcates from a faith so sweet and inward, that the scoffer is silenced and the caviler rebuked.

I have dwelt longer on this subject, because it forms so intimate and essential a part of the entire view of life which I find in these volumes — a view so pregnant and suggestive, that an expansive and liberal theory of morals must necessarily grow out of it.

Although Emerson claims no consistency for the speculations here presented to us, I do not find in the whole range of modern literature a mind that overlooks life from a point of view so high and commanding — that arrives so surely, by an induction so rapid and unerring, at the last results from the speculative reason. And moreover, notwithstanding (or I might rather say in consequence of) the large and free scope of his intellect, I find everywhere a pervasive consistency, a living unity of thought, which is never violated.

He has in truth no affinity with that class of thinkers described by Novalis[43] who construct a theory in order to free themselves from the weariness of thought, nor, on the other hand, with that barren Eclecticism, which, consisting only of a fortuitous collection of ideas and having no internal principle of growth, is, like fossil substances, capable of enlargement only by accretion. For whenever thought is genuine, proceeding from a true inner life, its most spontaneous and unpremeditated enunciation manifests something of that formative energy, that harmonious adaptation of parts which mark the development of organic structure.

We are told by one of Mr. Emerson's most discerning readers, that "it may be said of him that he has never written one good work if such a work be one where the whole commands more admiration than the parts — where, after an accumulation of materials, fire enough be applied to fuse the whole into one new substance." The Essays are said to resemble "a string of mosaics, or a house built of medals."[44]

It may be so; yet will I say of them as Andrew Marvell of his flower garden —

What Rome, Greece, Palestine e'er said,
I, in this light Mosaic, read.[45]

[43] If Whitman read Novalis's "The Apprentices at Sais" (1798) in German, the apparent source of this topic, it most likely would have been in the edition prepared by Tieck and Schlegel. Or she read the lengthy review by Thomas Carlyle in 1829 in his *Critical and Miscellaneous Essays*.
[44] Margaret Fuller. "Review of Emerson's *Essays [Second Series]*."
[45] Andrew Marvell. "Upon Appleton House, to My Lord Fairfax" (1651), ll.

<167>

They are in truth Sibylline leaves, whose price decreases not with their want of completeness in number or arrangement. They have the unity of nature, where the whole reappears in all its parts.

> Out of these scattered Sibyl leaves
> Strange prophecies my spirit weaves.[46]

A single aphorism often suggests the whole economy of being, and unlocks to us the secret passages of things. To me they breathe a harmony so pure and responsive that I recognize therein no jarring element.

They are faithful transcripts of thought, as it evolves itself in a mind of the ripest and most harmonious development, fragmentary only in so far as the view which every man takes of life must be fragmentary, and, as are the oldest and most costly scriptures, for life itself, as read or readable by man, is but a fragment — a "*Werden*," and not a "*Seyn*."[47]

In addition to his alleged want of unity and explicitness, we are told of his contra statements on every great question. His report is so faithful, he gives us so impartially all the aspects of things, that his meaning escapes us — "We get now one idea and then another, but seldom such a permanent and final result." Men prefer to have the bolted wheat prepared and garnered for their use. Yet always these antitheses, these apparent contradictions are coordinates of a single law, and spanned by a central principle. Through conscious dualism only do we pass to conscious unity.

THE GREAT TRUTH to which all Emerson's affirmations point is Absolute Identity — the unity of all things in God. This is the *mot d'enigme*[48] to his whole philosophy — it lies at the foundation of his entire theory of life, and is the secret alike of his singleness and his universality.

In giving such prominence to this idea he has shown himself an apt representative of the philosophical character of his age, a philosophy standing as yet far in advance of its popular and prosaic character, yet destined ultimately to determine, as it has already indicated, the point of view from which science, art, religion, law and social polity are to be contemplated.

581-882. John Greenleaf Whittier called attention to the stanza in which these lines appear in *Old Portraits and Modern Sketches* (p. 102).

[46] Ibid, ll. 577-578. Marvell's lines read "Out of these scattered Sybil's leaves/ Strange prophecies my fancy weaves."

[47] *Werden* versus *Seyn/Sein.* Becoming something (process) rather than being something (essence).

[48] *Mot d'enigme.* Key to the mystery.

<168>

The idea of Absolute Identity furnishes the type, in conformity with which thought develops itself in all the master spirits of the time. It suggested to Swedenborg his doctrine of correspondences[49] — to Fourier his theory of "universal unity" and "universal analogy"[50] — and to Schelling the parallelism that exists between the laws of nature and the laws of thought — or as Hegel has more intensively expressed it — *Die Absolute Einheit des Begriffs und der Objectivitat* — "the absolute oneness of thought and its object."[51] It inspired St. Simon[52] with his devout conception of the collective life of humanity, and revealed to him its harmonious and progressive development, thereby imparting to history an epic character which ennobles every phase of its progress. Under its influence science itself seems rapidly outgrowing its purely empirical limits, and approximating to a more large and poetic conception of the generic unity and dynamic power of nature. Perhaps, without falling back on the abhorrent theory of the materialists, we shall yet find that the mind has its physique and nature her Psyche. If the same law prevails in the natural as in the moral world — if the same primal energy informs them, then science becomes at once mystic and devout, — a portal through which we have access to the penetralia of that beautiful temple of nature, of which Heraclitus said, *"Enter, for here too are Gods."*[53]

The Pythagoreans taught that if the essence of all things admits of cognition, it is only in so far as the things of which the world consists, partake of it. With equal truth might we say, that if the things of which the world consists admit of cognition, it is only in so far as they partake of the essence of all things — *"Deus immundanus."*[54] Only through our

---

[49] Swedenborg. *Heavenly Arcana,* #912, 913, 5711.

[50] Charles Fourier (1772-1837), a pioneering libertarian socialist philosopher whose work inspired attempts at Utopian communities. Fourier originated the word "feminism" and advocated sexual freedom. He divided present human society into Savagery, Barbarism, and Civilization, having little regard for the lattermost. He anticipated a new age of voluntary work and association, and economic equality, called "Simple Harmony."

[51] Georg Wilhelm Friedrich Hegel (1770-1831), Kant's successor, whose ideas were first elaborated in *The Phenomenology of Spirit* (1807).

[52] Henri de Saint-Simon (1760-1825), political theorist and advocate for the working class. He advocated a mild Utopian socialism that did not entail class warfare.

[53] Heraclitus of Ephesus (c. 535 - c. 475 BCE), pre-Socratic Greek Philosopher. His work, *On Nature,* survives only in fragments. He is one of the first philosophers to discuss the nature of being. One of his ideas on the unity of things is "the path up and the path down are one and the same." When some visitors found Heraclitus, unphilosophically warming himself by a cooking fire, he welcomed them to join him, saying, "Here, too, are gods" (Fragment 74).

[54] *Deus immundanus.* God inside the world the reversal of the Deists' absentee-landlord God.

<169>

oneness with actual being can we assume the possibility of actual knowledge.

An able writer in the *Westminster Review*, in analyzing this great doctrine of Spinoza, says, "No believer in Ontology, as a possible science, can resist the all-embracing dialectic of Spinoza, but it is our strength that we reject all metaphysics as frivolous. Men can never arrive at a knowledge of things as they are in themselves. Turn it which way you will there is nothing in the consciousness but the consciousness itself — to know more would involve the necessity to be more."[55] Aye, verily! — but this identical fact of being more is that on which the believer in absolute cognition grounds his faith. No philosophy can explain the relation of thought to its object, which conceives of man as an isolated and detached particle of the great whole (a belief which we cannot even state without a paradox). But a more profound observation shows us the manifold, living and essential union which inwardly and invisibly unites all individuals with each other and with nature. Only through "a mystical union of all things resting in God"[56] can we explain the most familiar facts of experience — far less the subtle mysteries of those evanescent and abnormal states in which the soul, transcending the limits of time and space, holds commune with the invisible world, recalls the past and foresees the future — moods when

> We ebb into a former life, or seem
> To lapse for back in a confused dream
> To states of mystical similitude.[57]

The new Platonists, who regarded this class of phenomena as a kind of natural magic or divination, based the possibility of such powers on the essential connection and dependence of all things.

The great idea then which has exercised so vast an influence on the literature of the age is the *unity of being*, or as a recent critic on the "Teutonic Metaphysics or American Transcendentalism," has satirically expressed it, "everything is everything, and everything else is everything. and everything is everything else."[58] We cannot lie surprised at the vagueness and folly which this writer finds in a Philosophy which be

55 George Henry Lewes. "Spinoza's Life and Works," p. 212.
56 Mystical Union. A Hindu concept of union with Brahma, an idea which came West and found itself expressed in the writings of Fénelon in *Maximes des Saintes sur la Vie Intérieure* (Art. 29), and in William Blake's *Jerusalem*, "The Mystical Union of the Emanation in the Lord" (J53.24 E203).
57 Tennyson, "Early Sonnets, No 1." (1833). This poem has been read as a description of the hypnotic state, *i.e.*, Mesmerism. Whitman read articles about Mesmerism with intense interest, even mistaking Poe's "The Facts in the Case of M. Valdemar" for a journalistic account.
58 C.E. Stowe. "Teutonic Metaphysics," p. 75.

<170>

vainly attempts to grasp. The same plant will not grow in every soil. Yet is this "Each in all" philosophy no mere "Hall of Phantasy,"[59] no "Blind Man's Holiday"[60] or "Fool's Paradise,"[61] but a sure ground of holiest love, of sternest courage, of serenest patience, and above all of unfailing charity. Old as thought itself, it is necessarily modified by the psychical and physical culture of the ages in which it manifests itself. Dimly foreshadowed in the vast and gloomy Pantheism of India, it has shed a shimmering glory on the vistas of all the Poets of antiquity from Orpheus to Virgil. On the secret shrine of the Cabirii,[62] it cast a lurid and fitful gleam, flashed through the night of Egyptian darkness, and shot back a pale and reflex ray from the pages of the Talmud. In the medieval age it illumined the dream of the mystic and the theory of the naturalist, while in our own it animates and cheers with its full solar beam the whole hemisphere of thought. Receiving from the adamantine logic of Spinoza a scientific statement invulnerable to criticism, it remained for a long time without any perceptible influence on the literature and philosophy of the age. Spinoza gave to the theory of identity a complete anatomical structure, but it waited for Schelling to breathe into it the breath of life, to unfold the profound significance that was involved in it as a system that at once infused life into nature, while it recognized in humanity the control of laws as beneficent and inevitable as those which obtain in the natural world.

A T THE PERIOD immediately preceding his enunciation of this philosophy, society was evidently in a subversive or transition state.

Empiricism had done its work well, and proved a vigilant vassal in the temple of science, but it knew not how to avail itself of the stores it had aggregated with such tireless industry. It was overwhelmed with its own wealth, and waited for the hand of a master to dispose of its treasures. Not until philosophy had learned, like Deucalion, to cast behind it these stones of the earth could they become living forms. The Tree of Knowledge was heavy with golden fruit, but a flaming sword still barred the way to the Tree of Life.

---

[59] *Hall of Phantasy.* This may be an allusion to Nathaniel Hawthorne's short-story, "The Hall of Fantasy," published in 1843.

[60] *Blind Man's Holiday.* The period between dusk and the time of lighting candles, when it is difficult to see clearly or to do useful work.

[61] *Fool's Paradise.* A place where people too stupid to reason are sent after death. Described by Ariosto and Dante, its population is swollen by Milton to include monks and hermits.

[62] *Cabiri.* An ancient mystery cult centered at Lemnos and Samothrace. Sailors invoked the Cabiri generically as "the great gods," so Whitman may be citing them as a transcendant grasp of deities.

<171>

Kant was but the precursor and not (as is sometimes thought) the founder of the recent philosophy, for he left untouched the great idea of the essential union of God with Humanity, and regarding the reason as strictly subjective, he desired all knowledge of absolute truth, and analyzed the laws of mind only as subjective phenomena. His method was therefore purely experimental. Yet it must be confessed that he gave to empiricism the noblest character of which it is susceptible, and sought to arrange for it an honorable compromise with idealism. Nor can it be denied that he proved himself an able diplomatist; but he could not succeed in satisfying the large demands of the intellect, which asks nothing less than absolute cognition.

The Manichaean hypothesis which had been reaffirmed by Bayle,[63] and against which Leibniz[64] composed his *Théodicée*, had still many advocates. The ghost of Gnostic heresy (the belief in two principles) still walked the earth. The time was full of discord, and waited for the atonement, or reunion. The age of indeterminate although of healthful and impulsive action had long since yielded to an era of blind, unquestioning faith. With the introduction of printing, this blind faith of the Middle Ages was at an end, and the skeptical, critical, self-conscious life commenced. The development of new powers and the consciousness of new wants involved the age in moral and political conflicts. With inquiry came doubt and denial, speculation and negation. All the learning and intellect of the eighteenth century was unequal to the solution of the great controversial questions that had been transmitted to it. While it examined and tested all creeds and opinions, it regarded none as worthy of belief. The work of destruction was the only work to which it seemed appointed, and faithfully did it perform its mission.

Man had eaten to satiety of the fruit of the Tree of Knowledge, and had become familiar with change and death. All things seemed shadowy and unreal. Human life was a mere point in time compared to the vast periods of history — the endless aeons of science. The researches of the historian had opened interminable vistas into the twilight realms of mythical and traditionary story. Every spot of earth was hallowed by the footsteps of the departed, — every city was a mausoleum of the dead.

[63] Pierre Bayle (1647-1706), author of the *Dictionnaire Historique et Critique* (Historical and Critical Dictionary), a font of knowledge and skepticism that inspired Voltaire. Bayle argued for tolerance and found fault with the metaphysical ideas of Descartes, Spinoza, and Leibniz. Bayle's article on "The Origin of Evil" explores whether evil is accounted for by "two principles" or whether God permits and includes evil.

[64] Gottfried Wilhelm Leibniz's *Theodicy* (1710) placed the origin of evil in the freedom and imperfection of humans. He argued that the active evil of sin and the passive evils of pain and suffering are only apparent imperfections in a Divine scheme that is under God's control and is the best of all possible worlds.

<172>

The literature of the period, enriched with countless accessions from the distant and the past, and presenting such varied modes of apprehending life and nature, was calculated to stimulate to their highest action the reflective faculties, and particularly the faculty of comparison, thereby tending to induce that critical, self-conscious character which then began to distinguish it, and which Carlyle denounces as the unpardonable sin. Man had now learned that he must find repose in clear and adequate ideas of being, or find it not at all. Not by any grace of manner, any play of fancy, or novelty or incident, could he be lapt into forgetfulness of himself, — of his own mysterious being. For him there was no self-oblivion. He cannot be amused — he will not be deceived.

Literature was no longer an heroic song or a devotional anthem. It was introspective, self-involved, and meditative.

> Its sweetest songs were those
> That told of saddest thought[65]

The poet no longer dwelt with God in the garden of innocence, where the fruits and flowers or existence proffered their willing treasures, but was driven forth to delve wearily, and often ineffectually, for the "bread of life" in the thorny fields of the intellect.

In his eloquent lament we see only the fact that an ideal was unfolding to his awakened thought, to which he could as yet in no way conform the real — the soul meanwhile awaiting in bitter travail the birth of the new conceptions that had sprung to life within it.

In reviewing this period of the history of modern literature, we seem to stand with the immortal Florentine, looking down from the brink of an abyss "that receives the thunder of infinite lamentations."

> Vero e che in su la proda mi trovai
> Della valle d'abisso dolorosa,
> Che tuono accoglie d'infiniti quai.[66]

The heart of man was riven asunder with fierce conflicts; perplexed with inexplicable contradictions. The Sphinx had fixed on him her evil eye, torturing him with questions which he must answer or die. The aggregated treasures of science and learning seemed to mock the imperious demands of the restless intellect with their unavailing hoards; while History unrolled her vast scroll but to threaten or to warn, "for within and without it was written with lamentations, and mourning, and woe."[67] From the wide Orient echoed the cry of desolation and despair

---

[65] Shelley. "To a Skylark."
[66] Dante. *Inferno.* Canto IV.

<173>

— from Judea was the wail borne onward, "the wail of multitudinous Egypt"[68] — Greece and Rome swelled with their choral voices the ancient burden, till all articulate sounds were lost in the sullen boom of a cathedral bell, heard solemnly tolling throughout the long and dismal night of the dark ages. No beneficent purpose was yet detected in the annals of the race — the development of no inherent law, either recognized or divined therein — far less that plenary inspiration now claimed for the entire record of Humanity.

The old Gods had deserted the earth — Priests and lawgivers had lost their sanctity. Man listened in vain for the spheral harmonies — no voice, no tone from those eternal depths. The song of the stars was drowned in the Babel clamor of sophists and sciolists.

At the close of the eighteenth century there was no theory too visionary, no opinion too paradoxical, to find its advocates and disciples. Pyrrhonism and Materialism, Epicurianism and Stoicism had their successive culminations. The gay and mercurial, like Diderot and Voltaire, laughed and made merry with "the great humbug of the Universe," and sought only, like Aristippus, to win from the passing hour its full complement of pleasure. Amusement was their only aim — annihilation their only hope.

The severe and saturnine, affecting the masculine virtues and indomitable volitions of the Stoics, found a congenial system in the imperious ethics of Fichte,[69] and in his pure and proud faith in the omnipotence of the will, a pretence and a paradigm for their self-complacent egotism. Both Sybarite and Stoic expressing, under opposite forms, the extremes of sublimated self-seeking.

From this Chaos of partial and opposing systems, Schelling[70] freed himself by a daring and sublime hypothesis, a bold affirmation of ontological truth, which affected not to justify itself by any laborious

---

[67] Ezekiel 3:9-10.

[68] Ezekiel 32:18.

[69] Johann Gottlieb Fichte (1762-1814), unfairly dismissed as a mere stepping-stone between Kant and Hegel. After several versions of this evolving transcendental philosophy "Wissenschaftslehre" found their way into print, and he ventured into public advice to students and citizens, his work was condemned as "nihilist" and he was driven from his position at Jena in 1798. He is a foundational figure in German Idealism, a pioneer in exploring consciousness and self-awareness, and, unfortunately, a fierce pioneer of German nationalism.

[70] Friedrich Wilhelm Joseph Schelling (1775-1854), student of Fichte, and friend and rival to Hegel. Goethe was an advocate of his work on Natural Philosophy. His appeal to Carlyle and Emerson doubtless came from his 1797 treatise *Von der Weltseele* (On the World-Soul) and his 1800 *System des transcendentalen Idealismus* (The System of Transcendental Idealism). He is now regarded as a forerunner of Existentialism.

<174>

psychological analysis, but to the elucidation of which all recent discoveries in mental and physical science indubitably tend.

The fatal defect of the Kantian philosophy, the difficulty of imputing validity to our subjective conceptions, is here supplied by assuming the identity of that which knows, with that which is known; thus integrating all antagonisms, even the great antagonism of matter and spirit, the insuperable problem in every dualistic system.

In the philosophy of Schelling, the real and the ideal are equally represented. God and nature no longer appear as two conceptions fundamentally and essentially distinct, but all things are living and instinct with a divine energy. The idea of progress as the gradual development in Humanity of this inherent energy was now for the first time intelligibly and distinctly slated. Only recently have men begun to know that the destiny of the race is onward, forever onward. The successive forms, laws, creeds and institutions of society are no longer regarded as ultimate, and it is seen that any attempt to perpetuate the same beyond the time when they represent the average intelligence of society, can only lead to stagnation and paralysis. We have learned the significance of the proverb that says the new wine cannot be kept in the old bottles.

Intimately associated with the belief in progress, is that recognition of the true value of the present, which is so prominent a feature of our time.

In this despised present, men begin doubtfully to acknowledge a divinity — the last messenger of God to man — in whose bosom lies treasured the hoarded wealth of the past, and the possibilities of the infinite future.

To live well and happily in the moment is our perfect wisdom. "Five minutes to-day," says Emerson, "are as much as five minutes in the next millennium."[71]

An abandonment to this serene, instinctive and trustful life, is a virtue of our age, and a legitimate product of its philosophy. Jesus also taught men to live in the moment without anxiety or fear, but his disciples failed to imbibe his cheerful faith.

The Greek philosophers, almost without an exception, represented life under a gloomy aspect. Endurance and submission, rather than love and joy, were the virtues of their age.

The Germans, who have been the enunciators of so many great truths, were the first to give emphasis to the idea that man's immediate duty and true mission is to conform the present to his ever expanding ideal. If God is the "Life of the world," if he is in the process as well as

---

[71] Emerson, "Experience." *Essays II*, pp. 65-66.

<175>

in the form, then is he in every phase of the process, and every moment has its message and its import.

"Surprising, indeed, on whatever side we look" (says one of the young, Heaven-taught seers of our day), "is that revival of the individual consciousness of a living relationship with the All-Good. Our literature is every day more deeply tinged with the sense of the mysterious power which animates existence and governs all events."[72]

This philosophy of identity, under which are included all those views and opinions which are generally in New England classed under the name of Transcendentalism, perhaps we can nowhere find so pure and poetic an expression of these ideas, from which the intellect has derived at once inspiration and repose, as in the writings of Emerson. Yet, although the truths which inform his pages are essentially the same with those of the new German school, he seems to hold them rather after the manner of the Neo-Platonists than of the modern Germans. Plotinus and Proclus, Plutarch and Marcus Antoninus are evidently greater favorites with him than Schelling and Hegel. If I were inclined to look for a flaw in Emerson's crystalline intellect, I should probably find it in a want of that due appreciation of the real, the eternal and necessary correlative of the ideal, which constitutes one of the distinguishing merits of Schelling's system. Not the less true is it that the *Essays* contain the essential oil and expressed perfume of those truths which have infused a new spirit into the life and literature of the nineteenth century, while in their author we see a striking example of that serenity of soul which is a necessary result of his philosophy. "Beholding identity and eternal causation, the soul is raised above passion, and becomes a tranquillity out of the knowledge that all things go well."[73]

Goethe also tells us that he derived from the theory of identity, as he obtained it from Spinoza, the serenity which pervaded his maturer life. "After seeking in vain for a means of interpreting my strange moral being, I found in the Ethics of Spinoza a calm to my passions, a wide free view over the sensuous and moral world."[74]

By superficial observers, Emerson is often compared to Carlyle; but in Carlyle this all-harmonizing sense of the unity of being (the distinguishing characteristic of Emerson's intellect), is manifestly wanting; and notwithstanding his frequent allusions to the new German philosophy,

---

[72] William Henry Channing. *The Present*, Vol. 1. 1843, p. 153.

[73] Emerson. "Self-Reliance," *Essays, First Series*, p. 69.

[74] Goethe. *Autobiography*, Vol. 2, p. 26. This is reconfirmed in the *Conversations with Goethe*, where Eckermann writes, "Such a point Goethe early found in Spinoza; and he acknowledges with joy how much the views of that great thinker answered the wants of his youth. In him he found himself, and in him therefore could he fortify himself to the best advantage." Eckermann, Oxenford trans., p. 524.

<176>

as containing the secret of a higher revelation for those who are capable of receiving it, yet it is evident that the struggle of man with destiny entirely possesses and absorbs him. The mountain of reality presses heavily on his giant heart, and its Titanic throes cannot shake off the superincumbent weight. A fierce unrest consumes him. His incessant calls to labor sound in our ears like the dismal knell of the "work-house clock" summoning a benighted race to their hopeless toil. "For, man's highest blessedness," he tells us, "is that he toil and knows not what to toil at."[75] We recognize in him vast energies, impetuous volitions, a wit emanating from the consciousness of dissonance and disruption; a mirthfulness that makes us weep or shudder, but never do we see in him "the level glance, serene and steadfast, that marks the God."

Carlyle is still struggling with destiny, still overwhelmed and saddened by the contemplation of the "void and formless infinite," perplexed by the fearful antagonisms of good and evil, life and death, time and eternity.

The editor of the *Boston Quarterly* has been sometimes classed among the New England disciples or teachers of Transcendentalism, and he has, in fact, from time to time exhibited some predilections for its doctrines, as diluted by Cousin, but he has never found that point of view, from which alone these truths can be seen and comprehended as one harmonious system. He has by turns affirmed and denied the great truth of man's knowledge of the absolute, through the mystical union of God with humanity. Yesterday he believed in the impersonality of the reason; to-day to deny its personality, is to deny our own. In laboring to define human personality, and to demonstrate the exact nature and scope of its powers of cognition, will, &c., he involves himself in endless contradictions and inextricable difficulties, thus furnishing another evidence that nature abhors limitation, overflowing all our landmarks and annulling all our distinctions. In one of those aphorisms of Novalis, where a profound truth is often expressed under the form of a bold and startling paradox, he says, "men think it a vulgar error to represent God as a person, but we have yet to learn that man is not less impersonal than God."[76] When we attempt to separate man from his life in God, we have nothing left but Mr. Brownson's[77] "simple faculty of cognition," or the

[75] Carlyle. "Characteristics." *Essays and Miscellaneous Writings*, p. 300.
[76] Novalis (Frederic von Hardenburg) 1772-1801, short-lived poet and philosopher. His prose poems, aphorisms, and fragments were published in 1802. Whitman's selection seems to be a paraphrase of an aphorism reading "We think of God as a person, as we think of ourselves as persons. God is just as personal and individual as we are, for our so-called *ego* is not our own *ego*, but His reflection" (p. 221). Carlyle's long essay on Novalis in *The Foreign Review* in 1829 presents a number of Novalis prose fragments, but not this one. Carlyle called him the German Pascal (*Essays*, 186).
[77] Orestes Augustus Brownson (1803-1876), founder of the *Boston Quarterly*,

<177>

"*Tabula rasa*" of Locke. In his denial of the impersonal reason, in his review of Charles Elwood, April, 1842,[78] Mr. Brownson seems already to have forgotten "that life which is the light of the world, and in which we live, and move, and have our being," a gospel, which in 1841, he quoted as containing the only intelligible solution of these problems.[79]

Like a comet moving in a narrow ellipse, he sweeps athwart our hemisphere "with fear of change perplexing nations" — darts towards the central orb of truth, and is off again ere we can say "*Ecce Venit*" to the regions of outer darkness.

Carlyle, too, is to many readers but one of those nebulous meteors[80] that hide in their rapid and eccentric course the very stars of heaven from our bewildered gaze. But with Carlyle a sincere faith lies behind this apparent skepticism — and when a calm telescopic glance is turned upon this blazing glory — this mighty mass of phosphorescent splendor, through the very centre of its burning heart, these constant stars may be seen shining afar off in the serene depths of ether.

The fact that Schelling himself has apostatized from the large faith of his philosophic creed,[81] which has exercised so vast an influence on his age, does not in any way affect the truth of his doctrines and need not excite our surprise. Few men, says Menzel, are able to maintain themselves in a position so central, of such perfect equipoise and impartiality[82] — and a wiser than Menzel has said an index or mercury of intellectual proficiency is the perception of identity.

Schelling's theory of a God immanent in Nature and in Humanity, on which he rested the possibility of absolute cognition, was, as we have drifted from Transcendentalism and converted to Catholicism in 1844. After merging his journal with *The United States Magazine and Democratic Review* in 1842, he took it back under his own aegis in 1844 to espouse his new religious stance. Although the journal was abolitionist, Brownson renounced some of his other more radical views and promoted the idea of a Catholic-dominated United States.

[78] "Charles Elwood; or The Infidel Converted." *Boston Quarterly*, Vol. 5, No. 18. This book review includes an elaborate discussion of reason as an impersonal faculty including ideas from Cousin, Fichte, and Kant, concluding with "Whatever, then, the reason spontaneously reveals is revealed by God himself" (p. 169).

[79] Orestes Brownson, in a review of Theodore Parker's *A Discourse on the Transient and Permanent in Christianity*, in *Boston Quarterly Review*, Vol. 4, October 1841, p. 469.

[80] *Nebulous meteors . . .* Comets.

[81] *Schelling ... has aspostatized ...* After 1834, Schelling publicly turned against the philosophy of Hegel, and rebuked his own earlier ideas.

[82] Wolfgang Menzel (1798-1873), poet and literary critic. This is probably from his book, *German Literature* (p. 30). He was a poetic traditionalist and an opponent of Heine. Curiously, his literary criticism employs the same excesses of prejudice and opinion as Heine, but more often from the contrary point of view.

<178>

seen, but a sublime hypothesis, and the skeptic still proposes to the idealist, although in fainter tones, the eternal question respecting the validity of his intuitions. "How will you demonstrate, how legitimate the truth of these eternal truths?"

As well might we ask the seer to demonstrate his apocalyptic vision of the future — the poet his fine sense of beauty and of love! Can a soul not beautiful, asks Plotinus, attain to an intuition of beauty?[83]

The error seems to lie in the assumption, that all true conceptions and adequate ideas are capable of being immediately demonstrated as such to all minds. Unquestionably all the possibilities of humanity are latent in every individual of the race, but the degrees of actual development differ more than men are disposed to admit. No man can construct or accept a philosophy which transcends the level of his actual life. "The spring cannot rise higher than its source." *Alle Philosophie musse geliebt und gelebt werden.*"[84]

Although true being is everywhere present, it is, as Plotinus has said, more or less present in proportion to our ability of receiving it.

According to Sir James Mackintosh,[85] who is indeed no other than an agreeable Philistine, the theories of Fichte, Schelling, and Hegel, are so many attempts to fix the absolute as a positive in knowledge, while the absolute, like the water in the sieve of the Danaïdes,[86] has run through as a negative into the abyss of nothing.

If we could arrest and appropriate it, it would no longer be the absolute. The individual intellect is in truth a sieve through which it *passes*, but in which it can never be arrested or contained.

Plato, who was disposed lo seek the essence of our knowledge in ideas alone, did not attempt to enumerate these ideas, as if he shrank from subjecting them to a profane analysis. Schelling, as we have said, took his stand with Plato in the region of supra-sensible truths, where no partial results of observation could either confirm or refute him in his

---

[83] Plotinus (c. 204 - 270), Platonist philosopher. See *The Enneads* 1.6, "On Beauty."

[84] *Alle Philosophie* ... All Philosophy must be loved and lived. From Goethe's conversations with Jonannes Falk (Falk, p. 70, Austin, p. 74).

85 James Mackintosh (1765-1832), politician and historian, published a defence of the French Revolution and a history of England's Glorious Revolution. He took on philosophy late in life. His *Dissertation on the Progress of Ethical Philosophy* (1828) was included in the 7th edition of the *Encyclopædia Britannica.* His overview of German literature, intellectual life, and philosophy, in which he oversweeps Kant, Fichte and Schelling, is his "Review of Madame de Staël's 'De L'Allemagne'" (see pp. 267-268).

[86] Danaïdes. In Greek mythology, a group of 50 daughters, who protested being forced to marry 50 cousins; 49 of them murdered their husbands on their wedding night. Their punishment is to spend eternity carrying water in a sieve, unable ever to complete their task.

<179>

reasoning; yet his sublime hypothesis, in so far as it rests on the assumption of absolute identity, strictly coincides with the rigid deductions of experimental science.

Every new discovery in physics teaches that all difference is phenomenal. The integrity of being is detected under manifold disguises. The farther we push our inquiries into the different departments of science, the more obvious are the analogies subsisting between them. In nature all the lines blend and converge towards a common center. The moment we attempt to distinguish and define, to draw lines and affix boundaries, we are perplexed and baffled by her fluidity and sameness. In the crystal we already detect a paradigm of vegetable forms, in the vegetable an approach to the sentient instinct, while sensation and volition present strange and subtle analogies with electricity.

The discovery of the dependence of the chemical affinities of bodies on their electric states — the detection of electric forces in magnetic phenomena — the close analogies subsisting between light, heat, and sound, all point to one primal energy in nature, the agent in all natural phenomena, as in the mind that perceives them — for mind itself, in so far as we are acquainted with its mode of being, is but a subtle force vibrating to the impulsion of other forces external to itself.[87]

And what then is the omnipresent energy which determines alike the regular form of a crystal, the symmetrical structure of a flower, and the cyclic motions of a planet; — perhaps even the mysterious concords and harmonies of a human soul? — What is this invisible power, itself intangible and imponderable, from which all this bright apocalypse of visible nature is evolved? — which under certain ascertained conditions originates life in inanimate matter[88], which dissolves into airy nothing the substance of the most solid mountains, which makes and unmakes all things.

"Nature," says Emerson, "is the incarnation of a thought and turns to a thought again."[89] Paradoxical as this may seem, it is the affirmation of a simple fact. Berkeley, after all, was perhaps nearer the truth than has been imagined. For the question between him and his opponents was not whether the objects of perception have a *real* existence out of the mind, but simply whether they have a solid substantial existence — whether the things which affect us from without be matter or spirit?

---

[87] This allusion to what we know now as the electromagnetic spectrum, demonstrates how well-read Whitman was in contemporary science.

[88] Chambers, Robert. *Vestiges of the Natural History of Creation,* p. 141. Although science has come a long way toward understanding how life originated spontaneously in the conditions of the early earth, the traditional lore of spontaneous generation of insects and other animals were all observational errors.

[89] Emerson. "Nature." *Essays, Second Series.*

<180>

When Berkeley says that these objects and qualities are but the immediate effects of the ever-present Deity, he assumes a sublime truth in strict accordance with the results to which all modern researches into the internal structure and equilibrium of matter evidently point.[90]

All that we know of matter may be comprised in a statement of the laws by which certain forces emanating from certain centers act upon each other. None of our senses ever go behind these forces, and we are unable to determine whether they have a substantial basis or proceed simply from an ideal center.

Since Leibniz rejected the Newtonian theory of hard, impenetrable, insoluble atoms, and introduced his own hypothesis of monads, or simple, spiritual, inextended units, essentially possessed of attractive and repulsive forces, science has been slowly but surely approximating to a more spiritual apprehension of the material world and of the laws by which it is governed, — to a theory which should remove the great stumbling-block of matter which has proved so formidable an obstacle in the path of the cosmogonist, and which the Manicheans and their modern disciples have elevated into the rival and adversary of Deity.

This theory of Leibniz, when presented in a more finished state by Boscovitch, very generally superseded that of Newton.[91] His idea that the properties of bodies depend on certain forces emanating from geometric points, or points bearing certain relations to each other in space, has subsequently received a striking confirmation from the discovery that the chemical affinities of bodies depend on their electric states; and the physical philosopher already confidently anticipates the time when the chemical problem shall be changed into a mechanical problem — a question of forces, distance and time.

"But what, then," asks the materialist, "are these ultimate atoms — these inextended points — or, as Exley has recently more correctly designated them, these "spheres of force?" — in what do the powers and properties that pertain to them inhere?"[92]

---

[90] George Berkeley (1685-1753), Irish bishop, philosopher, and sometime resident of Newport, Rhode Island. His 1710 *A Treatise Concerning the Principles of Human Knowledge* and later writings present the argument that matter does not exist, except in the mind of the observer, and the subsuming mind of an omniscient, omnipresent deity. Some of his other speculations anticipate relativity theory.

[91] Leibniz vs. Newton. No scientist today subscribes to Leibniz's model of the structure of matter. Atoms do exist, and they are not infinitely divisible as Leibniz believed. Leibniz was correct only in the sense that atoms are indeed mostly empty space, and that the atomic weight, centered in the tiny nucleus, and the arrangement of the atom's captive electrons, determine the chemical properties of a substance.

[92] Thomas Exley proposed that "each atom of matter consists of an indefinitely extensive sphere of attraction, resting on a very small concentric sphere of

<181>

To this question science has returned no positive answer. All our inquiries into the laws of sensation and the phenomena which induce sensation have revealed to us only "an elastic fluid vibrating to the impulsion of elastic media."

"The intellect ignores matter." "Solidity is an illusion of the senses."

May we not then reasonably assume that the latent, yet immediate and inherent principle of the forces which represent matter is the great "caused entity" of Spinoza, which manifests itself under the two modes or attributes of "extension and thought." The life of "the world?" Thus are we again brought back to the great fact of unity in diversity — to the primal manifestation of that mysterious law of polarity which comprehends all phenomena — to that absolute identity which is the starting point and result of all philosophy. And thus is the mystic God-lore of an earlier age elucidated and justified by the scientific researches of our own.[93]

Let us not decry the age in which we live — it is rich in good gifts and instinct with an infinite hope. Though conversant in all prudential and practical arts, it is not deserted of the ancient wisdom. It is mystic and devout, yet patient and diligent in investigation and research. An age in which mighty secrets have been won from nature by the ceaseless questioning of her solitary votaries, in which science seems about to restore to us all that the imagination has from time to time surrendered to the narrow skepticism of the understanding. Already she has whispered to us the secret law of Nature's boldest miracles,— she has imparted to us a spell by which we may restore the oracles of the past, and has initiated us into the possible modes and conditions of a more spiritual and sublimated existence.

The limits of human knowledge, so accurately defined in the Augustan age of French literature, are now removed beyond even the range of conjecture.

---

repulsion, the force being every where, from the center, inversely as the square of the distance ... Are we absolutely to exclude solid atoms? I confess I can find no use for them." *Principles of Natural Philosophy* (p. xix). This idea persists to the end of the book, where Exley insists "[T]here is no imaginable use, as far as we can perceive, for a solid nucleus, which is not answered by this concentrated force." (p. 470). The text ends on a religious note that Leibniz would have approved of, on matter and force: "a wonderful act of the Ever-living God, who worketh all things according to the counsels of His Will. Every atom of matter . . . was created or brought into existence by an operation of the Almighty Power of God" (p. 470).

[93] Metaphysical claims to knowledge about physical reality become the most embarrassing relics of any age. Whitman's synthesis is earnest, but simply not true, as no theological wisdom has ever emerged from a physics lab. This lesson ought to be heeded by today's writers who go on about quantum theory and string theory, seeking a justification for spiritual urges.

<182>

But yesterday man pondered in blank over the origin of worlds; to-day we read the secrets of creation in the cavernous depths below and in the starry vaults above. We not only weigh the massive bulk of Jupiter or Saturn as in a balance with unerring precision, but by the sublime induction of Laplace,[94] we have ascended from investigations concerning the size, figure and motion of planets, to an intelligible theory of their birth. We see worlds in every stage of formation slowly evolving from an imponderable ether, and by the aid of the subtle process of analysis, invented by Newton and Leibniz, are enabled to map out the bright pathway of the stars on the vast blank of the unrecorded past and illimitable future! Science in these latter days has wonderfully enlarged our perspective.

Our range of observation both in space and time is infinitely expanded. The reflecting man is no longer in danger of mistaking his garden wall for the boundary line of the universe, nor the nineteenth century for the hour of doom.

The old fountains from which the great and good of past ages drank wisdom and power are reopened, and their sacred and long-sealed waters flow freely beside the dusty highways of life. Even the silent tombs of Etruria and the desolate temples of Egypt yield up their jealous secrets,[95] and teach through their eloquent anaglyphs the universality of our own mythology. The torch of science gleams athwart fretted altars and graven obelisks, and the old stones become vocal beneath its ray, and pour forth a Memnonian music. Yet in the very presence of the mighty past, men aspire to a future that shall confirm the great idea of unlimited progress. Everywhere they recognize a progressive life, a beneficent law; and know that to place themselves in harmony with these laws, to "fall into the divine circuits,"[96] is to find both freedom and repose.

---

[94] Pierre-Simon Laplace (1749-1827), author of *Mécanique Céleste* (Celestial Mechanics), published in five volumes from 1799 to 1825. It would be fair to call him the 19th century's Newton, and his work on astronomy introduced the nebular hypothesis of the origin of stellar systems, and even speculated about black holes.

[95] The Rosetta Stone had only recently been deciphered, so that Egyptian hieroglyphics could finally be read and translated. The study of ancient Etruria was only in its infancy, but lavishly-illustrated books about Etruscan art appeared as early as 1766 (Harcanville) and 1767 (Passeri), and Whitman might have read Mrs. Gray's *Tour to the Sepulchres of Etruria, in 1839,* as well as Betham's *Etruria-Celtica* (1842).

[96] "Let us take our bloated nothingness out of the path of the divine circuits. Let us unlearn our wisdom of the world." Emerson. "Spiritual Laws," p. 160.

Though baffled seers cannot impart
The secret of its laboring heart,
Throb thine with Nature's throbbing breast
And all is clear from east to west.[97]

In asserting that the fontal idea of Emerson's writings, as of the philosophy of the age, is absolute identity, I have not been careful to avert from them the imputation of Pantheism, Platonism, Spinozism, &c., &c. It matters little how we designate this manner of interpreting the phenomena of being, since it contains an inherent vitality which alike survives neglect and defies ridicule.

Superficial and timid men may decry these ideas as unintelligible or profane; but what rational ground of faith is left to him who doubts that God is over all and in all, that evil is but the absence and privation of good, and that all apparent evil must give way before a fuller development of the life that *is* within us? Only when the knowledge that the highest dwells ever with us becomes "a sweet enveloping thought,"[98] shall we be enabled to lead a single and trustful life, "to live in thoughts and act with energies that are immortal."[99]

---

[97] Emerson. From lines serving as an epigraph to "Nature." *Essays, Second Series.*
[98] Emerson. "The Over-Soul," p. 297.
[99] "So I come to live in thoughts, and act with energies which are immortal." Emerson. "The Over-Soul," p. 298.

<184>

WALTER SAVAGE LANDOR

A LETTER FROM BATH (1857)
by Sarah Helen Whitman

◇————————————————————◇

W E LEFT LONDON on the nineteenth in the express train for Bath, traveling more than a hundred miles in two hours and a half, without inconvenience or fatigue. The road is the best and the safest in England and the cars more luxurious than a private carriage.

The stately, sleepy old town lies softly cradled within an amphitheatre of lofty hills; its noble crescents and beautiful villas, all trellised and tapestried with flowers; its old walls and towers and terraces folded and curtained in heavy draperies of ivy, and steeped in the soft vapors of the "aquae solis," the old Roman name for its healing waters — "waters of the sun." As we rode through some of its terraced streets last evening, we did not wonder at its reputation as the most picturesque inland city of Europe. It looked magically beautiful by the soft, rosy twilight that at this season in England lingers far into the night.

Bath is still the favorite resort of invalids, idlers and aristocrats, of all who would enjoy the *dolce far niente*[1] in the midst of a perfumed and dreamy atmosphere.

Here were passed the last years of William Beckford,[2] the eccentric author of *Vathek*,[3] and the luxurious proprietor of Fonthill Abbey.[4] It was here that he sought to realize the last dreams of his marvelous fancy. It seems to have been his costly and mournful ambition to erect for himself a gorgeous "palace of art," in which he might live and die alone; but an eternal unrest consumed him, and one after another of his rare creations were, like his paradise at Cintra[5] (made memorable in Byron's beautiful description), abandoned to desolation and decay. That most grand and terrible conception of retribution and despair, "The Hall of Eblis"[6] might well have emanated from such a brain. Mr. Beckford was undoubtedly what would be called in our day "a medium" — the victim perhaps of some haunting, demoniac possession. His *Vathek* was written in French, at a single sitting of three

---

[1] *Dolce far niente*. Pleasant idleness.
[2] William Beckford (1760-1844), eccentric English novelist and art collector.
[3] Beckford's novel, *Vathek* (1786).
[4] Fonthill Abbey, a Gothic re-creation designed by architect James Wyatt, was finally completed for Beckford in 1807.
[5] Beckford's house in Sintra's Montserrat Gardens in Portugal, where he resided from 1793-1799. The lavish gardens included an artificial waterfall.
[6] A netherworld of doomed souls in *Vathek*. Beckford revealed that the interior architecture of Fonthill provoked this imaginary locale (Melville, p. 42).

<187>

nights and two days, and without intervening sleep or rest. May not his rare intellectual tastes, his lavish expenditure in architectural creation, and his solitary and restless life have suggested to Tennyson his wonderful "Palace of Art,"[7] and to Edgar Poe that strange and sumptuous fantasy, "The Domain of Arnheim," one of his most cherished and favorite conceptions?

William Beckford's Tower at Bath.

YESTERDAY WE ACCEPTED an invitation to take tea with Walter Savage Landor at his house in River street. Hardly less of a recluse than the author of *Vathek*, Mr. Landor ignores general society, professes not to know a dozen people in England, and politely expresses his enjoyment in the society of "foreigners." Mr. Emerson in his *English Traits*, speaks of Landor as one of the three or four persons whom he wished to see in visiting Europe. He still lives, as in Italy, among a "cloud of pictures." His rooms are hung from basement to attic with rare paintings by the best French, English, and Italian masters. Dutch pictures he does not like, and has carefully weeded them from his walls. He holds to the only orthodox creed in art, that beauty should be its sole and devout aim. Among his pictures was a beautiful portrait of the mother of Sheridan, by Romney.[8] It was full of riant, sparkling life, and showed the clear bright fountain from which sprang the vivacious wit of the brilliant orator and conversationalist. A picture of Europa, by Correggio,[9]

[7] Tennyson, "The Palace of Art" (1823), quotes Beckford's phrase "hearts of flame," l. 241.

[8] George Romney (1734-1802), British portrait painter.

[2] Although Correggio painted a series of scenes from Ovid's *Metamorphoses*, I

<188>

pleased me more than all the rest. With one hand she had grasped a horn of the stately animal she rode, while the other filled with roses, was pressed tenderly against her cheek. There was a strange ideal charm in her innocent playfulness and in the aerial lightness with which she seemed borne along through a solemn, mysterious atmosphere, whose lurid gloom beautifully relieved her soft pearly cheek and fluttering milk-white robes. I can never forget this picture. I afterwards found it was a great favorite with Mr. Landor, who said he would rather part with every picture in his collection than with this.

His conversation surprises by its freshness and novelty, and stimulates by its resistance. With all his fine taste and culture, he is too arbitrary in his opinions and too eccentric in his tastes to be a safe guide to others; but it is pleasant to talk with a man who has faith in his own fancies His manners are a singular compound of noble courtesy and abrupt, uncompromising protest and assertion. He said, "You have great writers in your country," and spoke in high praise of Emerson, recalling with evident pleasure their personal interviews in Italy many years ago. He objected to his style, as to that of many of the ablest English writers of the last half century; insisting on a classic directness and transparency of diction as one of the cardinal virtues.

Among others, he instanced Sydney Smith[10] and Washington Irving as examples of faultless style. But to assert that the colossal and shadowy dreams, the intricate and labyrinthian fancies of De Quincey could be adequately expressed in a style that is adapted to the racy humor and practical common sense of Sydney Smith, or to insist that the scope, the subtlety, the insight, the remote and star-like beauty of Emerson's thought can be told in the sweet familiar phrase of Irving, is simply to ask that which is, in the very nature of things, impossible. As well require that the bulbul and the nightingale should sing like the robin and the lark, or that the night-blooming cereus should yield the perfume of the day-lily and the violet. He praised with much emphasis, the writings of Miss Lynn — *Amymone, Azeth the Egyptian,* and some others.[11] He said they combined some of the finer attributes of Rousseau's genius, with the intellectual freedom of De Stael. I believe these works are just being published in America. He professed not to have heard of the author of *Christie Johnstone*,[12] whose last novel has so stirred the sympathies of all American

do not find a painting on *The Rape of Europa* among Correggio's extant paintings. It may be a misattribution.

[10] Sydney Smith (1771-1845), English cleric and writer, praised for his wit and prose style.

[11] Eliza Lynn Linton (1822-1898), British journalist and novelist. She was a friend of Landor, but it is fortunate that Whitman did not meet her: Linton was an avowed anti-feminist.

[12] *Christie Johnstone* (1853) is a novel by Charles Reade (1814-1884), later

<189>

readers. With the exception of Howitt's[13] last work, which has just been sent him by the author, I saw no books in his apartments.

He is said to give away his books as soon as he has read them; a most princely and gracious habit. Beautiful flowers were on the table, and bloomed in beds of earth on the broad stone ledges of the windows, an almost universal custom in Bath. He gave us moss roses and musk plants at parting, and we left him with pleasant memories of the hours passed in his society. He invited us to return on the morrow and see his pictures by the morning light. But today we went with a party of friends to Clifton, and tomorrow we leave Bath, with its grand old Abbey, — "the lantern of England," — its Temple of Minerva, its Roman ruins and its medieval relics, for "sunny France."

— June 20, 1857
Published in *The Providence Journal*
and in *Emerson's Magazine & Putnam's Monthly, October, 1857*

---

famed for *The Cloister and the Hearth* (1861).
[13] William Howitt (1792-1879), a British writer with some Spiritualist connections. He translated Joseph Ennemoser's *History of Magic* (1854), and compiled *The History of the Supernatural in All Ages and Nations* (1863).

<190>

◇——◇

A. BRONSON
ALCOTT

Tablets, by A. Bronson Alcott (1868)
Book Review by S.H.W.
[Sarah Helen Whitman]

A S WE OPEN the quaint pages of Mr. Alcott's unique volume,[1] we find them fragrant with the perfume of "sweet herbs" and "table plants"; we breathe the odorous air of orchards and gardens, seasoned with delightful talks about "rural culture," "modern teaching," "Socratic dialectic;" — about "vestiges," "symbols," "embryons," "temperaments;" — about the grand themes — always freshly and newly treated here — of "genesis," "metamorphoses," "immortality." The little book is hardly for the million; it will not be likely to pass through so many editions as the *Kathrina* of Dr. Holland,[2] or the *Proverbial Philosophy* of Mr. Martin Tupper. [3]There are words here of a meaning so profound, an import so vast and suggestive, that we read them with a kind of awe, as if listening to mysterious voices, such as in the old ancestral Edens, talked with man in the garden in the cool of the evening. There are, doubtless, some pages here which will make critics carp and sophists smile; a few problems suggested which literal readers had better not try to solve; a few paragraphs, perhaps, which may not please sectarians and formalists; as for instance, "Let us have unspoken creeds, and these quick and operative. Has not the drawl of sacred names been heard till sacred names seem profane, and it were devout to fall into silence?"[4] And again: "I imagine our Bible is more loosely read, least understood, of any book in the English tongue. Conceive a fresh generation coming to its perusal as to a volume just issued in modern type from a popular book store, and reviewed in its journals. How better acquit ourselves of the Bibles of the world, than by fairly measuring our private convictions with their spirit and teachings?"[5]

In the eventful days when the young advocates and apostles of anti-slavery cause used often to gather together for social converse and co-operation, in the hospitable old house at Pleasant Valley,[6] I remember

---

[1] A. Bronson Alcott. *Tablets*. 1868. Boston: Roberts Brothers.
[2] Josiah Gilbert Holland (1819-1881) was an editor, historian and poet who sold over three-quarters of a million books, in what a Scribner's blurb called "his appeal to the universal popular heart." *Kathrina* is a 267-page poem recounting pious matrimonial bliss and a widower's mourning.
[3] Martin Farquar Tupper (1810-1889), British writer and poet. His didactic *Proverbial Philosophy*, published in 1837, was reprinted more than 40 times. Its long-winded moralizing does not commend it to today's readers.
[4] Alcott. *Tablets*, p. 141.
[5] Ibid, p. 142.
[6] Pleasant Valley, at Peterboro NY, was the site of the founding of the New York

<193>

how Mr. Alcott, who was ever a welcome guest there, sometimes stirred and startled them by the innocent audacity of some of his theories, and by the platonic latitude of his speculations. He seems to have in him, like William Blake, the inspired English artist, that fine inner sense which receives impressions of truth and beauty as simply and sweetly as we smell the fragrance of the briar-rose and the woodbine; like Blake, too, he combines the innocence of the child with the mystic vision of the prophet and the seer, and casts around him a kindling influence — an atmosphere of life, full of the ideal. Those who are familiar with Gilchrist's fascinating life of Blake,[7] and those who have read Algernon Swinburne's recondite and erratic eulogium on his genius,[8] will recognize in Mr. Alcott many kindred traits and fantasies.

The Concord school of writers doubtless owed much of its characteristic freshness and sincerity to him, and derived much of its inspiration, courage and reality from his spiritual contact. We have heard Mr. Emerson avow that the most suggestive and vital words he ever listened to were from the lips of Alcott. But whatever may be the relative value of his thought, he unquestionably belongs in a marked and memorable manner to the intellectual history of the time, and must remain alike in mental quality and personal appearance, a conspicuous figure of delicate and venerable beauty among the group of poets and writers who have lent to our literature some of its noblest characteristics: Emerson, with his rare combination of secular sense and spiritual loftiness; Channing, with his catholic spirit and sweet, benignant faith, gleaming white and luminous as a star against a sublime and sombre background of Puritan theologies; Margaret Fuller, the Britomartis[9] of our letters; Thoreau, an Indian Dryad[10] turned bookman, solitary, sweet, severe, smelling through and through of the fir tree and the pine; Ellery Channing, with his muse of vagrant grace, whose liberties are laws; Longfellow, with his richly illuminated manuscripts and golden legends; Hawthorne, aureoled with dreams of mystic sweetness and terror; Wendell Phillips, "from brow to foot all noble;"[11] [Theodore] Parker, stalwart, intrepid, invincible. Nor

Antislavery Society. Peterboro philanthropist Gerritt Smith funded Underground Railroad activities. He ran for president for the Liberty Party and added woman suffrage to the doomed party's platform in 1848. In a failed resettlement effort, Smith acquired 100,000 acres of land designated to be given to freed slaves.

[7] William Gilchrist. *Life of William Blake.* 1863.

[8] Algernon Charles Swinburne. *William Blake: A Critical Essay.* 1868.

[9] *Britomartis.* A Cretan epithet, literally, "Sweet maid," a name used in Spenser's *Fairie Queene* for a powerful female knight.

[10] *Dryad.* A tree-spirit.

[11] William D. O'Connor used these words to describe Wendell Phillips in a letter not published until 1883, in Bucke's *Walt Whitman* (p. 78). Since SHW notes O'Connor's earlier essay defending Walt Whitman, it is possible that she

<194>

to these should we forget to add one of another and, it may be, an ampler order, a man whose serene and stately presence we have lately seen looming above the crowd of our own city, and known everywhere by his well-worn title of the "Good Gray Poet," conferred upon him in Wm. D. O'Connor's gorgeous and powerful pamphlet of vindication.[12]

Among these and other suggestive and sincere thinkers of our time, Mr. Alcott must ever be remembered, and, after all abatements and discriminations, must ever hold among them a high place of honor; yet like the sublime phantom of Wordworth's "Laodamia," he dwells, perhaps, in an atmosphere of thought too remote and sublimated for popular human sympathy and appreciation:

> He spake of love, such love as spirits feel
> In worlds whose course is equable and pure;
> No fears to beat away — no strife to heal —
> The past unsighed for, and the future sure;
> Speaks of heroic arts in graver mood
> Revived, with finer harmony pursued;
>
> Of all that is most beauteous — imaged there
> In happier beauty: more pellucid streams,
> An ampler ether, a diviner air,
> And fields invested with purpureal gleams;
> Climes which the sun, who sheds the brightest day
> Earth knows, is all unworthy to survey.

— *The Providence Journal*
October 30, 1868

---

heard or read O'Connor's praise for Phillips elsewhere.
[12] William D. O'Connor. *The Good Gray Poet: A Vindication* (1866). Although SHW had initially resisted Walt Whitman's poetry, she was finally won over, and she doubtless recognized in O'Connor's pamphlet a parallel to her own 1860 defense of Poe.

<195>

GEORGE GORDON, LORD BYRON

Byronism (1869)
by S.H.W (Sarah Helen Whitman)

◇————————————————————————————————◇

ERHAPS IN THE literary history of the world no single article ever created such an overwhelming and absorbing interest as that which appeared in the September [1869] *Atlantic,* entitled "True Story of Lady Byron's Life."[1] The profound sensation which it created is evidence of the slumbering yet powerful spell which Byron's genius has exercised over the educated world.

It has been urged by the friends of Mrs. Stowe that her manuscript was read and its publication approved by Mr. Curtis,[2] Mr. Parton[3] and Dr. Oliver Wendell Holmes;[4] and had Mrs. Stowe confined herself to the defense of Lady Byron's conduct as a wife, without avowing her deliberate intention to undermine, by her revelations, the influence of Lord Byron's writings, there would have been far less cause for criticism and censure. But when she assumes that the errors and depravities of Byron's life demanded that his works shall be prohibited, and when she tells us that it was to protect the youth of America from their brilliant seductive influence that she revealed the dark secret she had kept so long, we cannot but be amazed at the credulity of her judgment and the innocent audacity of its avowal.

It has for years been a habit with some of the critics of the periodical press to speak of Byron's literary reputation as a thing of the past, and to allude with supercilious flippancy and frivolity to the decline of the sardonic and sensational school.

Mr. Walter Edgar McCann, a writer in the June *Galaxy* for 1868, says: "Byronism seems to have completely disappeared."[5] If, at the time that Byron's Dream[6] was written, "people had only known what they

_____

1 Harriet Beecher Stowe. "True Story of Lady Byron's Life." *Atlantic Monthly.* Vol. 24, September 1869, pp. 295-313.
2 George William Curtis (1824-1892), editor of *Harper's Magazine.*
3 James Parton (1822-1891), a widely-read biographer who had published books on Jefferson, Greeley, Voltaire, and Benjamin Franklin.
4 Holmes and Stowe were among the co-founders of *Atlantic Monthly* in 1857.
5 "The thing [Byronism] seems to have completely disappeared." Walter Edgar McCann. "Byronism." *The Galaxy.* Vol. 5, June 1868, p. 777. McCall is really talking about the Byronic lifestyle emulated by his fans, rather than Byron as literature, akin to the fever that followed the publication of Goethe's Werther: "No mania was ever before carried so far into the confines of the ludicrous . . . young noblemen wrapped in the solitude of their own absurdity, seated all alone in some dismal corner, gloomy and misanthropic . . . it always broke out in open collars and flaring neckties" (p. 779).
6 Byron, "The Dream" (1816).

<199>

know now," namely that Byron was a "sublime coxcomb,"[7] Mr. McCann thinks there would never have been any Byronism at all.

Yet in September, 1869, knowing what people *now* know or what Mrs. Stowe thinks they *ought* to know, Byronism, or the sales of Byron's works is rapidly and continuously on the increase.

A writer in the New York *Tribune,* also, only eight weeks ago, says: "There has been little danger this many a year that Byron's literary influence over young men and women could ever again become what it was at a time Mrs. Stowe describes from memory; *henceforth there is none at all.*"[8]

More recently a writer in the same journal says: "Mrs. Stowe by unveiling a long carefully guarded secret has restored virtue and vice to their proper places, and in future it will be remembered that, through her courage, there was one imposture less in the world."[9] Assuredly Byron with all his faults was no impostor. He was the last man to assume a virtue though he had it not. On the contrary he was notoriously given to a habit of mystifying his friends by the assumption of mysterious imaginary vices.[10]

Whatever may be proffered against his private life, we may rest assured that "the blazing star of Byron"[11] will not wane and pale beneath this dark stigma. His sublime genius, seen beside its shadow, will only burn and glow with a more dazzling, and, it is to be feared, a more baleful and fatal splendor.

With all his fault of character and conduct, with all the wild insanities of his genius, we cold ill spare from his "land's language"[12] the elements

---

[7] Ibid, p. 778.

[8] "The Byron Scandal." *New-York Tribune,* August 18, 1869.

[9] I did not locate this quotation, but the *Tribune* published at least eight articles on the Lady Byron "scandal" between August and September, 1869. Most of the articles debunked details of Stowe's account and cast doubt on the veracity of the whole story. By early September, Lady Byron's executors had spoken and the story was regarded as unreliable, and Stowe was disgraced in the matter. The incest accusation, however, has never gone away. The damage was done. See the Bibliography under "Byron Scandal" for a list of the main articles. The scandal was also mentioned in the lead editorials for some days, and noted in passing in unrelated articles.

[10] *Mysterious imaginary vices.* One letter in the 1869 *Tribune* series, titled "Another Version of the Story" (August 27) hints at an unspecified scandal that could still not be named. It has been established now that Byron had sexual adventures with many young men, extending from his youth all the way to his final days in Greece, the unspeakable and unprintable "vice" that would have subjected him to prison and banishment from society.

[11] Thomas Moore. Diary for March 10-11, 1844. Vol. 7, p. 366.

[12] Lord Byron. *Childe Harold.* IV:ix, ll. 4-6. "I twine/ My hopes of being remember'd in my line/ With my land's language".

<200>

of power and strength and splendor with which he has enriched and ennobled it.

The sustained harmonies and winged ascensions of Wordsworth, the far-floating cloudy wefts of Shelley, the cunning sensuousness and the rich antique imagery of Keats, the range and subtlety of Browning, the toned and tempered luxuries of Tennyson, — none of these can atone for the breath and freedom and fullness of Byron's virile and resonant verse, whose large majestic movement sometimes, like

Dark Guadiana, rolls [his] power along,
In sullen billows, murmuring and vast;

and sometimes flows with an exulting and abounding motion,

[And] Tagus dashing onward to the deep[13]

Every land trodden by his footsteps, every city where he lingered, every sea whereon he sailed, was immortalized and enhaloed by his genius. Cadiz, Seville, Saragossa; Athenia, Albania, — Leucadia's far projecting rock of woe; dark Tomerit and Laos wide and deep; Belgium and the blue rushing of the arrowy Rhone; the castled crags of Crachenfels, Jura, Ehrenbreitzen, Geneva, Lake Leman, Clarens,

The winged Lion's marble piles,
Where Venice sat in state, throned on her hundred isles,
Ferrara with its wide and grass-grown streets,[14]

and, looming beyond all, the Eternal City, with its Coliseum

Where the stars twinkle through the loops of time,
And the low night wind waves along the air.[15]

To all these, Byron has "linked his name with his land's language."

With Mrs. Beecher Stowe, I well remember the breathless interest which in the zenith of his career his name and fame enkindled in the hearts of all readers.

The prestige of his genius, always so potent in Europe, acquired a still more mysterious and romantic fascination as it flared on us across the intervening ocean.

I passed the summer of 1814 at Jamaica, Long Island. The estate of Mr. C.I. Bogert, the relative at whose house I was visiting, adjoined that of Mr. Rufus King, whose eldest son, while Mr. King was our minister

---

13 *Childe Harold.* I:iv
14 *Childe Harold.* IV
15 Ibid.

<201>

at the Court of St. James, had been a classmate and chum of Lord Byron's at Harrow or Cambridge. I was, during that eventful summer, frequently a guest, with my relatives, at Mr. King's tea-table; and when it is remembered that, as Moore tells us, it was considered a distinction even to have seen the author of *Childe Harold*, it may readily be imagined with what interest I listened as an imaginative child to conversations and personal anecdotes concerning him. Mr. King had an unbounded admiration for the genius of Byron, and often read and quoted his favorite passages, and, as I have since been told, with fine critical analysis. I remember that he surprised me by saying to one of his guests that he preferred the "Giaour" to the "Corsair." I had read the latter with avidity and was sadly perplexed whether to name my favorite dolly Medora or Gulnare. I eventually decided on Gulnare, and sewed a "bare bodkin" to her girdle to represent a dagger.

Mr. King always pronounced the name of Byron as if it were spelled *Birron*. Childe Harold he pronounced as *Cheelde* Harold, and the Giaour as spoken with a soft G.

At these tea-table talks were sometimes present, my cousin, the beautiful Miss Bartlett, afterward the mother of Susan and Anna Warner,[16] the sister authoresses of *Queechy, The Wide, Wide World, Dollars and Cents, The Hills of the Shatemuc*, and other charming stories. Miss Mardenbro, afterwards Mrs. Rhoda Newcomb, of this city, the intimate friend of Miss Bartlett, was also an occasional guest there. Col. Ward, the grandfather of Mrs. Julia Ward Howe, a valued friend and near-neighbor of my uncle, frequently joined the circle assembled there.

The allied armies had recently entered Paris. The new novel of *Waverly* was exciting interest and conjecture,[17] great and important events were transpiring at home in Europe, but amid all the absorbing topics of the hour, the genius of Byron was always a favorite and engrossing theme.

Are we to be told that the interest he inspired was a factitious interest, that the fascination of his genius consisted in its "sublime coxcombry," its affected misanthropy, its levity, its effrontery, its profanity, its sardonic and sensational characteristics? We will not believe it. Yet with respect to this last attribute, I will quote a pertinent paragraph from Ruskin's "Lilies for Queen's Garden":

> I am not afraid of the word passion or sensation, still less of
> the *thing*. We have heard many outcries against sensation lately.
> It is not *less* sensation that we want, but *more*. The ennobling

---

16 Susan Bogert Warner (1819-1885) wrote a number of successful religious and children's books, some in collaboration with her sister Anna Bartlett Warner (1827-1915).

17 Sir Walter Scott published his novel, *Waverly*, anonymously, and succeeding books were attributed mysteriously to "The Author of *Waverly*."

<202>

difference between one man and another is precisely this, that one is more sympathetic than another — of keener apprehension and quicker feeling; in a word, more sentient and sensational.[18]

Let me quote here from the private letter of a poet and novelist words whose inspired eloquence will find an echo in many hearts:

Poor Byron! Poor Prometheus! Light-bringer; fire-bringer! He that glorified America when she had no other friend. He that aggrandized liberty and revolt against the tyrants in Europe. He that ever and always in every public issue, in all his poetry, served the generous idea, the good cause, and manfully took the human side! But his memory will yet be absolved.

Meantime, while Mrs. Stowe is awaiting her documentary proofs, in the lull of the storm, we may still remember with pitying tenderness the noble words of Mrs. Browning:

And poor, proud Byron, sad as grave
And salt as life; forlornly brave,
And quivering with the dart he drave.[19]

— *The Providence Journal*
October 18, 1869

---

[18] John Ruskin. "Of King's Treasuries." *Sesame and Lilies,* p. 36.
[19] Elizabeth Barrett Browning, "A Vision of Poets" (1844).

<203>

◇——◇

.

SELECTED
POEMS

The Abduction of Proserpine by Pluto. Fresco by Luca Giordano,
1684-86. Palazzo Medici, Florence.

PROSERPINE, ON EARTH,
TO PLUTO IN HADES

◇————————————◇

Nec repetita sequi curet Proserpina matrem
—Virgil, Georgics, I. 39[1]

I think on thee amid these spring-time flowers,
  On thee, my emperor, my sovran lord,
Dwelling alone in dim Tartarean[2] towers
  Of thy dark realm, by earth and heaven abhorred,
Wandering afar by that Avernian[3] river
Where dead kings walk and phantoms wail forever.

I think on thee in that stern palace regnant,
  Where no sweet voice of summer charms the air,
Where the vast solitude seems ever pregnant
  With some wild dream of untold despair.
Thy love, remembered, doth heaven's light eclipse;
I feel thy lingering kisses on my lips.

I languish for the late autumnal showers,
  The cool, cool plashing of the autumn rain,
The shimmering hoar-frost and fast-fading flowers,
  That give me back to thy dark realm again:
To thee I'll bring Sicilia's starry skies[4]
And all the heaven of summer in my eyes.

When from the earth's noontide beauty borne away
  To the pale prairies of that under world,
A mournful flower upon thy breast I lay
  Till round thy heart its clinging tendrils curled —
A frightened dove, that tamed its fluttering pinion
To the dear magic of thy love's dominion.

---

[1] Proserpine, reclaimed, cares not to follow her mother.
[2] Tartarus is the realm below Hades where the banished Titans dwell.
[3] Avernus. A lake, later a lake and a canal in Campania. A cave there was depicted as an entrance into the Underworld in Virgil's *Aeneid*.
[4] Sicilia. Proserpine's home may have been Sicily.

<207>

For thou wert grandly beautiful as night,
  Stern Orcus,[5] in thy realm of buried kings;
And thy sad crown of cypress in my sight
  Fairer than all the bright and flowery rings
Of wreathèd poppies and of golden corn
By Ceres on her stately temples worn.

I sat beside thee on Hell's dusky throne,
  Nor feared the awful shadow of thy fate;
Content to share the burden of thy crown,
  And all the mournful splendors of thy state;
Bending my flower-like beauty to thy will,
Seeking with light thy lonely dark to fill.

Wondering, I think how thy dear love hath bound me
  In a new life that half forgets the old;
All day I haunt the meadows where you found me,
  Knee-deep in daffodils of dusky gold,
Or sit by Cyane's[6] sad fountain, dreaming
Of the red lake by thy proud palace gleaming.

When, in her car by wingèd dragons borne,
  Pale Ceres sought me through the shuddering night,
With angry torches and fierce eyes, forlorn,
  Slaying the dark that screened me from her sight,
Like a reft lioness that rends the air
Of midnight with her perilous despair,

Jove, pitying the great passion of her woe,
  Gave back thy queen-bride to the mother's grief —
To Ceres gave — through summer's golden glow
  And all the crescent months, from spear to sheaf:
Alas, how sadly in Sicilian bowers
I pass this lonely, lingering time of flowers!

---

[5] Orcus. Etruscan name for Hades.
[6] Cyane. A Sicilian nymph, earthly companion of Proserpine.

<208>

In the long silence of the languid noons,
  When all the panting birds are faint with heat,
I wander listless by the blue lagoons
  To hear their light waves rippling at my feet
Through the dead calm, and count the lingering time
By the slow pulsing of their silver chime.

I languish for the late autumnal showers,
  The cool, cool plashing of the autumn rain,
The shimmering hoar-frost and fast-fading flowers,
  That give me back to thy dark realm again:
I have no native land from thee apart,
And my high heaven of heavens is in thy heart.

<209>

THE RAVEN

◇————————————————◇

Raven, from the dim dominions
   On the Night's Plutonian shore,
Oft I hear thy dusky pinions
   Wave and flutter round my door —
See the shadow of thy pinions
   Float along the moon-lit floor;

Often, from the oak-woods glooming
   Round some dim ancestral tower,
In the lurid distance looming —
   Some high solitary tower —
I can hear thy storm-cry booming
   Through the lonely midnight hour.

When the moon is at the zenith,
   Thou dost haunt the moated hall,
Where the marish flower greeneth
   O'er the waters, like a pall —
Where the House of Usher leaneth,
   Darkly nodding to its fall:

There I see thee, dimly gliding —
   See thy black plumes waving slow —
In its hollow casements hiding,
   When their shadow yawns below,
To the sullen tarn confiding
   The dark secrets of their woe:—

See thee, when the stars are burning
   In their cressets, silver clear —
When Ligeia's spirit yearning
   For the earth-life, wanders near —
When Morella's soul returning,
   Weirdly whispers "I am here."

<210>

Once, within a realm enchanted,
    On a far isle of the seas,
By unearthly visions haunted,
    By unearthly melodies,
Where the evening sunlight slanted
    Golden through the garden trees, —

Where the dreamy moonlight dozes,
    Where the early violets dwell,
Listening to the silver closes
    Of a lyric loved too well,
Suddenly, among the roses,
    Like a cloud, thy shadow fell.

Once, where Ulalume lies sleeping,
    Hard by Auber's haunted mere,
With the ghouls a vigil keeping,
    On that night of all the year,
Came thy sounding pinions, sweeping
    Through the leafless woods of Weir!

Oft, with Proserpine I wander
    On the Night's Plutonian shore,
Hoping, fearing, while I ponder
    On thy loved and lost Lenore —
On the demon doubts that sunder
    Soul from soul forevermore;

Trusting, though with sorrow laden,
    That when life's dark dream is o'er,
By whatever name the maiden
    Lives within thy mystic lore,
Eiros, in that distant Aidenn,
    Shall his Charmion meet once more.

<211>

NOON

◇————————◇

from *Hours of Life*

"The mysterious silence of full noon." — Bailey. *Festus*.[7]

"Combien de fois dans le silence de minuit, et dans cet autre
silence de midi, si accablant, si inquiet, si dévorant, n'ai-je pas
senti mon coeur se précipiter vers un but inconnu, vers un
bonheur sans forme et sans nom, qui est au ciel, qui est dans
l'air, qui est partout, comme l'amour! C'est l'aspiration sainte
de la partie la plus éthéreé de notre âme vers l'inconnu."

—*George Sand*[8]

Dream followed dream; and still the day
Floated on golden wings away;
 But in the hush of the high noon,
Touched by a sorrow without name,
Consumed by a slow fever-flame,
 I loathed my life's mysterious boon,
Unconscious of its end or aim;

Lost in a languor of repose—
 A luxury of gloom —
As when the curved, voluptuous rose
 Droops with its wealth of bloom.

---

[7] *Festus*, a giant 12-part poem on philosophy and theology, published in 1839
and expanded in 1845, by Philip James Bailey (1816-1902). Bailey's line is
"The imperious silence of full noon" (p. 443). Bailey's poem appears to be a
vast expansion and variation on *Faust*, with Festus/Faustus pitted against
Lucifer, with a "Helen," and God, as characters as well.
[8] *Combien de foi* . . . "How many times, in the silence of midnight, and in this
other silence of noon, so overwhelmed, so anxious, so consumed, did I not feel
my heart rushing towards an unknown goal, towards a formless and nameless
happiness, which is in the heavens, which is in the air, which is everywhere, like
love! It is the holy aspiration of the most ethereal part of our soul toward the
unknown." From George Sand's 1833 novel, *Lélia*, Chap. 18.

<212>

Decked as for a festival
Seemed the wide and lonely hall
Of Nature, but a mute despair
Filled the universal air; —
A sense of loneliness and void, —
A wealth of beauty unenjoyed, —
A sadness born mid the excess
Of life's unvalued loveliness.

Every pulse of being panting
    With a bliss it fain would share,
Still there seemed a presence wanting,
Still some lost ideal haunting
    All the lone and lustrous air.

Far off I heard the solemn chimes
    Of Life and Death, —
The rhythm of ancestral rhymes
    Above, — beneath!

"Light in shadow ever fading —
Death on Life's bright realm invading —
Pain with pleasure keeping measure,
Wasting care with golden treasure."
    So the ancient burden rang,
    So the choral verses sang.

Though beautiful on all the hills
    The summer noon-light lay,
Far in the west a single cloud
Lay folded like a fleecy shroud,
    Ready to veil its ray.
And over all a purple pall
    Seemed waiting for the day.

I heard far, phantom voices calling
    Over all the flowery wold, —
O'er the westering meadows falling
    Into slopes of gleamy gold; —

<213>

Still I heard them calling, — calling, —
   Through the dim, entangled glooms —
Far through sunless valleys falling
   Downward to a place of tombs.

Near me pressed a vassal throng,
Slaves to custom, serfs to wrong —
Hollow-hearted, vain and cold,
Minions of the earthly mold;
Holding in supreme derision
Memories of the life Elysian,
Reckless of the birthright lost,
Heedless of the heavenly host,
Traitors to the Holy Ghost!

Haunted by a nameless terror —
   Thrilled by a foreboding breath,
As the aspen wildly trembles
   When the winds are still as death, —
I sought amid the sadness drear
Some loved familiar face to cheer
The solitude, — some lingering tone
Of love ere love and hope had flown.

I heard a low voice breathe my name:
   Was it the echo of my own, —
   That weird and melancholy tone, —
That voice whose subtle sweetness came
Keen as the serpent's tongue of flame?
So near, its music seemed to me
The music of my heart to be.

Still I heard it, nearer, clearer,
   When all other songs had flown,
Floating round me till it bound me
   In a wild world of its own.

<214>

Suddenly a chill wind leapt
   Through its woven harmonies;
All its silver chords were snapt
   As a wind-harp's by the breeze.
A shudder through the silence crept
And death athwart the noonlight swept.

Then came the pall, the dirge, the knell,
As, dust to dust, the earth-clods fell,
Down crumbling on a coffin lid,
Within whose narrow casket hid, —
Shut from the cheerful light of day, —
Buried, yet quick, my own heart lay.

Graves closed round my path of life,
   The beautiful had fled;
Pale shadows wandered by my side,
   And whispered of the dead.
The far off hollow of the sky
   Seemed like an idle mockery. —
The vaulted hollow of the sky,
   With its blue depths of mystery
   But rounded Death's vast empery.

O'erwearied with life's restless change
   From ecstasy to agony,
Its fleeting pleasures born to die,
   The mirage of its fantasy,
Its worn and melancholy range
Of hopes that could no more estrange
   The married heart of memory,
Doomed, while we drain life's perfumed wine,
For the dull Lethean wave to pine,
And, for each thrill of joy, to know
Despair's slow pulse or sorrow's throe, —
I sought some central truth to span
   These wide extremes of good and ill —
I longed with one bold glance to scan
   Life's perfect sphere, to rend at will
The gloom of Erebus, — dread zone,

<215>

Coiled like a serpent round the throne
Of Heaven — the realm where Justice veils
Her heart and holds her even scales, —
Where awful Nemesis awaits
The doomed, by Pluto's iron gates.

In the long noon-tide of my sorrow,
I questioned of the eternal morrow;
    I gazed in sullen awe
Far through the illimitable gloom
Down deepening like the swift maelstrom,
    The doubting soul to draw
Into eternal solitudes,
Where unrelenting silence broods
    Around the throne of Law.

I questioned the dim chronicle
    Of ages gone before —
I listened for the triumph songs
    That range from shore to shore,
Where the heroes and the conquerors wrought
    The mighty deeds of yore, —
Where the footprints of the martyrs
    Had bathed the earth in gore,
And the war-horns of the warriors
    Were heard from shore to shore.

Their blood on desert plains was shed, —
Their voices on the wind had fled, —
They were the drear and shadowy DEAD!

Still, through the storied past, I sought
An answer to my sleepless thought;
In the cloisters old and hoary
    Of the mediaeval time —
In the rude ancestral story
    Of the ancient Runic rhyme.

<216>

I paused on Grecian plains, to trace
Some remnant of a mightier race,
Serene in sorrow and in strife,
Calm conquerors of Death and Life,
Types of the god-like forms that shone
Upon the sculptured Parthenon.

But still, as when Prometheus bare
   From heaven the fiery dart,
I saw the "vulture passions"[9] tear
   The proud Caucasian[10] heart —
The war of destiny with will
Still conquered, yet conflicting still.

I heard loud Hallelujahs
   From Israel's golden lyre,
And I sought their great Jehovah
   In the cloud and in the fire.
I lingered by the stream that flowed
"Fast by the oracle of God"[11]—
I bowed, its sacred wave to sip —
Its waters fled my thirsting lip.

---

[9] Placing the word "vulture" one line above "Caucasian" suggests the punishment of Prometheus in the mountains of "the Indian Caucasus," in Shelley's *Prometheus Unbound*, but Whitman's choice to place "vulture passions" in quotes leads to other possible sources. In Byron's 1819 *Prophecy of Dante*: "for the mind/ Succumbs to long infection, and despair,/ And vulture Passions flying close behind,/ Await the moment to assail and tear" (Canto III, ll. 172-175). Earlier still, a well-known American political tract by Tunis Wortman elaborates on the self-punishment of evil-doers: "[L]et corroding envy, sickening Jealousy, and vulture passions torture and prey upon my heart." (*Treatise*, p. 171). This in turn may be a paraphrase of lines in Thomas Gray's 1747 poem, "Ode on the Distant Prospect of Eton College": "These shall the fury Passions tear,/ The vultures of the mind." (ll. 61-62) —BR.

[10] *Caucasian heart.* Gustav Klemm, in a work entitled *Allgemeine Culturgeschichte der Menschheit [General Cultural History of Mankind]*, divides the human races into the active and passive: the former (embracing only the so-called Caucasian race) marked by restless activity and aspiration, progress and the spirit of doubt and inquiry; the latter (comprising all the remaining races), by an absence or inferiority of these characteristics — SHW. [Klemm (1802-1867), was an anthropologist and librarian, and his ten-volume production, not surprisingly, classed Germans as the highest type of Caucasians. The "passive" races were Mongoloids, Negroids, Egyptians, Finns, and Hindus. So much for 19th-century anthropology.—BR]

[11] "Fast by the oracle of God." Milton, *Paradise Lost*, I;12.

<217>

The serpent trail was over all
    Its borders — and its palms that threw
Aloft their waving coronal,
    Were blistered by a poison dew.

Serener elements I sought,
Sublimer altitudes of thought,
The truth Saint John and Plato saw,
The mystic light, the inward law;
The Logos ever found and lost,
The aureola of the Ghost.

I hailed its faint auroral beam
In many a Poet's Delphic dream —
On many a shrine where faith's pure flame
Through fable's gorgeous oriel came.

Around the altars of the god,
In holy passion hushed, I trod,
Where one the mighty voice of Jove
Rang through Dodona's haunted grove.[12]
No more the dove with sable plumes
Swept through the forest's gorgeous glooms;
The shrines were desolate and cold,
Their paeans hushed, their story told,
In long, inglorious silence lost,
Like fiery tongues of Pentecost.

No more did music's golden surge
The mortal in immortal merge:
High canticles of joy and praise
Died with the dream of other days;
I only heard the Maenad's wail —
That shriek that made the orient pale:

---

[12] "The priestesses of Dodona assert that two black pigeons flew from Thebes in Egypt; one of which settled in Libya, the other among themselves: which latter, resting on a beech tree, declared with a human voice that here was to be the oracle of Jove."— Herodotus, Book II, ch 55 — SHW.

<218>

Evohe! — ah — Evohe!
The mystic burden of a woe
Whose dark enigma none may know;
The primal curse — the primal throe.[13]

Evohe! — ah — Evohe!
Nature shuddered at the cry
Of that ancient agony!

Still the fabled Python bound me,—
Still the serpent coil inwound me,—
Still I heard the Maenad's cry,
Evohe! — ah — Evohe!

Where the Nile pours his sullen wave
Through tombs and empires of the grave,
I sought, 'mid cenotaphs, to find
The earlier miracles of mind:
Alas, beside the funeral urn
How drearily the death-lights burn;
On dim Denderah's sculptured lore
    How sadly the noonlight falls,
How mournfully the west wind sighs
    Through Karnak's mouldering halls!
No tongue shall tell their wondrous tale,
No hand shall lift the Isis veil;
The mighty pyramids that rise
So drear along the morning skies,
Guard well the secrets of the dead,
Nor break the sleep of ages fled.

---

[13] "The Maenads, in their wild incantations, carried serpents in their hands, and with frantic gestures cried out Eva! Eva! Epiphanius thinks that this invocation related to the mother of mankind; but I am inclined to believe that it was the word Epha or Opha, rendered by the Greeks, Ophis, serpent. I take Abbadon to have been the name of the same ophite God whose worship has so long infected the world. The learned Heinsius makes Abbadon the same as the serpent Python."—Jacob Bryant, *Analysis of Ancient Mythology.* — SHW. [Bryant's speculations may be safely dismissed. His writings from the 1770s are based on the assumption that all mythology is derived from Hebrew Scripture. His work, with elaborate "proofs" employing etymological guesswork influenced William Blake, who had illustrated Bryant's work. —BR].

"While Maenads cry Evoe, Evoe! That voice that is contagion to the world."— Shelley, *Prometheus Unbound* — SHW.

<219>

Their awful shadow passed, I stood
On India's burning solitude;
Where, in the misty morning of the world,
Life lay as in a dream of beauty furled.

I saw the mighty altars of the Sun, —
Before whose fires, the star-gods, one by one,
Paled like thin ghosts, — in lurid splendors rife;
I heard the Persian hail him Lord of Life!
I saw his altar flames rise wild and high,
Veiling the glory of the noon-day sky,
Hiding the holy heavens with their ensanguined dye.

I turned, and from the Brahmin's milder law
I sought truth's mystic element to draw,
Pure as it sparkled in the cup of Heaven, —
The bright Amreeta to the immortals given, —
To bathe my soul in fontal springs, that lie
Veiled from the careless and incurious eye.

Half wakened from the brooding sleep
Of Nature ere she felt the leap
Of sentient life, the Hindoo seemed
Sad as the faith his fathers dreamed;
Like his own rock-hewn temples, wrought
From some obscure and shadowy thought
Of ancient days — some formless dread,
In the gray dawn of ages bred, —
Prone on his native earth reclined,
To endless reveries resigned,
His dull song lapsing on the Lethean stream,
Lost in the dim world of a lotus dream.

<220>

Still, still the eternal mystery
The shadow of the poison-tree
Of Good and Evil haunted me.
In Religion's holy name,
Furies fed her altar-flame,
Sophists gloried in her shame.
Still the ancient mythus bound me,
Still the serpent coil inwound me,
Still I heard the Maenad's cry,
Evohe! — ah — Evohe!

Wearied with man's discordant creed,
I sought on Nature's page to read
Life's history, eye yet she shrined
Her essence in the incarnate mind;
Intent her secret laws to trace
In primal solitudes of space,
From her first, faint atomic throes,
To where her orbèd splendor glows
In the vast, silent spheres that roll
Forever towards their unknown goal.

I turned from dull alchemic lore
With starry Chaldeans to soar,
And sought, on fancy's wing, to roam
    That glorious galaxy of light
Where mingling stars, like drifting foam,
    Melt on the solemn shores of night;
But still the surging glory chased
The dark through night's chaotic waste;
And still, within its deepening voids,
Crumbled the burning asteroids.

Long gloating on that hollow gloom,
Methought that in some vast maelstrom
The stars were hurrying to their doom —
Bubbles upon life's boundless sea,
Swift meteors of eternity,
Pale sparks of mystic fire, that fall
From God's unwaning coronal.

<221>

Is there, I asked, a living woe
In all those burning orbs that glow
Through the blue ether? — do they share
Our dim world's anguish and despair?
In their vast orbits do they fly
From some avenging destiny —
And shall their wild eyes pale beneath
The dread anathema of Death? —
Our own fair earth — shall she too drift,
Forever shrouded in a weft
Of stormy clouds, that surge and swirl
Around her in a dizzy whirl: —
Forever shall a shadow fall
Backward from her golden wall,
Its dark cone stretching, ghast and gray,
Into outer glooms away? —

From the sad, unsated quest
Of knowledge, how I longed to rest
On her green and silent breast!

I languished for the dews of death
    My fevered heart to steep, —
The heavy, honey-dews of death,
    The calm and dreamless sleep.

I left my fruitless lore apart,
And leaned my ear on Nature's heart,
To hear, far from life's busy throng,
The chime of her sweet undersong.

She pressed her balmy lips to mine,
She bathed me in her sylvan springs;
And still, by many a rural shrine,
She taught me sweet and holy things.
I felt her breath my temples fan,
I learned her temperate laws to scan,
My soul, of hers, became a conscious part;
Her beauty melted through my inmost heart.

<222>

Still I languished for the word
    Her sweet lips had never spoken,
Still, from the pale shadow-land,
    There came nor voice nor token;
No accent of the Holy Ghost
Whispered of the loved and lost;
    No bright wanderer came to tell
If, in worlds beyond the grave,
    Life, love, and beauty dwell.

<223>

THE TRAILING ARBUTUS

There's a flower that grows by the greenwood tree,[14]
In its desolate beauty more dear to me,
Than all that bask in the noontide beam
Through the long, bright summer by fount and stream.
Like a pure hope, nursed beneath sorrow's wing,
Its timid buds from the cold moss spring;
Their delicate hues like the pink sea-shell,
Or the shaded blush of the hyacinth's bell;
Their breath more sweet than the faint perfume
That breathes from the bridal orange-bloom.
It is not found by the garden wall,
It wreaths no brow in the festal hall;
But it dwells in the depths of the shadowy wood,
And shines, like a star, in the solitude.
Never did numbers its name prolong,
Ne'er hath it floated on wings of song;
Bard and minstrel have passed it by,
And left it, in silence and shade, to die.
But with joy to its cradle the wild bees come,
And praise its beauty with drony hum;
And children love, in the season of spring,
To watch for its earliest blossoming.

In the dewy morn of an April day,
When the traveler lingers along the way;
When the sod is sprinkled with tender green
Where rivulets water the earth, unseen;
When the floating fringe on the maple's crest
Rivals the tulip's crimson vest,
And the budding leaves of the birch-trees throw
A trembling shade on the turf below;
When my flower awakes from its dreamy rest,
And yields its lips to the sweet southwest,
Then, in those beautiful days of spring,
With hearts as light as the wild bird's wing,

---

[14] *A flower that grows* ... The trailing arbutus or mayflower (*Epigaea repens)*, is a low shrub found especially near oak trees. It is the floral emblem of Massachusetts and of Nova Scotia.

<224>

Flinging their tasks and their toys aside,
Gay little groups through the wood-paths glide,
Peeping and peering among the trees
As they scent its breath on the passing breeze,
Hunting about, among the lichens gray,
And the tangled mosses beside the way,
Till they catch the glance of its quiet eye,
Like light that breaks through a cloudy sky.

For me, sweet blossom, thy tendrils cling
Round my heart of hearts as in childhood's spring;
And they breath, as it floats on the wandering air,
Wakes all the music of memory there,
Thou recallest the time when, a fearless child,
I roved all day through the wood-walks wild,
Seeking thy blossoms by bank and brae,
Wherever the snow-drifts had melted away.

Now as I linger, mid crowds alone,
Haunted by echoes of music flown;
When the shadows deepen around my way,
And the light of reason but leads astray;
When affections, nurtured with fondest care
In the trusting heart, become traitors there;
When, weary of all that the world bestows,
I turn to nature for calm repose,
How fain my spirit, in some far glen,
Would fold her wings 'mid thy flowers again!

<225>

TO THE ANGEL OF DEATH

Thou ancient Mystery! thy solemn night —
    Pierced by attempered rays from that far realm
That lies beyond, dark with excess of light —
    No more the shuddering spirit shall o'erwhelm.

No more thy charnel glooms the soul appall,
    Pale Azrael![15] awful eidolon of Death! —
The dawn-light breaks athwart thy glimmering hall,
    And thy dank vapors own the morning's breath.

Too long the terror of the dread unknown
    Hath the wrung heart with hopeless anguish riven;
The blasting splendors of the fiery throne
    "Burning within the inmost veil of Heaven —"[16]

The gloom of that great glory, which of old
Haunted the vision of the prophet's dream,
When the archangel of the Lord foretold
The day of doom, by dark Hiddekel's stream.[17]

In vain, through lingering years, I turned the page
    Rich with these sacred records of the past,
Hope languished, and no legend could assuage
    The rayless gloom thy awful shadow cast

In dread apocalypse, I saw thee borne
    On the pale steed, triumphant o'er the doomed,
Till the rent Heavens like a scroll were torn,
    And hollow earth her hundred isles entombed.

In vain I questioned the cold stars and kept
    Lone vigils by the grave of buried love,
No angel wing athwart the darkness swept,
    No voice vouchsafed my sorrow to reprove.

[15] Azrael is a Hebrew Angel of Destruction and the Muslim Angel of Death. Azrael is not mentioned in Christian scripture.
[16] Shelley. "Adonais."
[17] *Hiddekel's stream.* The Tigris River.

<226>

Was it the weight of that remorseless woe,
    The lonely anguish of that long despair —
That made thy marble lips at length forego
    Their silence at my soul's unceasing prayer?

Henceforth, the sorrowing heart its pulse shall still
    To solemn cadences of sweet repose,
Content life's mystic passion to fulfil
    In the great calm that from thy promise flows.

Welcome as the white feet of those who bring
    Glad tidings of great joy unto the world,
Shall fall the shadow of thy silver wing
    Over the weary couch of woe unfurled.

A heavenly halo kindles round thy brow;
    Beyond, the palms of Eden softly wave,
Bright messengers athwart the empyrean go,
    And love, to love, makes answer o'er the grave.

<227>

EVENING ON THE BANKS
OF THE MOSHASSUCK

Now to the sessions of sweet, silent thought,
I summon up remembrance of things past.
>—Shakespeare's Sonnets

Again September's golden day,
    Serenely still, intensely bright,
Fades on the umbered hills away,
    And melts into the coming night.
Again Moshassuck's silver tide
Reflects each green herb on its side,
Each tasseled wreath and tangling vine,
Whose tendrils o'er its margin twine.

And standing on its velvet shore,
    Where yester-night, with thee, I stood,
I trace its devious course once more,
    Far winding on, through vale and wood:
Now glimmering through yon golden mist,
By the last, glinting sunbeams kissed;
Now lost, where lengthening shadows fall
From hazel copse and moss-fringed wall.

Near where yon rocks the stream inurn,
    The lonely gentian blossoms still;
Still wave the star-flower and the fern
    O'er the soft outline of the hill;
While, far aloft, where pine-trees throw
Their shade athwart the sunset glow,
Thin vapors cloud the illumined air,
And parting daylight lingers there.

<228>

But ah, no longer thou art near,
　　This varied loveliness to see;
And I, though fondly lingering here,
　　To-night, can only think on thee.
The flowers thy gentle hand caressed
Still lie unwithered on my breast;
And still thy footsteps print the shore,
Where thou and I may rove no more.

Again I hear the murmuring fall
　　Of water from some distant dell;
The beetle's hum, the cricket's call,
　　And, far away, that evening bell.
Again, again, those sounds I hear;
But oh, how desolate and drear
They seem to-night! how like a knell
The music of that evening bell!

Again the new moon in the west,
　　Scarce seen upon yon golden sky,
Hangs o'er the mountain's purple crest,
　　With one pale planet trembling nigh;
And beautiful her pearly light
As when we blessed its beams last night;
But thou art on the far blue sea,
And I can only think on thee.

September, 1839.

<229>

THE PAST

◇————————◇

"So fern, und doch so nah."

— *Goethe.* 18

Thick darkness broodeth o'er the world:
    The raven pinions of the Night,
Close on her silent bosom furled,
    Reflect no gleam of Orient light.
E'en the wild Norland fires[19] that mocked
    The faint bloom of the eastern sky,
Now leave me, in close darkness locked,
    To-night's weird realm of fantasy.

Borne from pale shadow-lands remote,
    A morphean music, wildly sweet,
Seems, on the starless gloom, to float,
    Like the white-pinioned Paraclete.[20]
Softly into my dream it flows,
    Then faints into the silence drear;
While from the hollow dark outgrows
    The phantom Past, pale gliding near.

The visioned Past; so strangely fair!
    So veiled in shadowy, soft regrets.
So steeped in sadness, like the air
    That lingers when the day-star sets!
Ah! could I fold it to my heart,
    On its cold lip my kisses press,
This waste of aching life impart,
    To win it back from nothingness!

---

[18] *So fern* . . . So far, and yet so near. From Goethe's *Faust, Part II.* Lines of Helen of Troy: "Ich fühle mich so fern und doch so nah,/ Und sage nur zu gern: da bin ich! da!"
[19] *Norland fires.* The Northern Lights, or Aurora Borealis. New England experienced intense displays of the Northern Lights in the years 1835 to 1860.
[20] *Paraclete.* The Holy Spirit. Literally, advocate or helper. Whitman also cites this line in her review of Fuller's *Conversations with Goethe.*

<230>

I loathe the purple light of day,
    And shun the morning's golden star,
Beside that shadowy form to stray,
    Forever near, yet oh how far!
Thin as a cloud of summer even,
    All beauty from my gaze it bars;
Shuts out the silver cope of heaven,
    And glooms athwart the dying stars.

Cold, sad, and spectral, by my side,
    It breathes of love's ethereal bloom,
Of bridal memories, long affied
    To the dread silence of the tomb:
Sweet, cloistered memories, that the heart
    Shuts close within its chalice cold;
Faint perfumes, that no more dispart
    From the bruised lily's floral fold.

"My soul is weary of her life;"[21]
    My heart sinks with a slow despair;
The solemn, star-lit hours are rife
    With fantasy; the noontide glare,
And the cool morning, fancy free,
    Are false with shadows; for the day
Brings no blithe sense of verity,
    Nor wins from twilight thoughts away.

Oh, bathe me in the Lethean stream,
    And feed me on the lotus flowers;
Shut out this false, bewildering dream,
    This memory of departed hours!
Sweet haunting dream! so strangely fair
    So veiled in shadowy, soft regrets
So steeped in sadness, like the air
    That lingers when the day-star sets!

---

[21] *My soul is weary of her life.* Job 10:1.

<231>

The Future can no charm confer,
    My heart's deep solitudes to break;
No angel's foot again shall stir
    The waters of that silent lake.
I wander in pale dreams away,
    And shun the morning's golden star,
To follow still that failing ray,
    Forever near, yet oh how far!

February, 1846.

<232>

A NIGHT IN AUGUST

◇────────────────◇

"And thenceforth all that once was fair
Grew fairer."[22]

How softly comes the summer wind
   At evening o'er the hill,
Forever murmuring of thee
   When busy crowds are still;
The way-side flowers seem to guess
And whisper of my happiness.

The jasmine twines her snowy stars
   Into a fairer wreath;
The lily lifts her proud tiárs
   More royally beneath;
The snow-drop with her fairy bells,
In silver time, the story tells.

Through all the dusk and dewy hours,
   The banded stars above
Are singing, in their airy towers,
   The melodies of love;
And clouds of shadowy silver fly
All night, like doves, athwart the sky.

Fair Dian[23] lulls the throbbing stars
   Into Elysian dream;
And, rippling through my lattice bars,[24]
Her brooding glory streams
Around me, like the golden shower
That rained through Danäe's[25] guarded tower.

------

22 *And thenceforth all that once was fair/ Grew fairer.* From J.M. Legare, "A May Morn."
23 *Fair Dian.* Diana as moon-goddess.
24 *Lattice bars.* Probably the lattice-work of the rose-trellis at Whitman's Benefit Street home.
25 Danäe, princess of Argos, was locked in a tower to prevent her from marrying or producing a child. Zeus impregnates her as a rain-shower. Depicted in Ovid's *Metamorphoses*.

<233>

And when the waning moon doth glide
    Into the valleys gray;
When, like the music of a dream,
    The night-wind dies away;
When all the way-side flowers have furled
Their wings, with morning dews impearled,

A low, bewildering melody
    Seems murmuring in my ear, —
Tones such as the twilight wood
    The aspen thrills to hear,
When Faunus[26] slumbers on the hill,
And all the entrancèd boughs are still.

August, 1848

---

[26] Faunus, horned fertility god, also associated with Pan.

<234>

THE LAST FLOWERS

◇————————————◇

The undying voice of that dead time,
With its interminable chime,
Rings on my spirit like a knell.[27]

Dost thou remember that Autumnal day
    When by the Seekonk's[28] lonely wave we stood,
And marked the languor of repose that lay,
    Softer than sleep, on valley, wave and wood?

A trance of holy sadness seemed to lull
    The charmèd earth and circumambient air,
And the low murmur of the leaves seemed full
    Of a resigned and passionless despair.

Though the warm breath of Summer lingered still
    In the lone paths where late her footsteps passed,
The pallid star-flowers[29] on the purple hill
    Sighed dreamily "We are the last! the last!"

I stood beside thee, and a dream of heaven
    Around me like a golden halo fell!
Then the bright veil of phantasy was riven,
    And my lips murmured "Fare thee well! — farewell!"

I dared not listen to thy words, nor turn
    To meet the mystic language of thine eyes,
I only *felt* their power, and in the urn
    Of memory, treasured their sweet rhapsodies.

---

[27] Poe. "Tamerlane," ll. 22-24.
[28] Seekonk. Providence's main river, which runs along Swan Point Cemetery to downtown Providence and its harbor at the top of Narragansett Bay.
[29] *Star-flower*. An annual herb, *Borago officinalis,* usually with blue or pink flowers (but sometimes white). Pliny believed that the leaves were used in nepenthe, the elixir of forgetfulness. It has been used medicinally and as a garnish for drinks.

<235>

We parted then, forever — and the hours
    Of that bright day were gathered to the past —
But, through long, wintry nights, I heard the flowers
    Sigh dreamily, "We are the last! — the last!"

September, 1849.

<236>

THE PHANTOM VOICE

"*It is a phantom voice:*
Again!—again! how solemnly it falls
Into my heart of hearts!" — Poe, Scenes from *Politian*.

Through the solemn hush of midnight,
    How sadly on my ear,
Falls the echo of a harp whose tones
    I never more may hear!

A wild, unearthly melody,
    Whose monotone doth move,
The saddest, sweetest cadences
    Of sorrow and of love:

Till the burden of remembrance weighs
    Like lead upon my heart,
And the shadow, on my soul that sleeps,
    Will never more depart.

The ghastly moonlight, gliding
    Like a phantom through the gloom,
How it fills with solemn fantasies
    My solitary room!

And the sighing winds of Autumn,
    Ah! how sadly they repeat
That low, bewildering melody,
    So mystically sweet!

I hear it softly murmuring
    At midnight o'er the hill,
Or across the wide savannas,
    When all beside is still.

<237>

I hear it in the moaning
    Of the melancholy main;
In the rushing of the night-wind,
    The rhythm of the rain.

E'en the wild-flowers of the forest,
    Waving sadly to and fro,
But whisper to my boding heart,
    The burden of its woe.

And the spectral moon, now paling
    And fading, seems to say
"I leave thee to remembrances
    That will not pass away."

Ah, through all the solemn midnight,
    How mournful 'tis to hark
To the voices of the Silence,
    The whisper of the dark!

In vain I turn, some solace
    From the distant stars to crave:
They are shining on thy sepulchre,
    Are smiling on thy grave.

How I weary of their splendor!
    All night long, they seem to say,
"We are lonely — sad and lonely —
    Far away — far, far away!"

Thus, through all the solemn midnight,
    That phantom voice I hear;
As it echoes through the silence,
    When no earthly sound is near.

<238>

And though dawn-light yields to noon-light,
    And though darkness turns to day,
They but leave me to remembrances
    That will not pass away.

November, 1849

A NOVEMBER LANDSCAPE

How like a rich and gorgeous picture hung
In memory's storied hall seems that fair scene
O'er which long years their mellowing tints have flung!
The way-side flowers had faded one by one,
Hoar were the hills, the meadows drear and dun,
When homeward wending, 'neath the dusky screen
Of the autumnal woods, at close of day,
As o'er a pine-clad height my pathway lay,
Lo! at a sudden turn, the vale below
Lay far outspread, all flushed with purple light;
Gray rocks and umbered woods gave back the glow
Of the last day-beams, fading into night;
While down a glen where dark Moshassuck[30] flows,
With all its kindling lamps the distant city rose.

---

[30] Moshassuck, a river that begins in Lincoln, RI and ends in downtown Providence. During the Industrial Revolution, the river provided power to mills and connected to a canal. Even in Whitman's time the river was heavily polluted and blamed for cholera epidemics. Parts of it are now only a narrow ditch, and its silted lower waters were paved over in the 1960s. In the 1990s, the river was re-exposed in downtown Providence at Waterplace Park.

<239>

ARCTURUS, WRITTEN IN OCTOBER

"Our star looks through the storm."

Star of resplendent front! thy glorious eye
Shines on me still from out yon clouded sky, —
Shines on me through the horrors of a night
More drear than ever fell o'er day so bright, —
Shines till the envious Serpent slinks away,
And pales and trembles at thy steadfast ray.

Hast thou not stooped from heaven, fair star! to be
So near me in this hour of agony? —
So near, — so bright, — so glorious, that I seem
To lie entranced as in some wondrous dream, —
All earthly joys forgot, — all earthly fear,
Purged in the light of thy resplendent sphere:
Kindling within my soul a pure desire
To blend with thine its incandescent fire, —
To lose my very life in thine, and be
Soul of thy soul through all eternity.

1849.

<240>

RESURGEMUS

◇——————————◇

I mourn thee not: no words can tell
    The solemn calm that tranced my breast
When first I knew thy soul had past
    From earth to its eternal rest;

For doubt and darkness, o'er thy head,
    Forever waved their Condor wings;
And in their murky shadows bred
    Forms of unutterable things;

And all around thy silent hearth,
    The glory that once blushed and bloomed
Was but a dim-remembered dream
    Of "the old time entombed."[31]

Those melancholy eyes that seemed
    To look beyond all time, or, turned
On eyes they loved, so softly beamed,
    How few their mystic language learned.

How few could read their depths, or know
    The proud, high heart that dwelt alone
In gorgeous palaces of woe,
    Like Eblis on his burning throne.[32]

For ah! no human heart could brook
    The darkness of thy doom to share,
And not a living eye could look
    Unscathed upon thy dread despair.

I mourn thee not: life had no lore
    Thy soul in morphean dews to steep,
Love's lost nepenthe[33] to restore,
    Or bid the avenging sorrow sleep.

---

[31] *Old time entombed* . . . From Poe's "The Haunted Palace."
[32] The Hall of Eblis, from William Beckford's *Vathek* (1786).
[33] *Nepenthe*. A mythical elixir of forgetfulness.

<241>

Yet, while the night of life shall last,
    While the slow stars above me roll,
In the heart's solitudes I keep
    A solemn vigil for thy soul.

I tread dim cloistral aisles, where all
    Beneath are solemn-sounding graves;
While o'er the oriel, like a pall,
    A dark, funereal shadow waves.

There, kneeling by a lampless shrine,
    Alone amid a place of tombs,
My erring spirit pleads for thine
    Till light along the Orient blooms.

Oh, when thy faults are all forgiven,
    The vigil of my life outwrought,
In some calm altitude of heaven, —
    The dream of thy prophetic thought, —

Forever near thee, soul in soul,
    Near thee forever, yet how far,
May our lives reach love's perfect goal
    In the high order of thy star!

<242>

THE ROUT OF THE CHILDREN

FROM THE FRENCH OF VICTOR HUGO.

Little darlings, return to my desolate room!
Since I drove you away, it is mantled in gloom; —
Since I drove you away, with rude, menacing words; —
What harm had you done me, you dear little birds?
Little rosy-lipped bandits; — what mischief had hatched?
What gem from my casket of minerals snatched?—
What old, gothic missal, enriched by your hands,
With fantastic designs, you mischievous brigands?
Ah, none: you but stopped in my study a minute,
To plunder my desk of some papers within it —
Some manuscript verses devoted to Fame;
Which you threw in the fire, and fanned to a flame;
On the tissue of tinder all blackened and charred,
With wandering fire-sparks brilliantly starred,
To see, as you said, how the folks, one by one,
Go out of the church when the meeting is done.
Then, muttering vengeance, in menacing tone,
I shouted, "Begone imps, and leave me alone!
You have burnt up my verses, entitled 'To Fame:'
I shall die, and the world never hear of my name."

Great loss then, indeed! and great cause for dismay, —
A strophe, ill-born in the noise of your play!
Great Bobadil verses that puffed as they went,
And swaggered their impotent meanings to vent;
And long alexandrines, entangling their feet
Like a pack of rude school-boys, let loose in the street.
You did but redeem from a fate more obscure,
The rhyme that some newspaper waited to lure
To that cavernous cell, called the poet's own nook,
Where no reader of newspapers pauses to look.
For *this* have I raved! Ah, I blush to recall
How I sat, with my chair leaning back to the wall,

<243>

Still muttering vengeance, in menacing tone,
And repeating "Begone imps, and leave me alone!"

Alone! fine result, and great triumph! alone!
Forgotten — forlorn, like a toad in a stone!
And here have you left me — my eye on the door,
Grave, haughty, severe, — but you mind me no more;
For without you have found all you sought to obtain —
All the freedom, that here, you had sighed for in vain —
The fresh air, the streamlet that runs through the grass,
Where you fling in sweet blossoms and leaves as you pass;
The breezes, the flowers, the perfumes divine —
Ah, this poem of God is far better than mine!
You may pluck out the leaves of his book without fear,
Nor tremble the voice of the tyrant to hear: —
His roses and pinks you may rifle all day,
Nor regret the dull room whence I drove you away.
As for me, all the joy of my day has departed;
I sit in my chair — half asleep, heavy hearted,
While old Doctor Ennui, a Londoner, born
Of fogs and the Thames on a December morn,
Who waited to enter 'till you had gone out;
Has moped in my study all day in a pout,
And, usurping your corner, sits grouty and grim,
He gaping at me, and I gaping at him.

The pages I turned with such zeal to explore,
The books and the manuscripts please me no more:
I miss, o'er my shoulder, the sweet, peering face,
I miss the small finger to point out the place,
The nudge of the elbow, the sly little kiss,
The brow full of candor, that always said "yes,"
The great eyes of wonder, the frolicksome screams,
The sweet humming voices that lapt me in dreams.

<244>

Return little birds! — since I drove you away
I have lost all the sunshine and bloom of my day.
Take my tea-cups, enameled with butterflies wings —
All my Dresden and Sevres and beautiful things: —
You may twirl the round globe, the big map may unroll,
And sketch out new countries with crayon and coal.
My pictures and statues are waiting for you —
My vases of jasper and bright or-molu:[34]
Of my corals and shells you may gather your fill,
    And my malachite tables may mount at your will.
Your whooping and hiding — to all I agree;
    Your trooping and training are music to me.
Like heroes, returned from some great battle ground,
You may drag my old arm-chair in triumph around:
My great, painted Bible may turn o'er and o'er —
That book you ne'er touched but with terror before —
Where you see on the page, in fine colors displayed,
Dieu le pere, in an emperor's habit arrayed![35]
Then return, little doves! to my desolate room;
Since I drove you away, it is mantled in gloom; —
Oh return! you may ransack, and rifle, and reign,
    So you will but forgive me, and love me again.

---

[34] *Or-molu*. Ormolu, a process for gilding over bronze, for stands, handles, and other mounts for porcelain.
[35] *Dieu le pere*. God the father.

<245>

SHAKESPEARE HALL, 1838

Willard, in his *History of the Providence Stage*, gives the date of the opening of Shakespeare Hall as October 29, 1838. The theater is described thus: "The principal external decoration was a medallion bust of Shakespeare. The interior was beautifully decorated by accomplished artists; the ceiling representing a dome with a sun in the center, surrounded by the signs of the zodiac in gold ... The fronts of the boxes were exquisitely painted in panels. The auditorium contained, besides a pit, two tiers of boxes and a gallery of semi-circular form, and could seat about thirteen hundred spectators. The act-drop represented a moonlight view of the Capitol in Washington. The entire cost of the theater was twenty thousand dollars.

"An elegant prologue, written by Mrs. Sarah H. Whitman, was recited by Mrs. Maeder. The following lines heralding the advent of the drama, were enthusiastically received:"[36]

And now she comes with all her shadowy train
To hold her court within this gorgeous fane —
Here her bright banner fearlessly unfurls,
And scorns the pointless shaft the bigot hurls —
Pure are her means, her high intents sublime,
To cherish virtue and deter from crime.
With loftiest theme to rouse the languid heart,
And stern reproof with subtle grace impart;
To wake the noble love of well-earned fame,
And teach the glory of a deathless name.
She shows how heroes lived and martyrs died,
And fills the exulting breast with god-like pride,
That such high energies to man are given
To conquer earth, and ope the gate of Heaven.

---

[36] Willard, pp. 130-131.

<246>

THE DRAMA

◇——————————◇

SPOKEN AT THE OPENING OF THE THEATRE
IN PROVIDENCE, NOVEMBER 27, 1838.[37]

What new enchantment hovers in the air?
Soft music breathes and festal torches glare;
A roseate light illumes the storied wall,
And youth and beauty throng the lofty hall.

Lo, where the Drama, through the shades of night.
Bursts in soft splendor on the ravished sight;
Here lurks Thalia[38] with bewildering glance,
In the gay masque of Folly or Romance;

There proud Melpomene,[39] in pall and plume,
Trails her imperial purples through the gloom.
Immortal sisters in Art's fairy train,
Long lost, long mourned, resume your genial reign!

Can we forget when first in childhood's hour,
Our footsteps sought your vision-haunted bower?
When trembling, wondering 'mid the enraptured throng,
We quaffed the tide of eloquence and song;

While, stood revealed, the creatures of our dream,
Bright, breathing, palpable I scarce could we deem
   That earth confessed such beauty; — to abide
With these were life — vain shadows all beside.

O cold the hearts that from such witching sway
Could turn unmoved and passionless away.
Yet, though less genial prove our sordid age
To Art's bright reign than when the Grecian stage

---

37 Willard gives the date as October 29.
38 *Thalia.* The Muse of Comedy.
39 *Melpomene.* The Muse of Tragedy.

<247>

Enthroned the Drama's triumph and her pride,
To sacred rights and royal deeds allied;
When priests and scholars sought her scenic halls
And conquering heroes gathered to her walls,

While the vast area of her temples saw
Tumultuous Athens hushed in breathless awe;
Still do her structures rise, her altars blaze
Where late the savage tracked the pathless maze;

By many a stormy river of the West,
By many a lake that stays its mountain guest,
Far through the wild her festal notes are borne
Ere fade the echoes of the huntsman's horn.

Oft when the wint'ry storms shall hurtle round,
Or silent snow-flakes print the frozen ground;
When the cold rain comes. rattling on the blast,
And mantling clouds night's blazing host o'ercast,

Here shall we sit, in this enchanted hall,
Where breathing thoughts and burning words enthral,
Regardless of the cold world's sordid strife,
And all the hollow mimicries of life,

Where vainer actors idler pageants play,
    And wear their masks in the broad eye of day.
Here shall we see again, with martial stalk,
'The buried majesty of Denmark'[40] walk;

Macbeth shall shudder at the ghost of crime,
Nor spoil, for us, 'the pleasure of the time.'[41]
Here fair Hermione,[42] long tranced to stone —
Fixed like a statue on her marble throne

---

[40] *The buried majesty of Denmark.* In Shakespeare's *Hamlet,* I.1, l. 46: "In which the majesty of buried Denmark".
[41] *Macbeth,* III:4, l. 97.
[42] Hermione, heroine of Shakespeare's *The Winter's Tale.*

<248>

Descending from her pedestal; shall move
And breathe and tremble at the voice of love.
Here royal Katherine, love's sweet claim denied,
Shall plead the rights of an imperial bride;[43]

And with such haughty eloquence inspire,
'Our drops of tears shall turn to sparks of fire.'[44]
Manhood shall here cast off earth's coiling care,
And weary Age remember life was fair;

Entranced and spell-bound by her potent sway
Who 'calls each slumbering passion into play'[45]—
Exulting, trembling, as her accents flow
In varying strains of triumph or of woe —

Now decked in smiles, and now her brow o'erfraught
With the pale cast of melancholy thought.
Far through the twilight vistas of the past,
Where gathering years their cloudy mantles cast,

Oft turns her eagle eye, and, at its glance,
The shadows vanish from that drear expanse —
Lo, at her gaze, night melteth into day,
    And the dark mist of ages rolls away!

She hath 'called spirits from the vasty deep,'[46]
Roused kings and heroes from their dreamless sleep,
Restored the scenes of a chivalrous age
Where knightly forms heroic conflicts wage; —

---

[43] Katherine. Katherine of Aragon in Shakespeare's *All Is True (Henry VIII)*,
II:4.
[44] *Our drops of tears . . . Ibid*, II:4, ll. 70-71, "my drops of tears/ I'll turn to sparks
of fire."
[45] Thomas Campbell. *The Pleasures of Hope*. l. 26.
[46] Glendower, in *Henry IV, Part 1*, III:1, l. 51: "I can call spirits from the vasty
deep."

<249>

The victor's triumph on the ensanguined field,
The plume, the pennon, and the blazoned shield;
Bade the dead lover's clay-cold bosom glow,
And the slain warrior meet once more his foe;

And caused them, for a night, on earth to roam,
Then pass like spectres to their silent home.
And now she comes with all her shadowy train
To hold her court within this gorgeous fare;

Here her bright banner fearlessly unfurls,
Nor heeds the pointless shaft the bigot hurls.
She comes in living beauty to restore
The wondrous deeds of legendary lore,

Or, in light vaudevilles and comic mimes,
To paint 'the form and pressure of the times;'[47]
With lofty themes to rouse the languid heart,
Or stern reproof with subtle grace impart,—

To wake the noble love of well-earned fame
And teach the glory of a deathless name.
She shows how heroes lived and martyrs died,
In life dishonored and in death denied,

Yet nerved the powers of death and hell to scorn
When holy Honor sounds her bugle horn.
Such themes new vigor to the heart supply,
    Flush every cheek and light up every eye.

Whether in gorgeous drapery she is seen,
Moving before us like an empire's queen —
Or clothed in all the majesty of woe,
Bids beauty's tears like molten diamonds glow —

_____

[47] *The form and pressure of the times . . . Hamlet,* III:2, ll. 21-22. "[to show] the very age of body of the time his form and pressure."

<250>

Or wreathed in smiles, with soft, seducing glance,
Makes the warm life-blood through the pulses dance —
Still, ever beautiful, she meets the sight,
Taking all shapes to furnish new delight,

Forever changing, yet forever true
To one, fond aim — approving smiles from *you*.
Long may those smiles our virgin temple grace,
And Shakespeare's spirit hallow all the place.

<251>

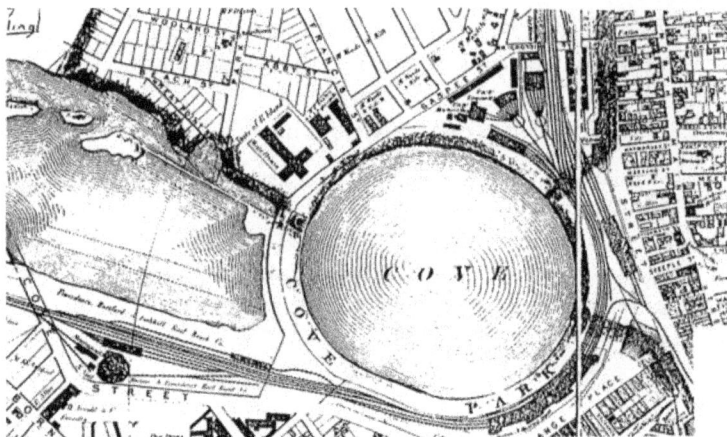
The Cove in downtown Providence, 1857.

ROGER WILLIAMS

WRITTEN FOR THE FIRST ANNUAL CELEBRATION
OF THE RHODE ISLAND HISTORICAL SOCIETY,
JANUARY 13, 1847.

Now, while the echoing cannon's roar
    Rocks our far frontal towers,
And bugle blast and trumpet's blare
    Float o'er the "Land of Flowers;"

While our bold eagle spreads his wing
    No more in lofty pride,
But sorrowing sinks, as if from Heaven
    The ensanguined field to hide;

<252>

Turn we from war's bewildering blaze,[48]
    And conquest's choral song,
To the still voice of other days,
    Long heard, — forgotten long.

Listen to his rich words, intoned
    To songs of lofty cheer,
Who in the howling wilderness,
    Mid forests wild and drear;

Breathed not of exile nor of wrong;
    Through the long winter nights,
But uttered in exulting song,
    The soul's unchartered rights.

Who sought the oracles of God
    In the heart's veiled shrine,
Nor asked the monarch nor the priest,
    His sacred laws to sign.

The brave, high heart that would not yield
    Its liberty of thought,
Far o'er the melancholy main,
    Through bitter trials brought;

But, to a double exile doomed,
    By Faith's pure guidance led —
Through the dark labyrinth of life,
    Held fast her golden thread.

Listen! The music of his dream
    Perchance may linger still
In the old familiar places
    Beneath the emerald hill.

---

[48] These opening stanzas seem to be about the 1841-42 Dorr Rebellion, still a touchy subject in 1847. Thomas Dorr, the governor elected on the suffrage ticket, repudiated, tried for treason and imprisoned, had been, ironically, Treasurer of the Rhode Island Historical Society, and had lived in a mansion on Providence's fashionable Benefit Street.

<253>

The wave-worn rock still breasts the storm
    On Seekonk's lonely side,
Where the dusky natives[49] hailed the bark
    That bore their gentle guide.[50]

The Spring that gushed amid the wild
    In music on his ear,
Still pours its waters, undefiled,
    The fainting heart to cheer.[51]

And the fair cove,[52] that slept so calm
    Beneath o'ershadowing hills,
And bore the exile's evening psalm
    Far up its flowery rills —

The wave that parted to receive
    The pilgrim's light canoe,
As if an angel's balmy wing
    Had stirred its waters blue —

What though the fire-winged courser's breath
    Has swept its cooling tide,
And fast before its withering blast,
    The rushing wave has dried,[53]

Still, narrowed to our crowded mart —
    A fair enchanted mere —
In the proud city's throbbing heart
    It sleeps serene and clear.

---

[49] Narragansett Indians who greeted Williams and helped him find a locale for settling, which would become the city of Providence.
[50] The Roger Williams landing place of 1636 is marked with a monument on Gano Street in Providence, near the Seekonk River.
[51] The Roger Williams spring is in the Roger Williams National Memorial in downtown Providence.
[52] The natural cove where Providence was established was gradually hemmed in by railroad tracks, and the Cove finally vanished. During its heydey it was a handsome artificial lake; in its decline it was probably quite noxious.
[53] Changes to the Cove to accommodate railroads were underway when this poem was written, and the work was finished in 1849. For a history of the changes to the Cove, see Holleran, "Filling the Providence Cove."

<254>

Or turn we to the green hill's side;
    There, with, the spring-time showers,
The white-thorn, o'er a nameless grave,
    Rains its pale, silver flowers.

Yet memory lingers with the past,
    Nor vainly seeks to trace
His foot-prints on a rock, whence time
    Nor tempests can efface;

Whereon he planted, fast and deep,
    The roof-tree of a home
Wide as the wings of Love may sweep,
    Free as her thoughts may roam;

Where, through all time, the saints may dwell,
    And from pure fountains draw
That peace which passeth human thought,
    In Liberty and Law.

When heavenward, up the silver stair
    Of silence drawn, we tread
The visioned mount that looks beyond
    The Valley of the Dead, —

Oh, may we gather to our hearts
    The deeds our fathers wrought,
And feed the perfumed lamp of love
    In the cool air of thought:

While HOPE shall on her ANCHOR lean,[54]
    May Memory fondly turn
To wreath the amaranth and the palm
    Around their funeral urn.

---

[54] The word "Hope" and the image of an anchor appear in Rhode Island's state motto.

<255>

LINES WRITTEN IN NOVEMBER

Farewell the forest shade, the twilight grove,
The turfy path with fern and flowers inwove,
Where through long summer days I wandered far,
Till warned of Evening by her folding star.
No more I linger by the fountain's play,
Where arching boughs shut out the sultry ray,
Making at noontide hours a dewy gloom
O'er the moist marge, where weeds and wild flowers bloom;
Till, from the western sun, a glancing flood
Of arrowy radiance filled the twilight wood,
Glinting athwart each leafy, verdant fold,
And flecking all the turf with drops of gold.

Sweet sang the wild bird on the waving bough
Where cold November winds are wailing now;
The chirp of insects on the sunny lea,
And the low, drowsy bugle of the bee,
Are silent all; closed is their vesper lay,
Borne by the breeze of Autumn far away.
Yet still the withered heath I love to rove,
The bare, brown meadow, and the leafless grove;
Still love to tread the bleak hill's rocky side,
Where nodding asters wave in purple pride,
Or, from its summit, listen to the flow
Of the dark waters, booming far below.
Still through the tangling, pathless copse I stray,
Where sere and rustling leaves obstruct the way,
To find the last, pale blossom of the year,
That strangely blooms when all is dark and drear:
The wild witch-hazel,[55] fraught with mystic power
To ban or bless, as sorcery rules the hour.
Then, homeward wending, through the dusky vale,
Where winding rills their evening damps exhale,
Pause by the dark pool, in whose sleeping wave
Pale Dian loves her golden locks to lave;

---

[55] The witch-hazel tree blossoms at unexpected times, more typically in
February, preceding all other spring blossoms. The blossoms, containing an oil
that resists freezing, can be seen even after a snowstorm.

<256>

As when she stole upon Endymion's rest,
And his young dreams with heavenly beauty blest.
And thou, "stern ruler of the inverted year,"[56]
Cold, cheerless Winter, hath thy wild career
No sweet, peculiar pleasures for the heart,
That can ideal worth to rudest forms impart?
When, through thy long, dark nights, cold sleet and rain
Patter and plash against the frosty pane,
Warm curtained from the storm, I love to lie,
Wakeful, and listening to the lullaby
Of fitful winds, that as they rise and fall
Send hollow murmurs through the echoing hall.
Oft, by the blazing hearth at even-tide,
I love to see the fitful shadows glide,
In flickering motion, o'er the illumined wall,
Till slumber's honey-dew my senses thrall;
Then, while in dreamy consciousness, I lie
Twixt sleep and waking, fairy fantasy
Culls, from the golden past, a treasured store,
And weaves a dream so sweet, hope could not ask for more.
In the cold splendor of a frosty night,
When blazing stars burn with intenser light
Through the blue vault of heaven; when the keen air
Sculptures in bolder lines the uplands bare;
When sleeps the shrouded earth, in solemn trance,
Beneath the wan moon's melancholy glance;
I love to mark earth's sister planets rise,
And in pale beauty tread the midnight skies;
Where, like lone pilgrims, constant as the night,
They fill their dark urns from the fount of light.
    I love the Borealis flames that fly,
Fitful and wild, athwart the northern sky;
The storied constellations, like a page
Fraught with the wonders of a former age,
Where monsters grim, Gorgons, and Hydras rise,
And "gods and heroes blaze along the skies."[57]

---

[56] *Stern ruler* . . . From the "Winter" section of Thomson's *The Seasons*.
[57] *Gods and heroes* . . . From William Hamilton Drummond. *The Giant's Causeway* (1811): "Lions and Centaurs, Gorgons, Hydras, rise,/ And gods and heroes blaze along the skies."

<257>

Thus Nature's music, various as the hour,
Solemn or sweet, hath ever mystic power
Still to preserve the unperverted heart
Awake to love and beauty; to impart
Treasures of thought and feeling, pure and deep,
That aid the doubting soul its heavenward course to keep.

OUR ISLAND OF DREAMS

*"By the foam
Of perilous seas, in faery lands forlorn."* —Keats.[58]

Tell him I lingered alone on the shore,
Where we parted, in sorrow, to meet never more;
The night wind blew cold on my desolate heart,[59]
But colder those wild words of doom, "Ye must part?"
O'er the dark, heaving waters, I sent forth a cry;
Save the wail of those waters there came no reply.

I longed, like a bird, o'er the billows to flee,
From our lone island home and the moan of the sea:
Away far away from the wild ocean shore,
Where the waves ever murmur, "No more, never more;"

Where I wake, in the wild noon of midnight, to hear
That lone song of the surges, so mournful and drear.
When the clouds that now veil from us heaven's fair light,
Their soft, silver lining turn forth on the night;
When time shall the vapors of falsehood dispel,
He shall know if I loved him; but never how well.

1849.

---

[58] Keats. "Ode to a Nightingale," ll. 69-70.
[59] Whitman suggested that this line, and some of the images of this poem, may have influenced Poe in his "Annabel Lee."

<258>

SONNETS

I.

To ———[60]

Vainly my heart had with thy sorceries striven:
It had no refuge from thy love, — no Heaven
But in thy fatal presence; — from afar
It owned thy power and trembled like a star
O'erfraught with light and splendor. Could I deem
How dark a shadow should obscure its beam? —
Could I believe that pain could ever dwell
Where thy bright presence cast its blissful spell?
Thou wert my proud palladium; — could I fear
The avenging Destinies when thou wert near? —
Thou wert my Destiny; — thy song, thy fame,
The wild enchantments clustering round thy name,
Were my soul's heritage, its royal dower;
Its glory and its kingdom and its power!

---

[60] The subject of these six sonnets is obviously Edgar Allan Poe.

<259>

II.

When first I looked into thy glorious eyes,
    And saw, with their unearthly beauty pained,
Heaven deepening within heaven, like the skies
    Of autumn nights without a shadow stained,
I stood as one whom some strange dream enthralls;
    For, far away, in some lost life divine,
Some land which every glorious dream recalls,
    A spirit looked on me with eyes like thine.
E'en now, though death has veiled their starry light,
And closed their lids in his relentless night —
As some strange dream, remembered in a dream,
Again I see, in sleep, their tender beam;
Unfading hopes their cloudless azure fill,
Heaven deepening within heaven, serene and still.

III.

Oft since thine earthly eyes have closed on mine,
    Our souls, dim-wandering in the hall of dreams,
Hold mystic converse on the life divine,
    By the still music of immortal streams;
And oft thy spirit tells how souls, affied
    By sovran destinies, no more can part, —
How death and hell are powerless to divide
    Souls whose deep lives lie folded heart in heart.
And if, at times, some lingering shadow lies
    Heavy upon my path, some haunting dread,
Then do I point thee to the harmonies
    Of those calm heights whereto our souls arise
Through suffering, — the faith that doth approve
In death the deathless power and divine life of love.

<260>

IV.

We met beneath September's gorgeous beams:
    Long in my house of life thy star had reigned;
Its mournful splendor trembled through my dreams,
    Nor with the night's phantasmal glories waned.
We wandered thoughtfully o'er golden meads
    To a lone woodland, lit by starry flowers,
Where a wild, solitary pathway leads
    Through mouldering sepulchres and cypress bowers.
A dreamy sadness filled the autumnal air; —
    By a low, nameless grave I stood beside thee,
My heart according to thy murmured prayer
    The full, sweet answers that my lips denied thee.
O mournful faith, on that dread altar sealed —
Sad dawn of love in realms of death revealed!

V.

On our lone pathway bloomed no earthly hopes: —
    Sorrow and death were near us, as we stood
Where the dim forest, from the upland slopes,
    Swept darkly to the sea. The enchanted wood
Thrilled, as by some foreboding terror stirred;
    And as the waves broke on the lonely shore,
In their low monotone, methought I heard
    A solemn voice that sighed, "Ye meet no more."
There, while the level sunbeams seemed to burn
    Through the long aisles of red, autumnal gloom, —
Where stately, storied cenotaphs inurn
    Sweet human hopes, too fair on Earth to bloom, —
Was the bud reaped, whose petals, pure and cold,
Sleep on my heart till Heaven the flower unfold.

<261>

VI.

If thy sad heart, pining for human love,
    In its earth solitude grew dark with fear,
Lest the high Sun of Heaven itself should prove
    Powerless to save from that phantasmal sphere
Wherein thy spirit wandered — if the flowers
    That pressed around thy feet, seemed but to bloom
In lone Gethsemanes, through starless hours,
    When all, who loved, had left thee to thy doom: —
Oh, yet believe, that, in that hollow vale,
    Where thy soul lingers, waiting to attain
So much of Heaven's sweet grace as shall avail
    To lift its burden of remorseful pain, —
My soul shall meet thee and its Heaven forego
Till God's great love, on both, one hope, one Heaven bestow.

<262>

ARCTURUS, WRITTEN IN APRIL

"Nec morti esse locum, sed viva volare
Sideris in numerum atque alto succedere coelo."
— Virgil, *Georgics*, IV. [61]

Again, imperial star! thy mystic beams
Pour their wild splendors on my waking dreams,
Piercing the blue depths of the vernal night
With opal shafts and flames of ruby light;
Filling the air with melodies, that come
Mournful and sweet, from the dark, sapphire dome, —
Weird sounds, that make the cheek with wonder pale,
As their wild symphonies o'ersweep the gale.
For, in that gorgeous world, I fondly deem,
Dwells the freed soul of one whose earthly dream
Was full of beauty, majesty and woe;
One who, in that pure realm of thine, doth grow
Into a power serene, a solemn joy,
Undimmed by earthly sorrow or alloy;
Sphered far above the dread, phantasmal gloom,
The penal tortures of that living tomb
Wherein his earth-life languished; who shall tell
The drear enchantments of that Dantean hell!

---

[61] "For there is no place of annihilation: but above, they mount up each into his own order of star, and take their high seat in the heavens." Virgil. *Georgics*, Book IV.

<263>

"Was it not Fate, whose earthly name is Sorrow,"[62]
That bade him, with prophetic soul, to borrow
From all the stars that fleck night's purple dome,
Thee, bright Arcturus! for his Eden home:
Was it not Fate, whose name in Heaven above,
Is Truth and Goodness and unchanging Love,
Was it not Fate, that bade him turn to thee
As the bright regent of his destiny?
For when thine orb passed from the lengthening gloom
Of autumn nights, a morning-star to bloom
Beside Aurora's eastern gates of pearl,
He passed from earth, his weary wings to furl
In the cool vales of Heaven: thence, through yon sea
Of starry isles, to hold his course to thee.

Now, when in April's cloudless nights, I turn
To where thy pharos[63] mid the stars doth burn,
A glorious cynosure, I read in thee
The rune of Virgil's golden augury;[64]
And deem that o'er thy seas of silver calm
Floats the far perfume of the Eden palm.

April, 1850.

---

[62] *Was it not Fate* ... From Poe's "To Helen."
[63] Pharos. Lighthouse, as in the great Pharos lighthouse in Alexandria. Since Arcturus, one of the brightest stars in the sky, is also used for navigation, the lighthouse metaphor is apt.
[64] As quoted in the poem's epigraph.

LEONORA

◇———————◇

FROM THE GERMAN OF BÜRGER.[65]

From heavy dreams, sad Leonore
    Rose with the dawning day;
Her heart oppressed by boding fears
    At Wilhelm's long delay.
With Frederic's force her soldier went
    To meet his country's foe;[66]
And since, no tidings had he sent
    To tell of weal or woe.

The king and the proud empress-queen,[67]
    Weary of endless war,
At length renounce their fruitless strife
    And welcome peace once more.
The weary, toil-worn warriors come,
    Rejoicing on their way;
With blare of trump and beat of drum,
    In oaken garlands gay.

And every way-side, every path,
    Is thronged with eager feet,
Of friends and kindred, hurrying forth
    The coming host to meet.
The lover greets his plighted bride;
    But ah! for poor Leonore,
No greeting to her pallid lips
    Shall bring the roses more.

---

[65] Gottfried August Bürger (1747-1794) was credited with creating the entire genre of the Romantic German ballad. "Leonore" or "Leonora," based on the English ballad, "Sweet William's Ghost," was the most famous ballad poem in Europe in the late 1700s. It was translated or adapted into English by William Taylor of Norwich, Sir Walter Scott, Matthew Gregory Lewis, and by numerous anonymous translators.

[66] The poem is set in Prague during the Seven Years' War (1756-1763). (The famous English translation by William Taylor of Norwich moves it back to the time of the Crusade of Richard I of England in 1190.) "Frederic" in this version is the Prussian king Frederick the Great.

[67] Austrian Empress Maria Theresa.

<265>

She wandered up and down the road,
    To frantic fears a prey,
And vainly questioned all that came,
    Throughout that weary day;
The army now had all passed by!
    She tore her raven hair,
She threw herself upon the earth,
    In desolate despair.

The mother folds her to her heart,
    And seeks with counsels vain
Some word of comfort to impart
    To soothe her darling's pain.
"Oh mother, what is lost is lost!
    Now Earth and Heaven may go.
There is no pitying God in Heaven —
    No love for aught below."

"Peace, peace! who know the Father's love,
    Knows he can aid impart; —
The blessed sacrament shall soothe
    Thy pierced and bleeding heart." —
"No balm upon this burning heart
    The sacrament can pour!
No sacrament to love and life
    The cold, cold dead restore.

"Oh mother, would my lamp of life
    Would sink in endless night!
How shall I loathe the midnight gloom
    And loathe the morning light!
And what, to me, is Heaven's bliss.
    And what, to me, is Hell;
With him, with him is happiness,
    And oh, without him, Hell!"

<266>

"Perchance, dear child, he loves no more,
    And wandering far and wide,
Hath sought, upon a foreign shore,
    To wed a foreign bride." —
"Oh mother, what is lost is lost!
    There is no pitying love —
No joy in life, no balm in death —
    No hope in Heaven above.

"Go out, life's light, — forever out;
    Die, die, in night and dread!
There is no pitying God in Heaven;
    Would, would that I were dead!"
Thus raged the frenzy of despair
    Within her burning brain —
Thus with God's righteous providence
    She strove in anguish vain.

She beat her breast and tore her hair
    Till the long day was done, —
Till in the West the silent stars
    Came twinkling one by one.
She sat within her lonely room,
    Nor marked the dying day,
Till the moon's light, o'er tower and height,
    In silver glory lay.

When lo! she hears a courser's hoofs
    Ring on the frozen ground:
A knight alights before the gate —
    His clanging arms resound.
And hark! a low and soft *"kling ling"*
    Sounds through the silent room![68]
And hark! a well known voice she hears
    Beside her in the gloom!

---

[68] This made a bit more sense in the 1839 original published in *The Knickerbocker*: "And now the portal bell doth ring,/ Its soft alarum, "Kling, ling, ling;'"

<267>

"What ho! Leonore: unbar the door;
    Art watching or asleep?
Doth my fair bride forget her vows,
    Or fear her vows to keep?" —
"Ah Wilhelm, thou! so late at night?
    Oh, I have watched and wept;
What from thy Leonora's side
    So long her love hath kept!"

"From far Hungarian fields I come
    On my lone midnight ride,
To bear thee to thy distant home;
    Away, away my bride!" —
"The wind blows through the hawthorn bush;
    In whistles loud and shrill;
Come in, and warm thee in my arms;
    Ah! why so cold and still?" —

"Let the wind through the hawthorn blow,
    Or howl across the mere;
The black horse paws, and clank the spurs,
    I dare not linger here.
Come, don thy snow-white robes with speed,
    And swiftly mount behind;
We ride a hundred leagues ere day,
    Our bridal bed to find!"

"And must we ride a hundred leagues
    To reach our bridal bower?
Hark! even now, the booming bell
    Tolls out the midnight hour." —
"Ha! dost thou fear? the moon shines clear;
    Soon will our course be sped!
I bear thee to our bridal home
    And to our bridal bed." —

<268>

"Ah! tell me where the bridal hall,
　　And where the couch is spread?" —
"Far, far from here; cold, narrow, drear,
　　Lies our low marriage bed!" —
"Hast room for me?" — "For thee and me;
　　Come, busk thee, darling bride;
The wedding guests are waiting,
　　The door stands open wide."

The maiden donned her bridal robes;
　　On the black steed she sprung,
And round the knight her snowy arms
　　In trembling silence flung.
And on they gallop, fast and far,
　　Nor mount nor stream their course can bar;
While horse and rider pant and blow;
　　The fire-sparks flashing as they go.

The crags shoot by, — the castles fly, —
　　The rattling hoofs resound;
The bridges thunder 'neath their tread,
　　And rings the hollow ground.
"Ha! doth my Leonora fear
　　With her true love to ride?
The midnight moon shines cold and clear
　　The dead ride swift, my bride!"

Hark! wailings float upon the air,
　　And hollow dirges ring!
Why tolls the bell that solemn knell,
　　Why flaps the raven's wing?
Lo, sweeping o'er the lonely moor,
　　A dark funereal train!
They chant a requiem o'er the bier,
　　A hoarse, sepulchral strain."

<269>

"Bury your dead when midnight's past,
    With wild lament and prayer;
To-night I wed a fearless bride,
    Our banquet ye shall share.
Come, priest and choir, and mourners all,
    Come, crone the marriage song;
Come, priest, and bless the bridal bed,
    And join the merry throng."

Now fades into the dusky air
    The coffin and the pall;
They sweep along, a ghostly throng,
    The mourners, priest, and all;
And faster, faster, still they speed,
    O'er wild morass and moonlight mead,
While horse and rider pant and blow,
    The fire sparks flashing as they go!

How swiftly, on the right and left,
    The mountains hurry by;
How swiftly, on the right and left,
    Town, tower, and forest fly!
"Doth my love fear? the moon shines clear;
Ah ha! dost fear the dead?
    The dead ride swift, — hurrah! hurrah!"[69] —
"Ah, speak not of the dead!"

Now, where the moonbeams faintly fall,
    Yon frantic rabble see;
How fearfully they wheel and spin,
    Beneath the gallows-tree!
"Halloo, halloo! ye grisly crew,
    Come here, and follow me;
Around us prance a fetter-dance,[70]
    And quit the gallows-tree."

---

[69] In Whitman's 1839 version, a more emphatic "huzza! huza!" is used.
[70] If the "rabble" consists of hanged men dangling from the gallows tree, their legs may still have been fettered with iron shackles.

<270>

And now, across the moonlit waste,
    They hurry on behind;
A sound like dry and withered leaves,
    Low rustling in the wind.
And onward, onward still they speed,
    Nor rock nor stock their course impede;
While horse and rider pant and blow,
    The fire-sparks flashing as they go!

Fast flies the quiet moonlight scene,
    Fast, fast and far, it flies;
Fast fly the fleecy clouds above,
    And fast the starry skies.
"Ah! dost thou fear? — the moon shines clear;
    And fast the dead can ride." —
"Oh, name the dead no more!" — "Ah, ha!
    Dost fear the dead, my bride?

"Methinks I smell the morning air,
    And hark! the cock doth crow!
Then onward speed, my trusty steed!
    Haste, haste! our sands run low.
Our race is run, our course is done,
    And we are at the goal;
Swift ride the dead, — hurrah, hurrah!
    Come, priest, bind soul to soul!"

Up to a gloomy portal now,
    With slackened rein they ride;
When lo! the massive bar and bolt
    Back from their staples glide.
And as the dark and sounding door
    Upon its hinges turns,
She sees, in the moon's glimmering light,
    Gray tombs and moldering urns.

<271>

Suddenly, from the rider's form,
  By some unearthly spell,
The welded armor, piece by piece,
  In shivered fragments fell.
She sees a hideous skeleton,
  A ghastly Horror, stand
Before her glazing eyes revealed, —
  An hour-glass in his hand.

High reared the fiery, frantic steed,
  And trembled with affright;
Then sank into the yawning earth,
  And vanished from her sight!
Wild howlings echoed through the air,
  And from the graves beneath;
While Leonora's throbbing heart
  Trembled 'twixt life and death.

Now round her, in the pallid light,
  The wheeling spectres fly,
And, as they vanish from her sight,
  In hollow murmurs cry:
"Repent; nor doubt the Father's love;
  Submit to Heaven's control:
We yield thy body to the earth:
  May God receive thy soul."

<272>

FROM GOETHE'S FAUST

◇————————————————◇

PART SECOND.
SCENE AT THE COURT OF THE EMPEROR.

MEPHISTOPHELES.
It seems that everywhere on this dull earth
Something is lacking; — *here* of gold is dearth.
'T is true we cannot sweep it from the floor,
But wisdom can unfathomed depths explore.
In mountain clefts and dungeons manifold,
Are piles of minted and unminted gold,
And I, by spiritual force and trust
In mighty nature, can obtain the dust.

CHANCELLOR.
Nature and spirit! — never Christian spake
Such words as these. We burn men at the stake
For such profanities. Foul words and evil!
Nature means sin, and spirit means the Devil;
And, between both, is nursed the abortive brood
Whose monster heresies mankind delude.

MEPHISTOPHELES.
By this I see what wiseacres ye are;
What ye can handle not seems miles afar:
What ye can grasp not is an empty shade;
What ye divine not must all search evade:
That which ye have not poised in weight is stinted,
And no coin current save what ye have minted.

<273>

THE LOST CHURCH

FROM THE GERMAN OF UHLAND.

In yonder dim and pathless wood
    Strange sounds are heard at twilight hour,
And peals of solemn music swell,
    As from some minster's[71] lofty tower.
From age to age those sounds are heard,
    Borne on the breeze at twilight hour;
From age to age, no foot hath found
    A pathway to the minster's tower.

Late, wandering in that ancient wood,
    As onward through the gloom I trod,
From all the woes and wrongs of earth
    My soul ascended to its God.
When lo! in the hushed wilderness
    I heard, far off, that solemn bell:
Still heavenward as my spirit soared,
    Wilder and sweeter rang the knell.

While thus in holy musings rapt,
    My mind from outward sense withdrawn,
Some power had caught me from the earth,
    And far into the heavens upborne —
Methought a hundred years had passed,
    In mystic visions as I lay,
When suddenly the parting clouds
    Seemed opening wide and far away.

No midday sun its glory shed, —
    The stars were shrouded from my sight, —
And lo! majestic o'er my head,
    A minster shone in solemn light.
High through the lurid heavens it seemed
    Aloft, on cloudy wings, to rise,
Till all its pointed turrets gleamed,
    Far flaming, through the vaulted skies;

---

[71] *Minster.* The church of a monastery.

<274>

The bell, with full, resounding peal,
    Rang booming through the rocking tower:
No hand had stirred its iron tongue,
    Slow swaying to the storm-wind's power.
My bosom beating like a bark
    Dashed by the surging ocean's foam,
I trod, with faltering, fearful joy,
    The mazes of the mighty dome.

A soft light through the oriel streamed,
    Like summer moonlight's golden gloom;
Far through the dusky arches gleamed,
    And filled with glory all the room.
Pale sculptures of the sainted dead
    Seemed waking from their icy thrall,
And many a glory-circled head
    Smiled sadly from the storied wall.

Low at the altar's foot I knelt,
    Transfixed with awe, and dumb with dread,
For blazoned on the vaulted roof
    Were heaven's fiercest glories spread.
Yet when I raised my eyes once more,
    The vaulted roof itself was gone;
Wide open was heaven's lofty door,
    And every cloudy veil withdrawn!

What visions burst upon my soul —
    What joys unutterable there,
In waves on waves, forever roll
    Like music through the pulseless air —
These never mortal tongue may tell:
    Let him who fain would prove their power
Pause when he hears that solemn knell
    Float on the breeze at twilight hour.

<275>

THE DYING HEROES

◇————————————————◇

FROM THE GERMAN OF UHLAND.[72]

The valiant Danes drive back the Swedish host
In wild confusion to the northern coast;
The sounding chariots clash, — the bright swords gleam,
The broad, round shields flash back the moon's cold beam;
On the red corse-field, mid the fierce affray,
Lies the young Sven and Ulf the warrior gray.

SVEN.
Alas! my father, in the power and bloom
Of life, grim Norna[73] calls me to the tomb:
In vain my mother, from the oaken bough,
Weaves a bright garland for her warrior's brow; —
From her high tower my Edith looks in vain
To see my chariot in the victor's train.

ULF.
In the gray night for thee her tears shall fall,
Till visioned sleep thine image shall recall;
Yet mourn not thus: the path which thou hast led,
Though dark the way, she will not fear to tread;
Soon shall she, smiling through her golden hair,
For thee at Odin's feast the bowl prepare.

SVEN.
No more the solemn chant my voice shall raise
Amid our warrior youth on festal days;
The deeds of kings and heroes sing no more;
Their conquering arms, their fates in love and war;
Through my neglected harp the wind shall sigh,
And wake low dirges as it wanders by.

---

[72] Johann Ludwig Uhland (1787-1862), from his earliest poem, "Die sterbenden Helden" (1804). In the German original, the speakers are simply "Father" and "Son," and Whitman's "Edith" is an unnamed woman.
[73] *Norna.* Norse goddess of Fate.

<276>

ULF.

High towers above us, like an eagle's nest,
The bright Valhalla of our fathers' rest;
The stars roll under it, and, far below,
Red meteors gleam and fiery comets glow; —
There, at the solemn feast, we meet again;
Lift up thy song to a triumphal strain![74]

SVEN.

Ah, heavy doom! thus from the bright world torn, —
From life and love in youth's unhonored morn;
While yet no proud deed of the battle-field —
No trophied arms, are sculptured on my shield:
Twelve fearful judges[75] sit enthroned on high;
How shall I shrink before each awful eye!

ULF.

One lofty deed their favor shall secure, —
One deed whose rays no shadow can obscure;
Pours not thy young heart, on this barren strand,
Its life-blood freely for our fatherland?
And see! our foemen yield: — the clouds are riven!
There lies our pathway to the halls of Heaven![76]

---

[74] In the 1839 original published in *The Knickerbocker*, titled "The Dying
Hero," Whitman wrote: "There shall we share with them the solemn feast;/
There raise they voice; on earth thy song has ceased."
[75] The twelve judges of Odin, who dwell in Gladheim.
[76] In the 1839 original, Whitman wrote: "See! Our foes yield! — now lift thy
languid eye —/ There lies our pathway, through yon radiant sky." The revision
doubtless avoided having the word "eye" as a rhyme in two successive stanzas,
but the original seems more powerful by its avoidance of the non-Norse
"heaven." On the other hand, Uhland does use the word "Himmel."

<277>

APPENDIX A
Spiritualism
On A Picnic, 1855

◆———————————————◆

New York Daily Times, September 12, 1855

SPIRITUALISM WENT TO Flushing yesterday, and enjoyed what they call, in Camp Meeting, a refreshing season. It went in three steamboats, or rather it was conveyed in three separate parcels, by one. The first parcel, or that portion of Spiritualism that gets out of bed first in the morning, was taken on board the Island City at 8 A. M., and by the aid of a train of cars, deposited within one mile of a certain spirit-haunted woods, in the western part of the good old town of Flushing, on Long Island. The second parcel, with numerous baskets of food, succeeded in getting on board the ten o'clock boat. The third got its clothes on and appeared in full feather just in time for the 12 P. M. trip. The whole comprised some three hundred persons. There was no extraordinary occurrence on the way to the wood, except that a horse ran away from near Winfield, at sight of the second installment of the company. This was the first undeniable evidence of the presence of spirits. Ever since Tam O'Shanter's gray mare Meg lost her tail by the hand of a witch,[77] all horses have had an excusable horror of the disembodied. They always run fast when they come near, and it was noticed that the horse yesterday kept its tail well down.

For some time after arriving on the ground, appearances were similar to those of ordinary pic-nic parties, but at about 12 o'clock a circle was formed and sundry severe twitchings of the arms and legs of several members informed us that there was a terrible struggle going on between the affected persons and stray spirits that were endeavoring to obtain control over them. A very powerful spirit wrestled with a young man, who resisted bravely, but after a rough and tumble of five minutes the spirit gave him a sudden trip-and-twitch, and down he went. He was vanquished. Considerable money changed hands outside the circle, when the result was announced. Another spirit took a fancy to the left leg of a lad, who appeared to be about 18 years of age. He danced on his remaining leg to the amusement of the undeveloped. But, while he was engaged at his single-toe-jig, there came a second spirit, more vicious than the first, and pulled vigorously at the right side of his mouth, causing him to show his teeth, in a very disagreeable manner. He held out stoutly against both of them, and finally they gave up the fight. The lad

---

[77] From the famous supernatural poem by Robert Burns, "Tam O'Shanter."

<278>

straightened his leg, adjusted his mouth, and triumphed. A very feeble attack was now made upon two females, but the hour for dining having arrived, the spirits retired in a most gentlemanly style, and the party dined. Our reporter had secured an introduction to the prettiest lady present, consequently we find nothing in his notes under head of dinner, except — good strong tea — taper fingers — two large cups — pretty song — three sandwiches — fine voice — encore.

After dinner, Mr. [Henry] SMITH, the gentleman who, when in the razor-strop line, always had one more left of the same sort, got upon a stump and announced in his peculiar way, that he had something of great importance to impart to all present. Having said this much he awaited the effect, and then proposed a collection for the benefit of the colored man who had brought water for making the tea, and furnished planks for seats. Mr. SMITH went into the merits of the colored man extensively, repeating them every time he received a sixpence with untiring industry.

Mr. SMITH was followed by Prof. [Samuel Byron] BRITTAN, who in a very pleasing speech, introduced Prof. FOWLER, of Poughkeepsie, as a gentleman who would entertain the audience with a logical disquisition on the great subject in which millions are now interested.

Mr. FOWLER mounted a table, and after stating that if any one expected anything extraordinary from him, he would be disappointed, spoke with much eloquence on the wonderful power of the human mind. He did not attempt an explanation of the alleged discoveries of the spiritualists, but rather left it to be inferred that as they were yet beyond human comprehension, explanation was not yet to be expected. After we could account satisfactorily for dreams — tell how it is that when the mortal part is slumbering, the mind wanders toward and converses with old and far distant friends and even forms new acquaintances — how it revels in strange pleasures, sees sights never seen before, and enjoys sensations that are new, we might think of arriving at some solution of the mysteries of spiritualism.

He was followed by Mr. BRITTAN, who spoke in the same strain, and was equally well received.

Mr. [Russell Perkins] AMBLER was next introduced, and, professedly, under spiritual influence, recited a poem, the chief merits of which were sound and gesticulation. There were several others who addressed the audience, but the above were the most important.

<279>

A LARGE CIRCLE WAS now formed, and all prepared for interesting manifestations. Nearly seventy persons joined the circle, and the developed mediums present were requested to take a position inside. Some eight or ten entered, among them Mr. SMITH, before mentioned as having become notorious in the razor-strop line. Mr. SMITH made a very sensible speech, in which he claimed that as those within the circle were honest, respectable persons, they would not behave in a ridiculous manner, if they could help it. He then behaved very strangely, to say the least. He crooked his shoulders, as if he thought he had a bag of shavings on his back; screwed up his face to the sticking point and in a loud yet familiar voice, declared he had a letter which he wished some one to read for him, as he could not read a word himself. A very bold lady, with some wildness of eye, asked, as she swept the sky with her right hand, if the letter was in an unknown tongue.

Mr. SMITH, still maintaining the bag of shavings position, thought that was the most ridiculous question he ever heard. How the deuce could tell whether it was in an unknown tongue or not, when he could not read any tongue. He held up both hands, as if the letter were there; several persons outside the circle promised to read the document, if he would hand it over, but instead of doing that he pitched into the entire party on account of its ignorance, not excepting even the developed mediums. Spiritualism was literally up a stump. Here was an imaginary letter to be read, and no one equal to the task. Mr. SMITH, strange though it may seem, rejoiced exceedingly.

Spiritualism was in a quandary. At length Mr. [Pascal Beverly] RANDOLPH came forward, and in a few minutes was sufficiently under the influence to read the troublesome document. Mr. RANDOLPH is, perhaps, the best developed medium in this country. The letter was from a person now in the other world, who, when a child in this, was very beautiful, but had a very bad heart. He had done about all the evil possible, and died. The letter was warning to Mr. SMITH not to follow in his footsteps.

Mr. RANDOLPH was so much exhausted by his efforts that he was for a considerable time afterwards not able to stand. As soon as he left the circle, he who had previously been vanquished by a spirit, tried to break down a young tree but, failing in that, he commenced dancing around it in such a manner that the reputation of his dancing master was in great peril.

Several mediums now went about wildly, uttering short sentences, and throwing their arms about as loosely as if they were superannuated pump-handles.

<280>

HOW LONG THEY would have continued there is no knowing, had not the spirit of Paddy Somebody entered a down town clerk, who was at a distance, and, in a rich Irish brogue drawn off the spectators. Paddy is as quare a boy in the spirit as he was in the flesh. He gave a very bad report of the whereabouts of the spirit of his priest, illustrated spiritual progression through the spheres by a dark hole with no light in it, which he performed with a small gimbal, and finally made light of.

When Paddy's medium jumped off the table, the spirit of Paddy did not resent the affront, and the assembly moved to where a man without his coat was getting himself in a sweat over the withered arm of a lady. He tried to restore it whole as the other, but did not succeed.

It was now nearly time for the late home-train; and spiritualism, delighted with the way in which it had spent the day, packed up its tea kettles and other dishes, and proceeded homeward. Private circles will be continued as normal in New-York and Brooklyn.

<281>

BIBLIOGRAPHY

Adams, George. *The Rhode Island Register for the Year 1856*. Vol. 2. 1856. Providence: Gladding & Brother; George Whitney.

Alcott, A. Bronson. *Tablets*. 1868. Boston: Roberts Brothers.

Austin, John O. "One Line of the Power Family." *Narragansett Historical Register*. January 1889 (pp. 17-23). [Monograph of the same title at Rhode Island Historical Society Library genealogy collection is actually a reprint of this article.]

Austin, Sarah. *Characteristics of Goethe*. 1833. London: Effingham Wilson. 3 vols. [Translations from Falk, Müller and others.]

Bailey, Philip James. *Festus*. 1839. London: William Pickering. Fifth edition, 1852.

Baker, Noelle A. *Sarah Helen Whitman's Literary Criticism: A Critical Edition*. Dissertation. 1999. Georgia State University.

Barrett [Browning], Elizabeth. Letter to Edgar A. Poe. April 1846. "Poe in New York: Selections from the Correspondence of Edgar Allan Poe." Edited by George Woodberry. *The Century Illustrated Monthly Magazine*. Vol. 48, 1894 (pp. 854-56).

———. *The Poetical Works of Elizabeth Barrett Browning*. "From the Last London Edition." 1870. New York: T.Y. Crowell & Co. [Includes "A Vision of Poets" and "A Drama of Exile"].

Bayle, Peter [Pierre]. "Evil (Origin of)." *An Historical and Critical Dictionary*. Vol. 2. 1695-97. London: Hunt and Clarke. 1826 (pp. 52-81).

Bayne, Peter. *Essays in Biography and Criticism*. First series. 1857. Boston: Gould and Lincoln. 1867.

Bean, Judith Mattson. "Margaret Fuller's (Unsuccessful) Plan for Papers on Literature and Art." *ANQ: A Quarterly Journal of Short Articles, Notes and Reviews*. Vol. 14 No. 2, Spring 2001 (pp. 26-31).

Beckford, William. [Vathek,] *An Arabian Tale, From An Unpublished Manuscript*. 1786. London: J. Johnson.

Benton, Richard P. "Friends and Enemies: Women in the Life of Edgar Allan Poe" in *Myths and Reality*. 1987. Baltimore: The Edgar Allan Poe Society.

Berkeley, George. *The Works of George Berkeley, D.D.* Edited by Alexander Campbell Fraser. 1871. Oxford: Clarendon Press. 4 vols. [Vol. 1 includes the 1710 essay "A Treatise Concerning the Principles of Human Knowledge."]

Betham, William. *Etruria-Celtica: Etruscan Literature and Antiquities Investigated*. 1842. Dublin: Philip Dixon Hardy and Sons. 2 vols.

<283>

Bhagavat-Geeta, or Dialogues of Krishna and Arjoon. Translated by Charles Wilkins. 1849. Bangalore: Wesleyan Mission Press.

Bhagvat-Geeta, or Dialogues of Krééshna and Arjóón. Translated by Charles Wilkins. 1785. London: East India Company.

Blake, William. *Jerusalem: The Emanation of the Giant Albion.* 1804. London: Wiliam Blake.

Bowen, Francis. "Review of Vestiges." [Unsigned review.] *North American Review.* Vol. 60, April 1845 (pp. 426-478).

Bowen, Richard LeBaron. *Index to the Early Records of the Town of Providence, Volumes I-XXI.* 1949. Providence: Rhode Island Historical Society. [Includes references to the Power family.]

Boyd, A.K.H. ["K.P.I."] "Edgar A Poe." *Fraser's Magazine.* Vol. 55, June 1857. London: John W. Parker and Son (pp. 684-700).

Browne, Thomas. *Religio Medici.* 1643. London: The Clarendon Press. 1909. Accessible on line at: penelope.uchicago.edu/relmed/relmed.html

Brownson, Orestes. "A Discourse on the Transient and Permanent in Christianity." [Book review of sermon by Theodore Parker]. *The Boston Quarterly Review.* Vol. 4, No. 16, October 1841 (pp. 436-474).

————. "Charles Elwood; or the Infidel Converted." [Book review and essay.] *Boston Quarterly Review.* Vol. 5, April 1842 (pp. 129-182).

Bryant, Jacob. *A New System, or An Analysis of Antient Mythology.* 1774-1776. London: F. Payne. 3 vols. [Third edition in 6 vols in 1807, London: J. Walker et al.]

Bucke, Richard Maurice. *Walt Whitman.* 1884. Glasgow: Wilson & McCormick. [Includes the 1866 pamphlet by William D. O'Connor, "The Good Gray Poet," and an 1883 letter by O'Connor.]

Bulwer-Lytton, Edward. "A Brief Sketch of the Life of Schiller." *The Poems and Ballads of Schiller.* 1843. Leipzig: Bernhard Taupnitz. 1844.

————. *England and the English.* 1833. London: Richard Bentley.

Burke, J. Bernard. *Anecdotes of the Aristocracy, and Episodes in Ancestral Story.* 1849. London: Henry Colburn. 2 vols. ["The Poers or Powers of Waterford"].

Byron, George Gordon. *The Works of Lord Byron, Including the Suppressed Poems.* 1826. Paris: A. and W. Galignani.

"The Byron Scandal." [Unsigned.] *New-York Tribune,* August 18, 1869, p. 2. First of a series of articles and notices, including "The Byron Slander," by R. Shelton Mackenzie, August 21, p. 5; "The Byron Scandal: The Separation" [Unsigned], August 23, p. 2; "Mrs. Stowe's 'True Story of Lady Byron's Life': An Author's View of It" [Unsigned], August 27, p. 6; "Another Version of the Story"

<284>

[Unsigned], August 27, p. 6; "Great Britain: The Byron Scandal" [Unsigned], September 7, p. 1; "The Byron Story" by B. F. Butler, September 7, p. 5; "Literary Items: Mrs. Stowe Met With Tender Treatment" [Unsigned], September 8, p. 6.

Campbell, Thomas. *The Pleasures of Hope, With Other Poems*. 1800. New York: John Furman.

Capron, E.W. *Modern Spiritualism: Its Facts and Fanaticisms, Its Consistencies and Contradictions*. 1855. Boston: Bela Marsh.

Carlyle, Thomas. "Characteristics." *Critical and Miscellaneous Essays*. 1845. Philadelphia: Carey & Hart (pp. 296-310). [Reprinted from *Edinburgh Review*, No. 103, 1831].

———. "Diderot." *Critical and Miscellaneous Essays*, Vol. 3. 1899. London: Chapman and Hall. [Reprinted from *Foreign Quarterly Review*, No. 22, 1833].

———. "Goethe's *Faust*." [Unsigned review.] *New Edinburgh Review*. Vol. 2 No 4, April 1822 (pp. 316-334)

———. "Jean Paul Friedrich Richter." *Critical and Miscellaneous Essays*. 1845. Philadelphia: Carey & Hart (pp. 7-15). [Reprinted from *Edinburgh Review*, 1827).

———. "Novalis." *Critical and Miscellaneous Essays*. 1845. Philadelphia: Carey & Hart (pp. 167-186). [Reprinted from *Foreign Review*, No. 7, 1829).

———. "Preface." *Essays by R. W. Emerson*. 1841. London: James Fraser.

———. "State of German Literature." *Critical and Miscellaneous Essays*. Vol. 1. 1838. Boston: James Munroe & Company (pp. 28-94). [Reprinted from *Edinburgh Review*, No. 92. 1827].

Chambers, Robert. *Vestiges of the Natural History of Creation*. 1844. New York: Wiley and Putnam. 1845.

Channing, William Ellery. *The Works of William E. Channing, D.D.* 1899. Boston: American Unitarian Association. [Includes The Franklin Lecture, "Self-Culture" from September 1838, pp. 12-36.]

Channing, William Henry. "Call of the Present, No. 3 — Oneness of God and Man." *The Present*. Vol 1, No. 5, December 15 1843 (pp. 145-155).

"Characteristics of Goethe." [Unsigned book review]. *Edinburgh Review*. Vol. 62, July 1833 (pp. 371-403).

Chaucer, Geoffrey. *The Riverside Chaucer*. Edited by Larry D. Benson. Third Edition. 1987. Boston: Houghton Mifflin.

Coleridge, Samuel Taylor. *The Complete Works of Samuel Taylor Coleridge*. 1853. New York: Harper and Brothers. 1884. 7 vols. [Volume 4 includes the "Notes on Othello" (pp. 177-185)].

<285>

———. *Coleridge's Poetry and Prose*. 2004. New York: W.W. Norton.

Conrad, Susan P. *Perish the Thought: Intellectual Women in Romantic America 1830-1860*. 1976. New York: Oxford Univ. Press

Daniel, John Moncure. "Edgar Allan Poe." *Southern Literary Messenger.* Vol. 16 No. 3, March 1850 (pp. 172-187).

Davidson, James Wood. "Edgar A. Poe." *Russell's Magazine*. Vol. 2 No 2, November 1857 (pp. 161-173).

Deffand, Marquise. *Letters of the Marquise du Deffand to the Hon. Horace Walpole (1766-1780), to Which Are Added Letters of Madame du Deffand to Voltaire (1759-1775)*. 1810. London: Longman, Hurst, Rees, and Orne.

Diderot, Denis. *Encyclopédie ou Dictionnaire Raisonné des Science, des Arts et des Métiers*. Vol. 11. 1782. Lausanne: Sociétés Typographiques.

"A Discourse on Goethe and the Germans." [Unsigned article]. *Blackwood's Magazine,* Vol 45, 1838 (pp. 247-256).

Drummond, William Hamilton. *The Giants' Causeway*. 1811. Belfast: Joseph Smyth.

Dwight, John S. [editor and translator]. *Select Minor Poems, Translated from the German of Goethe and Schiller*. 1839. Boston: Hillard, Gray and Company.

Eckermann, Johann Peter. *Conversations with Goethe*. Translated by Gisela C. O'Brien. 1964. New York: Frederick Ungar Publishing. Milestones of Thought in the History of Ideas. [Selections, with introduction and index by Hans Kohn.]

———. *Conversations with Goethe In the Last Years of His Life*. Translated by S. M. Fuller. 1839. Boston: Hilliard, Gray, and Company. [First English-language translation of this work.]

——— and Frédéric Soret. *Conversations of Goethe with Eckermann and Soret*. Translated by John Oxenford. 1847. London: George Bell & Sons. 1875 new edition.

"Edgar Allan Poe." [Unsigned review of *The Works of Edgar Allan Poe*, edited by John Ingram.] *British Quarterly Review*. Vol. 62, July 1875 (pp. 89-101).

"The Editor's Chair." *Harper's New Monthly Magazine*. Vol XIII, No 73. June 1856 [Criticism of Poe's "The Bells" and "The Raven."]

Emerson, Ralph Waldo. *An Address Delivered Before the Senior Class in Divinity College, Cambridge, Sunday Evening, July 15, 1838*. 1838. Boston: James Munro and Company.

———. *The Early Poems of Ralph Waldo Emerson*. 1899. New York: Thomas Y. Crowell.

<286>

———. *Essays, Second Series.* 1844.

———. *Nature.* 1836. Boston: James Munroe and Company.

"Emerson *Essays.*" [Unsigned book review]. *Athenaeum,* No 730, October 23 1841 (pp. 803-804).

"Emerson *Essays.*" [Unsigned book review.] *New York Review.* Vol. 8, April 1841 (pp. 509-512).

Ennemoser, Joseph. *The History of Magic.* Translated by William Howitt. 1854. London: Henry G. Bohn. 2 vols.

Euripides. *The Bacchae,* in *Ten Plays.* Translated by Paul Roche. 1998 New York: Signet Classics.

Exley, Thomas. *Principles of Natural Philosophy: Or, A New Theory of Physics.* 1829. London: Longman, Rees, Orme, Brown, and Green.

Fairfield, Francis Gerry. "A Mad Man of Letters." *Scribner's Monthly,* October 1875 (pp. 690-699).

———. "A New Solution to an Old Puzzle." *Scribner's Monthly,* Vol. 9, Part 1 Jan 1875 (pp. 333-342); Part 2 Feb 1875 (pp. 483-488).

———. "Dream Life and Day Life." *Poems by Henry Sylvester Cornwell, Francis Gerry Fairfield, Luther Granger Riggs, and Ruth G.D. Havens.* 1875. West Meriden CT: Luther G. Riggs and Company (pp. 167-68).

Falk, Johannes Daniel. *Goethe aus näherem persönlichen Umgange dargestellt.* 1832. Leipzig: F.A. Brockhaus.

———. "Goethe, Pourtrayed from Familiar Personal Intercourse." Translated by Sarah Austin. *Characteristics of Goethe.* 1833. London: Effingham Wilson.

"Faust: A Dramatic Poem by Goethe." [Unsigned book review of Hayward's prose translation]. *Edinburgh Review.* Vol 62, April 1833 (pp. 107-143).

Fénelon, François. *Maximes des Saintes sur la Vie Intérieur.* 1697. Paris: Bloud. 1911

Field, Edward. *State of Rhode Island and Providence Plantations at the End of the Century: A History.* 1902. Boston: Mason Publishing Company. [Includes lengthy chapters on the history of printing, newspapers, and libraries in Rhode Island.]

Fontenelle, Bernard Le Bovier. *Dialogues of the Dead.* 1653. Translated by John Hughes. Dublin: R. Reilly. Third edition, 1735.

Fuller, Margaret. "Present State of German Literature." [Book review.] *The American Monthly Magazine.* New Series Vol 2, July 1836 (pp. 1-13).

<287>

Fuller, Margaret. "Review of Emerson's Essays" [Second Series]. *The New York Tribune*. December 1 1844.

Gardiner, Alonzo. *How to Draw a Map*. London: Hughes & Co. 6th revised ed, 1879.

Gibbon, Edward. *The Decline and Fall of the Roman Empire*. 1776-1788. New York: Modern Library. n.d. 3 vols.

Gilchrist, William. *Life of William Blake, With Selections from His Poems and Other Writings*. 1863. London: Macmillan and Co. 2nd edition, 1880. 2 vols.

Gilfillan, George. *A Third Gallery of Portraits*. 1854. New York: Sheldon, Lampoert and Blakeman. 1860.

Goethe, Johann Wolfgang. *The Autobiography of Goethe: Truth and Poetry, From My Own Life*. Volume 1. Translated by John Oxenford. London: George Bell and Sons. 1891.

———. *The Autobiography of Goethe: Truth and Poetry, From My Own Life*. Volume 2. Translated by A. J. W. Morrison. 1849. London: Henry G. Bohn.

———. *Faust*. Translated by Walter Kaufmann. 1961. New York: Doubleday. [All of Part 1 and selections from Part 2, facing-pages German and English].

———. *Faust. Der Tragödie zweiter Teil*. 1832. Stuttgart. [Part 2 of Faust, also known as "Helena."]

———. *Faustus*. 1834. London: Hodgson, Boys & Graves. [Anonymous translation of scenes from *Faust*, by Samuel Taylor Coleridge, plus "An Appendix, containing the May-Day Night Scene, translated by Percy Bysshe Shelley"].

———. *Memoirs of Goethe, Written by Himself*. 1824. London: Henry Colburn. 2 vols.

———. *Wilhelm Meister's Apprenticeship*. Translated by Thomas Carlyle. 1839. London: The Anthological Society. 1892.

Gordon, John. "The Doctrines of Drs. Gall and Spurzheim." [Unsigned review]. *Edinburgh Review*, Vol. 25, June 1815, pp. 227-268.

Gray, Elizabeth Caroline Johnstone. *Tour to the Sepulchres of Etruria, in 1839*. 1843. London: J. Hatchard and Son.

Gray, Thomas. *The Works of Thomas Gray*. 1825. London: Harding, Triphook and Lepard. 2 vols.

Griswold, Rufus. Letter to William J. Pabodie. June 8, 1852. University of Indiana Lilly Collection. Poe, Box 2.

Harcanville, Pierre d'. *Antiquités étrusques, grecques et romaines: ou les beaux vases étrusques, grecs et romains, et les peintures rendues avec les couleurs qui leur sont propres*. 1787. Paris. 5 vols.

———. *Antiquités étrusques, grecques et romaines, tirées du cabinet du chevalier William Hamilton*. 1766-1767. Naples. 3 vols.

<288>

Hannay, James. "Life and Genius of Edgar Allan Poe." *The Poetical Works of Edgar Allan Poe.* Edited by James Hannay. 1852. London: C. Griffin & Co. pp. 13-32.

Hawthorne, Nathaniel. "The Hall of Fantasy." *The Pioneer.* February 1843. Boston: Leland and Whiting (pp. 49-55).

Hawthorne, Nathaniel. *Passages from English Note-Books.* 1870. Boston: Fields, Osgood & Co.

Hazlitt, William. "Fine Arts. British Institution." *The Collected Works of William Hazlitt.* Edited by A.R. Waller and Arnold Glover. Volume 11: Fugitive Writings. Feb, 5, 1814. London: J.M. Dent. 1904 [Source of SHW's quote on Turner.]

Heine, Heinrich. *The Romantic School.* 1833. Translated by S.L. Fleishman. New York: Henry Holt & Co. 1882.

Hemans, Felicia. *The Works of Felicia Hemans.* "Edited by her Sister." 1840. New York: C.S. Francis & Co. 3 vols. 1845.

———. *The Poetical Works of Mrs. Hemans.* "The Chandos Poets," n.d. London: Frederick Warne and Co.

Heraclitus. *The Fragments of the Work of Heraclitus of Ephesus, On Nature.* Translated by G. T. W. Patrick. 1889. Baltimore MD: N. Murray.

Heraclitus. *Heraclitus.* Translated by Philip Wheelwright. 1959. Princeton NJ: Princeton University Press.

Hetherington et al. *The Trial of Thomas Paterson, for Blasphemy before the High Court Justiciary, Edinburgh, with . . . the Trials of Thomas Finlay and Miss Matilda Roalfe (for Blasphemy) in the Sheriffs' Court. With Notes and a Special Dissertation on Blasphemy Prosecutions in General, by the Secretary of the "Anti-Persecution Union."* London: Anti-Persecution Union. 1844.

Higginson, Thomas Wentworth. "Poe." *The Recognition of Edgar Allan Poe: Selected Criticism Since 1829.* Edited by Eric W. Carlson. 1966. Ann Arbor: Univ. of Michigan Press. [Originally published in *Literary World,* March 15, 1879.]

Hirst, Henry B. "The Poets and Poetry of Philadelphia Number 11." *Philadelphia Saturday Museum.* March 4, 1843. [Source for phrenological description of Poe, to which Poe himself may have contributed].

"Histoire de la Litterature Allemande." [Unsigned review]. *Foreign Quarterly.* Vol 23, April 1839 (pp. 65-79).

Holland, Josiah Gilbert. *Kathrina, Her Life and Mine in a Poem.* 1867. New York: Charles Scribner's Sons. 1895.

Holleran, Michael. "Filling the Providence Cove: Image in the Evolution of Urban Form." *Rhode Island History.* Vol. 48 No. 3, August 1990 (pp. 65-85).

<289>

Howitt, William. *The History of the Supernatural in All Ages and Nations, and in All Churches, Christian and Pagan, Demonstrating a Universal Faith*. 1863. London: Longman, Green. 2 vols.

Hudson, David. *Memoir of Jemima Wilkinson, A Preacheress of the Eighteenth Century*. 1844. Bath, NY: R. L. Underhill & Co.

Jacobi, Friedrich Heinrich. *The Main Philosophical Writings, and the Novel Alwill*. Translated by George di Giovanni. 1994. Montreal: McGill-Queen's University Press.

Klemm, Gustav Friedrich. *Allgemeine CulturGeschichte der Menschheit (General Cultural History of Mankind)*. 1843-47. Leipzig: Teubner. 10 vols.

Kunce, Catherine. *The Correspondence of Sarah Helen Whitman and Julia Deane Freeman: Writer to Writer, Woman to Woman*. 2014. Newark, DE: University of Delaware Press.

Lancaster, Jane. *Inquire Within: A Social History of the Providence Athenaeum Since 1753*. 2003. Providence, RI: The Providence Athenaeum.

Landor, Walter Savage. *Gebir, Count Julian, and Other Poems*. 1831. London: Edward Moxon.

Lathrop, George Parsons. "Poe, Irving, and Hawthorne." *Scribner's Monthly*, Vol. 11, April 1876 (pp. 799-808).

Legare, J.M. "A May Morn." *The Southern and Western Literary Messenger and Review*. Vol 13, September 1847.

Leibniz, Gottfried Wilhelm. *Theodicy: Essays on the Goodness of God, the Freedom of Man, and the Origin of Evil*. 1710. Translated by E. M. Huggard. BiblioBazaar. 2007.

Letter from Anna Marsh Bartlett to Sarah Helen Whitman. April 1817. Ms. 204. Manuscript Collection of John Hay Library, Brown University, Providence, RI HA1388

Letter from Anna Marsh Bartlett to Sarah Helen Whitman. June 1817. Ms. 204. Manuscript Collection of John Hay Library, Brown University, Providence, RI HA1387

Lewes, George Henry. *The Life and Works of Goethe*. 1856. Boston: Ticknor and Fields. 2 vols.

———. ("G.H.L."). "Spinoza's Life and Works." *Westminster Review*. Vol 39. May 1843 (pp. 198-217). [Also reprinted in August 1843 in *The Eclectic Museum of Foreign Literature*, New York, 1843 (pp. 530-549).

Livy (Titus Livius). *The Early History of Rome*. Translated by Aubrey de Selincourt. 1960. New York: Penguin Books.

Lloyd, Rosemary. *Mallarmé and His Circle*. 1999. Ithaca NY: Cornell University Press.

<290>

Longfellow, Henry Wadsworth. Letter included in "The Late Edgar A. Poe." *Southern Literary Messenger,* November 1849 (p. 696). [The editor includes Longfellow's letter with an apology for "publishing what was intended as a private correspondence"].

Lowell, James Russell. "Edgar A. Poe." in *Works of the Late Edgar Allan Poe.* Volume 1: Tales. 1849. New York: J. S. Redfield. Edited by Rufus Griswold. 1859 printing by Blakeman & Mason.

Mackintosh, James. *The Miscellaneous Works of the Right Honorable Sir James Mackintosh.* 1846. New York: D. Appleton & Co. Three vols in one. 1870. [Includes "Dissertation on the Progress of Ethical Philosophy, Chiefly During the Seventeenth and Eighteenth Centuries" (pp. 94-197), and Review of Madame de Staël's 'De L'Allemagne" (pp. 260-270)]

Madden, R.A. *The Literary Life and Correspondence of The Countess Blessington.* 1855. London: T.C. Newby. 3 vols.

Magrath, Mary Gabriella. *A History of the Poe-Controversy in Periodical Literature of the Second Half of the Nineteenth Century.* 1955. Master's Thesis. Paper 1138. Loyola University. [Thorough review of the periodical responses pro and contra Griswold, and of the campaign to erect the Poe memorial in Baltimore. Magrath also solves some of the attribution questions for unsigned articles]. Retrieved from ecommon.luc.edu/luc_theses/1138

Marvell, Andrew. "Upon Appleton House." 1651. *Seventeenth-Century British Poetry: 1603-1660.* Edited by John R. Rumrich and Gregory Chaplin. 2006. New York: W. W. Norton & Company (pp. 559-581).

Maudsley, Henry, "Edgar Allan Poe." [Asylum] Journal of Mental Sciences, Vol. 60, 1860 (pp. 328-369).

McCann, Walter Edgar. "Byronism." *The Galaxy.* Vol. 5, June 1868 (pp. 778-781).

Melville, Lewis. *The Life and Letters of William Beckford of Fonthill.* 1910. New York: Duffield & Co.

Menzel, Wolfgang. *German Literature.* Translated by C. C. Felton. 1840. Boston: Hilliard, Gray and Co. 3 vols.

Miller, John Carl, ed. *Poe's Helen Remembers.* 1979. Charlottesville, VA: University Press of Virginia.

Milnes, Richard Monckton ("R.M.N."). "American Philosophy — Emerson's Works." *London and Westminster Review,* Vol. 33, March 1840 (pp. 345-372).

Moore, Thomas. *Memoirs, Journal and Correspondence of Thomas Moore.* Vol 7. 1853. London: Longman, Brown, Green, and Longmans.

<291>

Moulton, Louse Chandler. "Sarah Helen Whitman." *London Athenaeum*, No. 2669. Dec 21, 1878 (p. 804).

Mudford, William. "The Iron Shroud." *Tales from Blackwood*. Vol. 1. 1858. Edinburgh: William Blackwood & Sons. [The Mudford story anthologized here, first appeared in *Blackwood's Magazine* in August 1830. It has great similarities to Poe's "The Pit and the Pendulum."]

Müller, Karl Ottfried. *Attica and Athens: An Inquiry into the Civil, Moral and Religious Institutions of the Inhabitants*. Translated by John Leitch. 1842. London: Richard Groombridge.

———. *The History and Antiquities of the Doric Race*. Translated by Henry Tufnell. Second edition, 1839. London: John Murray. 2 vols.

———. *History of the Literature of Ancient Greece to the Period of Isocrates*. 1840. London: Baldwin & Cradock.

Müller-Wille, Stefan. "The Economy of Nature in Classical Natural History." *Studies in the History of Biology*. 2012. Vol. 4 No 4. [Discussion of "economy of nature" concept used in Whitman's essay on Shelley.]

Nichols, Mary Sargeant Gove. "Reminiscences of Edgar Allan Poe." *Six Penny Magazine* (London), Vol. 4 No. 20, February 1 1863 (pp. 471-474).

———. *Reminiscences of Edgar Allan Poe*. With a prefatory letter by T.O. Mabbott. 1931. New York: Union Square Bookshop. [A reprint of the article from *Six Penny Magazine*.]

Novalis [Georg Philipp Friedrich von Hardenberg]. *Novalis: His Life, Thoughts, and Works*. Translated by M.J. Hope. 1891. Chicago: A.C. McClurg.

———. *Novalis Schriften*. Edited by Ludwig Tieck and Friedrich Schlegel. 1802. Fourth edition. Berlin. 1826.

O'Connor, William D. *The Good Gray Poet: A Vindication*. 1866. New York: Bruce & Huntington.

Ollier, Edmund. *Poems from The Greek Mythology and Miscellaneous Poems*. London: John Camden Hotten. 1867 [First book publication of the poem "Eleusinia" quoted by SHW].

"Our Goosy" [Broadside lampooning William J. Pabodie's unsuccessful attempt to found a literary magazine, *The Argosy: A Semi-Monthly Critical Journal of Literature and Art*]. 1840. Brown. HB21163 Cav. 1986.

Parker, Theodore. *A Discourse of Matters Pertaining to Religion*. 1842. Boston: American Unitarian Association. 1907.

Passeri, Giovanni Battista. *Picturae Etruscorum in vasculis nunc primum in unum collectae explicationibus, et dissertationibus inlustratae*. 1767. Rome: Johannes Zempel. 3 vols.

<292>

Pitman, Joseph S. *Report on the Trial of Thomas Wilson Dorr, for Treason Against the State of Rhode Island*. 1844. Boston: Tappan & Dennet.

Plotinus. *The Ethical Treatises, Being the Treatises of the First Ennead*. 1917. London: The Medici Society. 1926.

Poe, Edgar Allan. *Eureka: A Prose Poem*. 1848. New York: Geo. P. Putnam.

———. *The Last Letters of Edgar Allan Poe to Sarah Helen Whitman*. Edited by James A. Harrison. 1909. New York: G.P. Putnam's Sons.

———. "The Poetic Principle." *The Complete Poems and Stories of Edgar Allan Poe*. Edited by Arthur Hobson Quinn and Edward H. O'Neill. 1946. New York: Alfred A. Knopf. (Vol 2, pp. 1021-1040).

———. *The Poetical Works of Edgar Allan Poe, with Original Memoir*. 1853. Illustrated. New York: J. S. Redfield. 1858. [Unsigned "Original Memoir" by Charles F. Briggs. With engravings based on the work of F. R. Pickersgill, John Tenniel, Birket Foster, Felix Darley, Jasper Cropsey, P. Duggan, Percival Skelton, and A. M. Madot.]

———. "A Tale of the Ragged Mountains." *The Complete Poems and Stories of Edgar Allan Poe*. Edited by Arthur Hobson Quinn and Edward H. O'Neill. 1946. New York: Alfred A. Knopf. Vol 1 (pp. 514-522).

———. *Tales*. 1845. New York: Wiley & Putnam.

———. *Tales of the Grotesque and Arabesque*. 1840. Philadelphia: Lea and Blanchard. 2 vols.

———. "Undine" [Marginalia M098]. *Democratic Review*. December 1844 (p. 588). Accessed from eapoe.org/works/misc/mar1244.htm

———. *The Works of Edgar Allan Poe. Vol. 1: Memoir — Tales*. Edited by John Ingram. 1874. Edinburgh: Adam and Charles Black.

———. *Works of the Late Edgar Allan Poe. Volume 1: Tales*. 1849. New York: J. S. Redfield. Edited by Rufus Griswold. 1859 printing by Blakeman & Mason. [This volume contains in the infamous "Memoir" of Poe by Griswold; "Edgar A. Poe" by James Russell Lowell; and "Death of Edgar A. Poe" by Nathaniel Parker Willis, which includes quotations from Griswold's "Ludwig" obituary of Poe.]

———. *Works of the Late Edgar Allan Poe. Volume 2: Poems and Tales*. 1849. New York: J. S. Redfield. Edited by Rufus Griswold. 1859 printing by Blakeman & Mason.

———. *Works of the Late Edgar Allan Poe. Volume 3: The Literati*. 1850. New York: J. S. Redfield. Edited by Rufus Griswold. 1859 printing by Blakeman & Mason.

<293>

————. *Works of the Late Edgar Allan Poe. Volume 4: Arthur Gordon Pym et al.* 1856. New York: J. S. Redfield. Edited by Rufus Griswold. 1859 printing by Blakeman & Mason.

Powers, Franklin E. *A genealogical record of the Powers(s) Families.* 1974. Aurora, Colorado: Powers. At Rhode Island Historical Society Library Genealogy Collection.

Proctor, Bryan W. "Edgar Allan Poe." *Edinburgh Review,* April 1858 (pp. 419-442).

Providence. City Council. Census Committee. [1855] *Census of the City of Providence.* 1856. Providence, RI: Knowles, Anthony & Co.

De Quincey, Thomas. *Confessions of an English Opium-Eater and Suspiria de Profundis.* 1821. Boston: Ticknor, Reed, and Fields. 1851.

Quinn, Arthur Hobson. *Edgar Allan Poe: A Critical Biography.* 1941. New York: D. Appleton-Century Co.

Richards, Eliza. "Lyric Telegraphy: Women Poets, Spiritualist Poetics, and the 'Phantom Voice' of Poe." *Yale Journal of Criticism,* Vol. 12 No. 2. 1999 (pp. 269-294).

Richter, Jean Paul. *Titan.* Translated by Charles Timothy Brooks. 1862. Boston: Ticknor.

Ritter, Heinrich. *The History of Ancient Philosophy.* Translated by Alexander J.W. Morrison. 1838. Oxford: Talboys. 4 vols.

"Ritter's *History of Philosophy*." [Unsigned review]. *Brownson's Quarterly Review.* Vol 3, third series, January 1855. Boston: Benjamin H. Greene.

Rousseau, Jean-Jacques. *Œuvres Complètes.* Vol. 2. 1852. Paris: Chez Alexandre Houssiaux. [Includes *La Nouvelle Héloise.*]

Ruskin, John, *Sesame and Lilies: Three Lectures.* 1865. Sunnyside, Orpington, Kent: George Allen. 1876.

Rutherford, Brett. *Last Flowers: The Romance Poems of Edgar Allan Poe and Sarah Helen Whitman.* 1985. Providence: The Poet's Press. Revised 4th edition, 2011.

Schiller, Friedrich. *Poems and Ballads.* Translated by Edward Bulwer Lytton. 1844. Leipzig: Bernhard Tauchnitz Jr. [Includes "The Artists," pp. 209-230.]

Scott, Walter. *Ivanhoe; A Romance.* Edinburgh: Archibald Constable. 1820. 3 vols.

Shelley, Percy Bysshe. "The Necessity of Atheism." Pamphlet, 1811. [An expanded version of this text was included in Shelley's *Queen Mab* in 1813.]

————. *Posthumous Poems.* 1824. London: John and Henry L. Hunt.

<294>

Silverman, Kenneth. *Edgar A. Poe: Mournful and Never-Ending Remembrance.* 1991. New York: HarperCollins Publishers.

Smith, E. Vale. "The Works of the Late Edgar Allan Poe." [Unsigned book review]. *North American Review.* Vol. 83 No. 173, October 1856. Boston: Crosby, Nichols & Co. (pp. 427-455).

Smith, Elizabeth Oakes. "Autobiographic Notes. Edgar Allan Poe." *Beadle's Monthly,* February 1867 (pp. 147-156).

———."Edgar A. Poe." [Unsigned article]. *United States Magazine.* Vol 4 No 3, March 1857 (pp. 262-268).

———. "Recollections of Poe." *Home Journal.* March 15 1876 (pp. 1-2).

Spinoza, Baruch. *Ethics.* Translated by R.H. M. Elwes. Accessed online from faculty.umb.edu/gary_zabel/Courses/Spinoza/Texts/Spinoza/index.html

Spurzheim, Johann. *The Physiognomical System of Drs. Gall and Spurzheim.* 1815. London. 2nd ed.

Stallo, J.B. *General Principles of the Philosophy of Nature, with An Outline of Some of Its Recent Developments Among the Germans, Embracing the Phuilosophical Systems of Schelling and Hegel, and Oken's System of Nature.* 1848. Boston: W. M. Crosby and H. P. Nichols,

Swedenborg, Emanuel. *Arcana Coelestia: The Heavenly Arcana.* 1747-1757. London: The Swedenborg Society. 1891.

Swinburne, Algernon Charles. *William Blake: A Critical Essay.* 1868. London: John Camden Hotten.

Tennyson, Alfred. *The Complete Poetical Works of Tennyson.* 1898. Cambridge MA: Houghton Mifflin.

———. *The Palace of Art and Other Poems.* Edited and annotated by E.H. Turpin. 1898. New York: Maynard, Merrill & Co. [Last revision of the title poem, along with useful annotations].

Thompson, John Reuben. "The Late Edgar Allen [sic] Poe." *Southern Literary Messenger.* Vol 15 No 11, November 1849 (pp. 694-697).

Thoreau, Henry David. *A Week on the Concord and the Merrimack Rivers.* 1849. Boston: Houghton Mifflin. *The Writings of Henry David Thoreau,* Vol 1. 1906.

Ticknor, Caroline. *Poe's Helen.* 1916. New York. Charles Scribner's Sons.

Tupper, Martin Farquhar. *Proverbial Philosophy: A Book of Thoughts and Arguments, Originally Treated.* [First and second series.] 1838, 1842. New York: Baker and Scribner. 1849.

Turnbull, John D. *The Wood-Daemon, or, The Clock Has Struck!* 1808. Boston: D. True. [Drama based on M.G. Lewis, in which David Poe took part in Boston].

<295>

Vanderhoof, E.W. *Historical Sketches of Western New York*. 1907. Buffalo: Privately printed. [Includes chapters on Jemima Wilkinson and on the beginnings of the Spiritualist movement with the Fox sisters].

Voltaire, Francois Marie. *Oeuvres Complètes de Voltaire*. 1784. [Volume 61, *Correspondence Général*, contains Voltaire's letters to Madame du Deffand.]

Wallace, Horace Binney. *Literary Criticisms and Other Papers*. 1856. Philadelphia: Parry and McMillan. [Likely source of SHW quote from George Herbert].

Whitman, Sarah Helen. "Alcott's Tablets." [Book review]. *The Providence Journal*. October 30, 1868.

———. "Byronism." *The Providence Journal*. October 318, 1869.

———. "Character and Writings of Shelley." [Signed as "Egeria"]. *The Literary Journal, and Weekly Register of Science and the Arts*. 1:32 (Providence, Sat Jan 11 1834) (pp. 252-253).

———. "The Dying Hero." (Translation from Uhland.) *The Knickerbocker: or, New-York Monthly Magazine*. Vol. 13, February 1839, pp. 134-135.

———. *Edgar Poe and His Critics*. 1860. New York: Rudd & Carleton.

———. *Edgar Poe and His Critics*. 1860. Providence, RI: Tibbitts and Preston. Second edition. 1885.

———. *Edgar Poe and His Critics*. Edited by Oral Sumner Coad. 1860. New Brunswick NJ: Rutgers University Press, 1949. [A reprint of Whitman's essay, published for the Poe Centennial Year, with a preface and notes by O. S. Coad.]

———. *Hours of Life, And Other Poems*. 1853. Providence: George H. Whitney.

———. "Introductory Letter." July, 1876. *The Life and Poems of Edgar Allan Poe*. E. L. Didier, ed. 1877. New York: W. J. Widdleton.

———. "Leonora, A Tale of the Battle of Prague." (Translated from Bürger). *The Knickerbocker: or, New-York Monthly Magazine*. Vol. 13, March 1839, pp. 197-198.

———. "The Lost Church" (Translation from Uhland). *The Knickerbocker: or, New-York Monthly Magazine*. Vol. 14, November 1839, pp. 430-431.

———. "On the Character and Attributes of Genius." [Signed "Egeria"]. *The Boston Pearl*, Vol. 5 No. 15, December 19, 1835 (pp. 107-108, 111).

———. "Our Window." *Emerson's Magazine and Putnam's Monthly*. Vol. 5 No. 4, October 1857 (pp. 540-542). [Reprint of letter from *The Providence Journal* about SHW's 1857 visit to Walter Savage Landor].

<296>

———. *Poems.* 1879. Boston: Houghton, Osgood and Company. [Reprinted in 1916.]

———. "Stanzas, A September Evening on the Banks of the Moshassuck." *The Knickerbocker: or, New-York Monthly Magazine.* Vol. 14, November 1839, p. 419.

———. "To Edgar Allan Poe [The Raven]" *Home Journal.* March 18, 1848.

———. [Signed as "Helen"] "To the Spirit of Poetry." *Ladies' Magazine (1828-1829).* October 1 1828 (pp. 457-458).

Whittier, John Greenleaf. *Old Portraits and Modern Sketches.* 1849. Boston: Ticknor, Reed, and Fields.

Willard, George R. *History of the Providence Stage, 1762-1891.* 1891. Providence: Rhode Island News Company.

Willis, Nathaniel P. ["N.P.W"]. "Letter About Edgar Poe." *Home Journal.* October 30, 1858.

"The Works of the Late Edgar Allan Poe." [Book review]. *The Edinburgh Review.* Vol. CVII. April, 1858 (pp. 419-442).

Wortman, Tunis. *A Treatise Concerning Political Inquiry, and the Liberty of the Press.* 1800. New York: George Forman.

Wright, Thomas. *Narratives of Sorcery and Witchcraft, from the Most Authentic Sources.* 1851. New York: Redfield. 1852.

<297>

ILLUSTRATIONS

Cover: Painting of Sarah Helen Whitman by Giovanni Thompson. Providence Athenaeum.

Frontispiece: Newspaper engraving of downtown Providence and College Hill from 1844.

Page 12: Nicholas Power, Jr. From Ticknor (1916). From a miniature by Malbone at The Providence Athenaeum.

Page 14: The Power family house at 88 Benefit Street. Photograph by Brett Rutherford.

Page 15: John Winslow Whitman. From Ticknor (1916).

Page 31: Sarah Helen Whitman in séance attire. Date unknown.

Page 33: Sarah Helen Whitman house on Power Street. Photograph by Brett Rutherford.

Page 35: Porch and entrance of The Providence Athenaeum, built in 1838. Photograph by Brett Rutherford.

Page 40: Daguerreotype of Edgar Allan Poe by Samuel W. Hartshorn, 1848. Original in Brown University Library.

Page 52: From a wood engraving depicting Poe's cottage at Fordham, as it was in 1874.

Page 71: "Edgar Allan Poe Walking High Bridge." The New York Public Library Digital Collections. 1930. (The Miriam and Ira D. Wallach Division of Art, Prints and Photographs: Print Collection, The New York Public Library.)

Page 72: High Bridge and Aqueduct, circa 1900.

<298>

Page 106: Portrait of Shelley by Curran (1819), oil on canvas. National Portrait Gallery.

Page 114: *Laocoön and His Sons*. Marble, copy after an Hellenistic original from c. 200 BCE. Found in the Baths of Trajan in 1506 CE. Photograph by Marie-Lan Nguyen. Wikimedia Commons. Museo Pio-Clementino, The Vatican.

Page 122: Portrait of Goethe in 1828 by Joseph Karl Stieler. Wikimedia Commons.

Page 149: Margaret Fuller in the 1840s.

Page 156: From a portrait of Emerson by Samuel Rowse. Library of Congress.

Page 186: Stipple engraving portrait of Walter Savage Landor by J. Brown. Original at National Library of Wales.

Page 188: William Beckford's tower at Bath. From a steel-plate engraving.

Page 192: Engraving portrait of A. Bronson Alcott, undated. New York Public Library Digital Gallery.

Page 198: Portrait of Lord Byron by Henry Pierce Bone. Wikimedia Commons.

Page 206: *The Abduction of Proserpine by Pluto*. Luca Giordano. Fresco, 1684-1686. Palazzo Medici, Florence.

Page 252: The Cove in downtown Providence in 1857. Smithsonian.

Page 298. Sarah Helen Whitman dressed as Athena. Date unknown.

<299>

ABOUT THIS BOOK

The body type for this book is set in Plantin, a typeface designed for Monotype in 1912, based on Renaissance Roman letter-forms found in the Plantin-Moretus Museum in Antwerp. The original designers were Frank Pierpont and Fritz Stelzer. The face moved into the digital era around 2001, and the Poet's Press has chosen it for its new standard typeface for print and ebooks, replacing Aldine.

Main titles and section titles are set in Geo Slab. Slab-serif typefaces began appearing early in the 19th century, and are still employed occasionally to evoke that era. Small titles are set in Century 725 Condensed, designed by Heinrich Hoffmeister, based on the classic Century family first created in 1894 by Linn Boyd Benton for American Type Founders, for use in *The Century Magazine*. It is used here in headlines, including small capitals and extra letterspacing, to suggest the days of metal typesetting.

<300>

◇———◇

www.ingramcontent.com/pod-product-compliance
Lightning Source LLC
Chambersburg PA
CBHW022005080426
42733CB00007B/473